Association

Registered as a charity (No. 266754)

The Association was formed by Philip and Mary Carter in 1973,
to promote the interests of users of the South West Coast Path

SOUTH WEST COAST PATH ASSOCIATION
Bowker House, Lee Mill Bridge, Ivybridge, Devon PL21 9EF
Tel: 01752 896237 Email: info@southwestcoastpath.org.uk
Visit our website at www.southwestcoastpath.org.uk

CHAIRMAN - ANDREW LACK
421 Bury Street West, London, N9 9JR
Tel: 0208 360 8423 Email: chair@southwestcoastpath.org.uk

TREASURER - GEORGE COLES
Bowker House see above. Email: treasurer@southwestcoastpath.org.uk

SECRETARY - STEVE CHURCH
4 Wheal Speed Road, Carbis Bay, St Ives TR26 2QG
Tel: 01736 791777 Email: secretary@southwestcoastpath.org.uk

ADMINISTRATOR - KATE HOLLAND
Bowker House see above

Published by: The South West Coast Path Association

All rights reserved. No part of this book may be reproduced or utilised in any form or by any means,
electronic or mechanical, including photocopying, recording or by any information storage and retrieval system,
without permission in writing from the South West Coast Path Association.

© South West Coast Path Association 2015
Designed by Ingrid Kendall, Paignton. Printed by Latimer Trend, Plymouth
ISBN: 978-0-907055-21-1

Jacket photography:
Lamorna Cove photographer - Fiona Barltrop
Burgh Island Tractor photographers - Pete & Judith Gibbins
Radar Memorial at St Aldelm's Head photographers -
Pete & Judith Gibbins
Minehead SWCP Marker photographer - Peter Gates

Welcome to the Annual Guide

Welcome to the South West Coast Path Association's Annual Guide to the wonderful experience of England's longest National Trail. This superb walk encircles the coastline of the entire South West Peninsula of England. In its 630 miles it encompasses high cliffs, breezy dunes, wooded estuaries, saltmarshes, picturesque fishing ports, sedate seaside towns, holiday resorts and all the interest of the major seaside city and naval port of Plymouth.

No matter what your interest, be it in the landscape, wildlife, history or just a wish to get away from it all, the South West Coast Path has the answer.

This Guide has been produced by the South West Coast Path Association, the charitable body set up to represent the interests of all those who walk on the Coast Path. It doesn't matter whether you're an afternoon stroller or a long-distance walker who intends to walk all 630 miles, or has done so, the Association is there for you.

The Association campaigns for the best possible standards for the Coast Path and its immediate corridor and financially assists where appropriate to ensure the best possible experience for those using the route. And, of course, it also provides help and information to walkers, including this Guide and the other publications mentioned in these pages.

So, if you've not already done so, why not join 5,000+ Coast Path enthusiasts and become a member. Then –

- your subscription will help the Association promote, protect and enhance the Coast Path, including providing funds for specific improvement projects;
- you will receive your copy of the Annual Guide free and keep up to date with what's happening on the Path via our two free Newsletters each year plus regular e-newsletters.
- you will be part of the "family" of those who love the Coast Path by knowing that your input is important to the Path's well-being.

Funding provided by members' subscriptions has enabled the Association to play a vital part in getting bridges replaced, re-constructing the Path when it has been lost to cliff falls, improving its alignment and a host of other improvements. That's all thanks to the Association's members....well done everyone!

The Association has now become heavily involved in raising funds from as many sources as possible to help improve the Coast Path. Following our incredibly successful 40th anniversary "Great South West Walk" event in 2013, which succeeded in raising over £650,000 for improvements, a smaller scale event took place in autumn 2014. A number of circular walks was organised around the line of the Coast Path, and sponsorship income was shared with a partner organisation, Children's Hospice South West. This new venture proved a good experience for the Association in working together with another charity and was beneficial to both organisations.

In addition, the Association took the lead in achieving a grant of £1 million for the Coast Path from the Coastal Communities Fund. The Fund is financed by the Government through the funding equivalent of 50% of the revenues of the Crown Estate's marine activities. The successful application means that 32 locations along the Coast Path will benefit from funds for repairs and improvements, some necessary because of the last two unusually bad winters, with the remainder of the funding being used for a major marketing, information and events programme, to include brand development, building relationships with businesses, partners and path users, and investment in new information for walkers at key locations. None of this would have been achievable without the moral backing and financial help, through subscriptions, of the Association membership.

Approaching Kynance Cove, Lizard Peninsula

Contents

Photographs courtesy of:
Lynne Adams, Mary Alice, Becky Avant, Debbie Bakewell, Adrian Ballisat, Ralph Buscher, Sally Davie, Pete & Ann Gibbins, Alan Greene, Richard Henson, Roger Hollingsworth, Lucy Masterton, Andrew McLoy, Paul Melling, Andrew Morris, Paul Moulton, Andrew Nicholson, Steve Pattemore, Baz Richardson, Jennifer Rowlandson, Audrey Rowlatt, Becky Stares, Richard Tapscott, Ann Warren, Dave Westcott, Doreen White and Robert Wright.

Introduction to The South West Coast Path

The South West Coast Path National Trail is a 630-mile adventure around the coastline of the south-west peninsula. From Minehead in Somerset all the way to Poole Harbour in Dorset, it is simply the best way to enjoy the scenery, wildlife and heritage of this wonderful coastline.

The sheer variety of the South West Coast Path means that there are plenty of gentle stretches as well as dramatic headlands and steep coastal valleys where the going can be strenuous and demanding. Relaxation, challenge, tranquillity or inspiration - the choice is yours!

National Trails are walking routes (and some also for riding) through the country's finest scenery and heritage. They are created and mainly funded by Natural England and managed by Highway Authorities and the National Trust. They receive a high standard of care and are the flagships of the rights of way network. No one in England and Wales lives more than 50 miles from a National Trail.

A detailed survey of the full length of the Coast Path has been carried out using global positioning systems, as a result of which we have access to very precise distances. This survey showed that the Coast Path is 630 miles (1014km) in length. This length includes the circumnavigation of the Isle of Portland, officially part of the Coast Path since 2003.

During a survey in 2011-12 of the entire Coast Path, an Association member used a sophisticated altimeter to calculate that the walker who has completed the whole Coast Path will have climbed 115000 feet (35024m), which is just a little short of walking the height of Mount Everest from sea level four times!

The path passes through some of the finest coastal scenery anywhere, and has enormous variety and contrast between bustling resorts and quiet coves. The path is the longest National Trail in the country; we think it is the finest, and hope you will too. We know of no other that has as much contrast and variety as ours and urge you to try it.

So here it is - England's longest and most beautiful walking trail - read about it, then go for it!

Dedicated to helping everyone enjoy the path

The Association was formed in 1973 by a group of enthusiasts to encourage the development and improvement of the South West Coast Path. This is still one of the main aims of the Association, and it works closely with Natural England, local authorities, the National Trust and other more general user groups such as the Ramblers' Association and the Long Distance Walkers' Association.

Padstow

www.southwestcoastpath.org.uk

The South West Coast Path Association

The Association is now an integral member of the South West Coast Path Partnership, the body whose role is to take collective responsibility for providing a high quality trail as defined by national Quality Standards. The Partnership includes all those organisations responsible for providing the Coast Path as well as the users.

Since its foundation the Association has continuously campaigned for maintenance, signing and alignment improvements. Of primary importance is to have the Coast Path removed from roads. There have been many improvements as long-standing members will know, and the Association has strongly influenced the implementation of these.

The Association has been instrumental in the placing of markers at each end of the trail, and also a half-way marker.

Today one of the Association's functions is to assist and advise all those who wish to walk along this wonderful coastline - whether in short, relaxing strolls around a headland, or by more demanding long distance walks lasting several days, or by heroic attempts at covering the whole length of 630 miles (1014km) in one go!

The Association currently has a programme of funding improvements to the Coast Path and encourages all who walk and enjoy the trail to join as members and support this very important work. To see how Association funding grants have helped improve the South West Coast Path in recent years see page 182.

Funding provided by our members' subscriptions have enabled the Association to play a vital part in a range of necessary Coast Path projects, including getting bridges replaced, improving the path alignment, replacing the path where it has been lost to cliff falls and other general enhancements. That's all thanks to our members... well done everyone!

And remember, the Association represents ALL Coast Path walkers, not just the hardy long-distance walkers. Whether you plan to walk all 630 miles, or have already done so, or are happy to stroll along the coast on a Sunday afternoon or a couple of days a year when on holiday, if you love the Coast Path the Association is for you.

The more members the Association has, the more influence it has when lobbying for improvements and repairs and the better chance it has of winning funding such as that achieved in 2014 (see page 4).

Crossing the Erme

Aims and Objectives

1. To secure the protection, improvement and preservation of an acceptable South West Coast Path and public access thereto in order to improve the conditions of life of the users of the South West Coast Path.

2. To educate users of the South West Coast Path to a greater knowledge of, respect and care for the coast and the countryside.

In furtherance of these objectives the Association aims to work for and assist in:

1. Providing information about the South West Coast Path and its corridor to the public;

2. The organisation directed at the improvement and maintenance of the South West Coast Path.

3. Providing a forum in which different interests connected with the South West Coast Path (including its corridor) and its use can discuss problems of mutual concern.

Membership

Members receive an Annual Guide as part of their membership plus two Newsletters and regular E-newsletters each year, with up-to-date information on the state of the path and special offers.

Subscriptions

Single	£14.50
Joint	£16.00
Life Membership	£220.00
Joint Life Membership	£250.00
Non-UK Membership	£22.00

Payment may be made at www.southwestcoastpath.org.uk or by telephoning 01752 896237 or by using a cheque or postal order made payable to the South West Coast Path Association.

We can accept the credit/debit cards shown below.

A Word to Beginners

Long distance path walking

These words are not for those hardy veterans who have all the gear, have done several paths already, and know all about it. However, we do get a number of letters each year from those who have not ventured before on long distance paths and need some advice. This we are pleased to try and provide and we do hope those who read this will find it helpful. However, it is easy to miss out things that folk wish to know, so if you who are new read this, and are still baffled, please contact us and we will try to provide the answers. As well as perhaps helping you, it will enable us to improve this section for another year and so be of help to more people.

Newcomers to the Coast Path

To get the feel of the Coast Path you are advised to take some day walks along it - there are some very good ones on the coast. Better still, look for the sections marked 'Easy' - start at one end and stop and turn back before you have half had enough. We say before half because it is always better to do a bit less and really enjoy it.

You can soon progress to setting out to walk a whole section either by using two cars or using public transport. One point here - if possible use the public transport to go out and walk back to your car or base; this means that you do not get yourself in a position of having to race the clock if you should take a bit more time than you thought.

If you are walking on your own, do please take additional care, for as you will appreciate, if you fall or twist an ankle there can be problems. If you are on your own therefore, you should leave a note with someone to make sure that you arrive at your destination. Not everyone is happy walking on their own and can feel lonely. There is also an added problem that you may try to do too much, so please bear this in mind.

There is no need to buy expensive equipment for the easy sections at the start; a pair of stout shoes and a rainproof jacket is all you need. As you progress, a small rucksack for 'eats' will be needed next.

Obviously if you can join a walking club and go out with them you will collect lots of friendly advice on all sorts of gear you may care to purchase as you become more serious about walking. Maps, guides, etc., are all listed in their appropriate sections.

For those who have walked, but not on long distance trails

Having stated the two big points, we will elaborate. You will not be able to accomplish in daily distance the same amount you normally cover in a day walk; you will have to settle for less. The first reason is that you will be carrying more equipment; you must for instance, have a complete change of clothing and footwear, possibly nightwear and toilet kit. For this you need a bigger rucksack so you will be carrying quite a bit more weight than you normally do. Secondly, there is what we call the 'wear' factor. For the first few days until you are really fit, it is just simply more tiring having to walk each day. The last point could be called the 'interest' factor. Usually, if you are walking a long distance path, you are further from your home base, in fresh fields and pastures new; there is more to see so you will need more time to look around.

If you usually accomplish 15 miles (24km) a day, aim, say, for 12 miles (19km). This is particularly important if you are booking ahead. You can find yourself tied to a treadmill which you cannot get off. Booking ahead has the advantage that you know there is a bed ahead. On the other hand, it does mean even if you are tired, have developed blisters, and the weather is diabolical, you have to go on. Be guided

Zennor

too by our `Trail Description' section and the terrain you are tackling. 6 miles (10km), say, of a `Severe' section can equal in effort 10-12 miles (16-19km) of an 'Easy' one.

Planning Your Walk

We have stated you must carry more gear and this is true. Having said that, think long and hard about every item you imagine you may need. You will be surprised - you may find you will not want it at all. Watch particularly those extras such as cameras and binoculars - they are often a source of considerable weight. One little additional point, many rucksacks, even modern ones, are not as waterproof as you think. A plastic liner, which can be obtained quite cheaply from rambling shops, etc., as an additional inner layer, may save you that most unpleasant discovery after a long day spent in the rain that your only change of clothing is no longer dry. We would also recommend that in addition to this liner, your dry clothing should then be enclosed in further plastic bags to ensure dryness. Trainer shoes are useful for wearing at the end of the day and can be worn on some parts of the path.

A sensible idea before undertaking a long walking holiday is to take, say, a weekend of two or three days first, walking continuously as a practice.

Another point to watch especially on our Coast Path is the availability of refreshments. At main holiday times, you will get them nearly everywhere, except for the few places we especially mention in our 'Coast Path Walk' section. Out of season, you will find them in surprisingly few places on long stretches of coast. The usual remarks about carrying stand-by supplies, therefore, certainly apply; better to carry an extra couple of bars of chocolate than to go hungry.

Walking alone

The Association has long had a scheme that enables single female members who are a little nervous about walking alone to team up with other single female members.

Contact the Administrator for information.

It has also been suggested that we start a similar Men's Walking Companion scheme. If you'd like to find out more, contact the Administrator.

Guides

Path Descriptions

These Path Descriptions give detailed accounts on a variety of aspects of short sections of the Coast Path. They cover in details what cannot be included in our Annual Guide. They are currently being updated and some are now in colour with excellent interim distance information and 'reverse' walking information.

- Minehead to Porlock Weir (9.5 miles/15.3km)
- Porlock Weir to Lynmouth (12.3 miles/19.8km)
- Lynmouth to Ilfracombe (18 miles/30km)
- Ilfracombe to Croyde Bay (13.6 miles/21.9km)
- Croyde Bay to Barnstaple (14.4 miles/23.1km)
- Barnstaple to Westward Ho! (19.1 miles/30.7km)
- Westward Ho! to Clovelly (11.2 miles/18km)
- Clovelly to Hartland Quay (10.3 miles/16.6km)
- Hartland Quay to Bude (15.4 miles/24.8km)
- Bude to Crackington Haven (10.2 miles/16.4km)
- Crackington Haven to Tintagel (12 miles/20km)
- Tintagel to Port Isaac (8 miles/13km)
- Port Isaac to Padstow (11.7 miles/18.9km)
- Padstow to Porthcothan (13.6 miles/21.8km)
- Porthcothan to Newquay (11.1 miles/17.9km)
- Newquay to Perranporth (10.8 miles/17.5km)
- Perranporth to Portreath (12.2 miles/19.7km)
- Portreath to Hayle (12.4 miles/19.9km)
- Hayle to Pendeen Watch (19.5 miles/31.3km)
- Pendeen Watch to Porthcurno (15.6 miles/25.2km)
- Porthcurno to Penzance (11.5 miles/18.5km)
- Penzance to Porthleven (14 miles/22.5km)
- Porthleven to The Lizard (13.9 miles/22.3km)
- The Lizard to Coverack (10.6 miles/17.1km)
- Coverack to Helford (13.1 miles/21.1km)
- Helford to Falmouth (10 miles/16.1km)
- St Mawes to Portscatho (6.2 miles/9.9km)

- Portscatho to Portloe (8 miles/12.8km)
- Portloe to Mevagissey (12.3 miles/19.7km)
- Mevagissey to Charlestown (7.2 miles/11.5km)
- Charlestown to Fowey (10.3 miles/16.5km)
- Fowey to Polperro (7.1 miles/11.5km)
- Polperro to Looe (5 miles/8km)
- Looe to Portwrinkle (7.6 miles/12km)
- Portwrinkle to Cawsand (9.6 miles/15.4km)
- Cawsand to Cremyll (3.5 miles/5.6km)
- Admiral's Hard to Barbican (3.5 miles/5.6km)
- Barbican to Mountbatten (5 miles/8km)
- Mountbatten to Warren Point (7.3 miles/11.7km)
- Noss Mayo to Mothecombe (9.5 miles/15.2km)
- Mothecombe to Thurlestone (9 miles/14.4km)
- Thuelestone to Salcombe (9.5 miles/15.2km)
- Salcombe to Torcross (12.9 miles/20.8km)
- Torcross to Kingswear (10 miles/16km)
- Kingswear to Brixham (11 miles/17.6mile)
- Brixham to Torquay (8.4 miles/13.5km)
- Torquay to Shaldon (10.8 miles/17.3km)
- Shaldon to Exmouth (7.9 miles/12.7km)
- Exmouth to Sidmouth (13.1 miles/21km)
- Sidmouth to Lyme Regis (17 miles/27km)
- Lyme Regis to West Bay (9.7 miles/15.6km)
- West Bay to Abbotsbury (9.4 miles/15.2km)
- Abbotsbury to Ferry Bridge (10.9 miles/17.5km)
- Isle of Portland (13.2 miles/21.3km)
- Ferry Bridge to Lulworth Cove (13.2 miles/21.3km)
- Lulworth to Kimmeridge, Lulworth Range (7 miles/11km)
- Kimmeridge to South Haven Point, Poole Harbour (20.9 miles/33.6km)
- Alternative Inland Route, West Bexington to Osmington Mills (18 miles/28km)

These Path Descriptions are all available to buy on our web site at www.southwestcoastpath.org.uk or by phone on 01752 896237.

The Reverse Guide

The Association has written a description of the Trail for those walking in the Poole to Minehead direction. It deals only with the path so this Annual Guide will be necessary for all the other information. Price £4.00 plus postage.

Maps

We are sometimes asked if you require a map sheet as well as a guide book and our advice is certainly yes. One does not get as badly lost on the Coast Path as you can on inland paths, but a map is an asset nonetheless. Furthermore many walkers derive much interest from looking at their route in relation to the rest of the countryside on ordinary walks, and the same applies just as much, if not more so, on our Coast Path. The National Trail Guides offer a partial solution with their maps, but even these are not as useful as a map.

A-Z Adventure Maps

The A-Z Map Company has now mapped the entire 630 miles of the South West Coast Path and covered the entire route in five new and convenient Adventure Atlases.

The maps use 1:25,000 mapping, updated by A-Z cartographers, and each one includes a comprehensive index, outdoor information and QR barcodes to provide an instant connection to the latest local information including weather and tide times.

The five maps cover North Devon and Somerset (Minehead to Bude), North Cornwall (Bude to Land's End), South Cornwall (Land's End to Plymouth), South Devon (Plymouth to Lyme Regis) and Dorset (Lyme Regis to Poole). The maps cost £7.95 each — check them out and order them on our web site at www.southwestcoastpath.org.uk

South Devon

Harvey Maps

Walk for a week with just one map - those who have walked in the Scottish Highlands or the Lake District will know of Harvey Maps.

Produced at a scale of 1:40 000 the walkers' maps for the South West Coast Path are ideal for this National Trail which, because it is following a geographic feature, i.e. the coast, route finding does not usually present any real difficulties.

Six maps cover the entire route of the Coast Path compared with fourteen OS Landranger maps or seventeen OS Explorer/Outdoor Leisure maps. The maps have a similar amount of detail as Landranger maps for the walker yet without the administrative symbols that sometimes obscure the detail.

Another useful feature is the provision on areas of the map not needed for walking (in this case the sea) of much important information about the Trail and services along the way like camping, accommodation and food. There are also Ranger Service contact numbers and enlargements of towns/villages showing facilities available and tips on weather and clothing.

Map 1 Minehead to Bude
Map 2 Bude to Portreath
Map 3 Portreath to Lizard
Map 4 Lizard to Plymouth
Map 5 Plymouth to Sidmouth
Map 6 Sidmouth to Poole

They are priced between £10.95 and £12.95 or £62.75 for the set of 6 and are available on their web site at www.harveymaps.co.uk or by phone on 01786 841202.

1:50 000 Ordnance Survey Maps

The Metric 1:50 000 Landranger Series needed to cover the coast from Minehead in Somerset to Poole Harbour in Dorset are as follows, working round the coast from Minehead.

181	Minehead & Brendon Hills
180	Barnstaple & Ilfracombe
190	Bude & Clovelly
200	Newquay & Bodmin
204	Truro & Falmouth
203	Land's End & Isles of Scilly
204	Truro & Falmouth
200	Newquay & Bodmin
201	Plymouth & Launceston
202	Torbay & South Dartmoor
192	Exeter & Sidmouth
193	Taunton & Lyme Regis
194	Dorchester & Weymouth
195	Bournemouth & Purbeck

1:25 000 Ordnance Survey Maps

In path order, from Minehead the Coast Path is on 2½" maps.

- **Outdoor Leisure 9** Exmoor
- **Explorer 139** Bideford, Ilfracombe and Barnstaple
- **Explorer 126** Clovelly and Hartland
- **Explorer 111** Bude, Boscastle and Tintagel
- **Explorer 109** Bodmin Moor (depicts Coast Path from Boscastle to Portgaverne)
- **Explorer 106** Newquay and Padstow
- **Explorer 104** Redruth, St Agnes, Camborne and Perranporth
- **Explorer 102** Land's End, Penzance & St Ives
- **Explorer 103** The Lizard
- **Explorer 105** Falmouth and Mevagissey
- **Explorer 107** St Austell and Liskeard
- **Explorer 108** Plymouth & Tavistock
- **Explorer OL20** South Devon
- **Explorer 110** Torquay and Dawlish
- **Explorer 115** Exmouth and Sidmouth
- **Explorer 116** Lyme Regis and Bridport
- **Outdoor Leisure 15** Purbeck and South Dorset

All A-Z, Harvey and OS maps can be obtained from most bookshops. They, including Harvey Maps, may also be obtained from KenRoy Thompson Limited, 25 Cobourg Street, Plymouth PL1 1SR
Tel: 01752 227693
Email: maps@kenroythompson.co.uk
Website: kenroythompson.co.uk

POST FREE TO UK MEMBERS OF THE SOUTH WEST COAST PATH ASSOCIATION (Credit cards accepted).

Books

This list is not exhaustive; there are a number of other books available but we have tried hard to list all those which are really useful and even those not really useful that you might think would be.

South West Coast Path - Minehead to South Haven Point

An excellent pocket sized book by Paddy Dillon (March 2003). We can recommend it as most useful. It has stunning photographs and OS maps. Available from www.cicerone.co.uk at £14.95 and many bookshops. Reprinted 2013. 978-1-85284-379-3.

National Trail Guides -

published by Aurum Press in association with Natural England. They are available from bookshops, or in case of difficulty, from Aurum Press, 74-77 White Lion Street, London, N1 9PF. These are good guide books with good maps. An excellent venture by those involved.

Minehead to Padstow
by Roland Tarr (May 2013)

Padstow to Falmouth
by John Macadam (April 2013)

Falmouth to Exmouth
by Brian Le Messurier (May 2013)

Exmouth to Poole
by Roland Tarr (May 2013)

Most Tourist Information Centres (see our Accommodation section) have good supplies of leaflets and books relating to their local areas. We suggest you telephone or write to them and ask what is available.

Please also see the Association's shop on pages 186-189 and remember that Tourist Information Centres (see page 179) are a source of local leaflets and books.

Railways

Help in planning your journey to the south west can be obtained at www.traveline.info

Throughout the year there is a regular service of direct First Great Western High Speed services linking London Paddington with Taunton, Exeter St. David's, Newton Abbot, Plymouth and Cornwall. There are also regular Arriva Cross Country Trains services linking Birmingham, the North West, North East and Scotland with Taunton, Exeter St. David's, Plymouth, Cornwall and Bournemouth.

There is also a First Great Western overnight sleeper service between Paddington and Penzance.

During the high season (May to September), demand for seats is high so it is recommended that seats are reserved in advance to ensure a comfortable journey. There is a half hourly South West Trains service linking London Waterloo, Woking, Basingstoke and Southampton with Bournemouth, Poole, Wareham (for Swanage), Dorchester (for Bridport and Lyme Regis) and Weymouth for those intending to walk the Dorset end of the Coast Path.

East Devon is also served by South West Trains with an hourly service from London Waterloo to Exeter St David's calling at Woking, Basingstoke and Salisbury to Axminster (for Lyme Regis & Seaton), Honiton (for Sidmouth), and Exeter Central (for Exmouth branch).

First Great Western West offers long distance and most local trains in the South West. The long distance trains link Cardiff and Bristol with Exeter, Penzance, Plymouth, Portsmouth, Salisbury, Southampton and Weymouth. The local services on the branch lines of Devon and Cornwall offer connections into and out of First Great Western and Arriva Cross Country services, and South West Trains at Exeter for the Exmouth branch.

For those walking the Coast Path in the far west, why not consider using the First Great Western night sleeper service from Paddington to Penzance? This is a unique way to arrive on the Coast Path ready to walk fully refreshed.

First Great Western West local routes run Sunday services on the routes listed below

- **Westbury - Yeovil - Weymouth**
- **Liskeard - Looe**
- **Exeter - Barnstaple**
- **Par - Newquay**
- **Exeter - Exmouth**
- **Truro - Falmouth**
- **Newton Abbot -Torquay - Paignton**
- **St Erth - St Ives**
- **Plymouth - Gunnislake**

The web address for First Great Western High Speed and West services is **www.firstgreatwestern.co.uk**

To obtain train information, book tickets and reserve seats call the National Rail Enquiries Service on 08457 484950 (24 hours a day) or via the website **www.nationalrail.co.uk** or go to **www.thetrainline.com**

The web address for Arriva is **www.crosscountrytrains.co.uk**

The web address for South West Trains is **www.southwesttrains.co.uk**

Bus Services

A National Transport Enquiry Service has been established. For all timetable enquiries in South West England, call Traveline on 0871 200 2233 or www.travelinesw.com

Tourist Information Centres can be very helpful with bus enquiries. For details of all coastal TICs see our Accommodation section at the back of this book.

Access to the start of the Path

Access to the start of the path can be made locally and from outside the region, with a bus service linking Minehead to the mainline railway station at Taunton.

Airports

There are airports in or near towns close to the Coast Path. In path order, they are:

Newquay Airport

Daily flights from London Gatwick and year round flights from Manchester and Isles of Scilly. Many more seasonal destinations.
St Mawgan, Newquay TR8 4RQ
nqyinfo@newquaycornwallairport.com
Tel: 01637 860600
www.newquaycornwallairport.com

Land's End

For flights to the Isles of Scilly:
Information from Isles of Scilly Travel,
Steamship House, Quay Street,
Penzance TR18 4BZ
Tel: 0845 710 5555
www.islesofscilly-travel.co.uk

Exeter

Exeter International Airport,
Exeter, EX5 2BD
www.exeter-airport.co.uk

Bournemouth

Bournemouth Airport Ltd.,
Christchurch, Bournemouth BH23 6SE
Tel: 01202 364000
www.bournemouthairport.com

Sea Transport & Coastal Cruises

Brittany Ferries provide a ferry link as follows to the South West Coast Path:
Plymouth/Roscoff; Poole/Cherbourg (Not Dec - Feb); Plymouth/Santander.
Tel: 0871 244 0744
www.brittany-ferries.co.uk, or contact by mail to Brittany Ferries, Millbay, Plymouth, Devon, PL1 3EW

The famous pleasure steamers Waverley and Balmoral provide both cruises and transport, to and from the Exmoor Coast.

From May until September these sea-going ships provide transport to South Wales, Bristol, North Somerset, Lundy Island and the Exmoor Coast.

Sailings are to and from llfracombe & Minehead. The timetable is subject to the Bristol Channel tides which have the second highest rise and fall in the world. Free copies of the full programme are available from:
Waverley Excursions Ltd.,
The Waverley Terminal,
36 Lancefield Quay, Glasgow G3 8HA
www.waverleyexcursions.co.uk
Tel: 0845 1304647, or from Tourist Information Centres in West Somerset and North Devon.

View From Fowey Town Quay

Planning your walking holiday in the south west can be helped at www.travelinesw.com or telephone 0871 200 2233.

Private Branch Line Railways

Bishops Lydeard to Minehead

The West Somerset Railway runs steam trains through 20 scenic miles (32 km) to Minehead. Bishops Lydeard is 4 miles (6 km) outside Taunton and easily accessible by bus. The service operates between February & December. For details contact the company at 'The Railway Station', Minehead TA24 5BG Tel: 01643 704996 Book online at www.west-somerset-railway.co.uk

Paignton to Kingswear (Dartmouth)

For the rambler who is also a railway enthusiast, the Paignton and Dartmouth Steam Railway is a `must'. This most attractive line runs from Paignton to Goodrington, Churston and Kingswear and operates preserved Great Western steam locomotives and rolling-stock. The line passes through some delightful coastal and river scenery, and a trip on the railway could easily be combined with a walk to make a very pleasant day out. Steam trains operate on selected dates in Feb & March, April - Oct; Daily April to October; Santa specials in December. For details contact Queens Park Station, Torbay Road, Paignton TQ4 6AF Tel: 01803 555872 www.dartmouthrailriver.co.uk

The Bodmin & Wenford Railway

runs between Bodmin Parkway to Bodmin General is a service that could prove useful for those requiring bus transport to the coast. Tel: 01208 73555 www.bodminrailway.co.uk

The Swanage Railway

which links a large park and ride facility at Norden, north west of Corfe Castle to Swanage, could also prove useful for those requiring car parking (not long stay) with access by rail to the Coast Path. If you require information contact the enquiry line on Tel: 01929 425800 www.swanagerailway.co.uk

Bus Information

Listed below, in path order, are details of services and information available from County Councils and local bus operators; it is intended for guidance use only. All information provided is correct at the time of going to print; responsibility for any inaccuracies or changes cannot be accepted by County Councils or bus operators. For up to date bus service information, telephone the relevant numbers given in the following paragraphs.

Somerset

For service 28 from Taunton to Minehead and services 30/30A from Taunton to Lyme Regis and Weymouth via Axminster (change buses) contact First, The Bus Station, Tower Street, Taunton, TA1 4AF Tel: 0871 200 2233 www.firstgroup.com

For service 18 from Taunton to Minehead, service 10 from Minehead to Porlock contact sales@webberbus.com 0800 096 3039 or 01278 452086 www.webberbus.com

Somerset County Council produces booklets detailing the timetables of all public bus services in Somerset which can be downloaded at www.somerset.gov.uk/timetables, or requested from Transporting Somerset, County Hall, Taunton, TA1 4DY Tel: 0845 345 9155 Email: generalenquiries@somerset.gov.uk www.somerset.gov.uk

North Devon

The North Devon coast has a range of bus services which may be of use to coastal walkers. The greatest choice of coastal destinations is provided from Barnstaple.

First Devon & Cornwall's X9 service will help those walking between North Devon and North Cornwall.

For timetable enquiries telephone Traveline on 0871 200 2233 or go online at www.travelinesw.org.uk

Alternatively the Devon County Council web site has a variety of options. There is an interactive bus map to look at and also Area Bus Timetable Booklets to download:

www.journeydevon.info They do advise that previously printed timetables will vary from these digital guides, but that the digital guides are the most up to date.

If you find yourself at a bus stop and want to know when the next bus is coming along, find the 8 letter reference number on the stop and text it to 84268. You will receive a reply with the times of the next 3 buses to come past that stop.

Cornwall

Cornwall Council have an informative web site at www.cornwallpublictransport.info with up to date and full timetables and frequency guides for all the different operators. There are weekday, evening and weekend timetables. You can also call 0300 1234 222 if you prefer. On the site there is an Interactive Cornwall County Map, which shows all the bus lines and their numbers. All the main towns have bus routes to and from them but do check the times especially out of the main holiday times. We have not listed as much detail here as in previous years simply due to the changing nature of the timetables and technology making the information more readily available to people.

Also, use the information for Traveline - 0871 200 2233 or go online at www.travelinesw.org.uk

Other local operators are www.firstgroup.com or www.westerngreyhound.com (01637 871871). Their information is included on the Cornwall Council site too.

Stagecoach run service X9 from Exeter to Bude, if you are coming to the South West by train this may be useful.

South Devon

The coastline between Plymouth and Exeter is accessible by bus from many inland towns. As for North Devon, the Devon County Council web site has a variety of options. There is an interactive bus map to look at and also Area Bus Timetable Booklets to download: www.journeydevon.info Also as for North Devon, when you are at a bus stop, use the 8 letter reference number on the bus stop and text it to 84268. You will receive a reply with the times of the next 3 buses to come past that stop.

For more timetable enquiries telephone Traveline on 0871 200 2233 or go online at www.travelinesw.org.uk The main operators are Stagecoach, First Group and Tally Ho

For Plymouth Citybus map and services go to www.plymouth.gov.uk and follow links for the transport section.

East Devon

The East Devon coastline is accessible by bus from Exeter, Ottery St. Mary, Honiton and Axminster. Trains from London Waterloo stop at Axminster, Honiton & Exeter or the quicker train from London Paddington stops at Exeter as do trains coming from Bristol.

Please note, as previously, that the summer and winter timetables do vary a lot.

See the North and South Devon sections for web site and telephone number information.

Dorset

The Dorset Coast is accessible by bus from various inland points with train connections for the distant traveller. For a complete and up to date list of bus routes, timetables and bus numbers go to www.dorsetforyou.com and follow the links for Transport. You can download the timetables for local services whose operators are as follows - First Hampshire & Dorset 0870 010 6022, Damory Coaches 01258 452545, Wilts and Dorset Bus Company 0845 0727 093 and Yellow Buses 01202 636110.

There is also a helpful map of where to find the bus stops. The main towns from which the transports leaves are Lyme Regis, Weymouth, Poole, Dorchester, Swanage, Bournemouth and Wareham.

SOUTH WEST WATER

South West Water is delighted to team up with the South West Coast Path Association to support one of the region's major tourist attractions.

The South West Coast Path offers a fantastic walking experience, scenic views of some of Europe's cleanest beaches and coastal waters, as well as access to many of those beaches and waterways.

Over the last two decades we've undertaken a massive clean-up of Devon and Cornwall's bathing waters and this has helped to transform the fortunes of the tourism industry in the South West. We're spending more this year to deliver even cleaner seas at seven locations across our area.

Transforming our region's bathing waters from polluted seas 25 years ago to some of the finest beaches in Europe today has been our focus for a quarter of a century. We continue to make improvements to ensure we meet the ever-higher standards set by the European Union for bathing water cleanliness. But nowadays, we love seeing people enjoy the fruits of that work: walking the Coast Path, playing on the beaches, swimming in the sea and taking advantage of all the opportunities afforded by living or visiting our stunning coastline.

The South West Coast Path is the path to the sea, giving access and enjoyment to millions. It feels very natural for us to support the Association and help it go from strength to strength as it protects this precious asset for the future.

We look forward to helping to promote this jewel in the region's tourism crown and all the good work done by the Association.

Ferries & River Crossings

The nature of the Coast Path means that many ferries must be used to cross estuaries along the length of the path. It is recommended the ferry operator be contacted direct for the service to be used. Please do this especially when a fairly late timing is expected and it is necessary to confirm the time of the last run. Also do this when using outside the main tourist season or if use by a party of walkers is planned. Full ferry details are shown here. Less detailed ferry information is also included in the relevant Walk Section text.

The walker tends to view feet as the only certain method of progress - and why not? Unfortunately, the absolute purist would need to be an olympic-class swimmer not to have to use ferries on the South West Coast Path. However, a certain amount of scepticism is helpful, absolute reliance on ferries is not advised. There are other ferries available on the path which walkers may wish to use for diversions or shortcuts. We have attempted to list those directly necessary.

The ferry crossings encountered, in path order, are: River Torridge (Instow/Appledore) (optional); River Camel (Rock/Padstow); River Gannel (Newquay/Crantock); Helford River (Helford/Helford Passage); Fal Estuary (Falmouth/St Mawes and St Mawes/Place); River Fowey (Fowey/Polruan); River Tamar (Cremyll/Plymouth); River Yealm (Wembury/Noss Mayo); River Avon (Bigbury-on-Sea/Bantham); River Dart (Dartmouth/Kingswear); River Teign (Shaldon/Teignmouth); River Exe (Starcross/Exmouth, Turf/Topsham); Weymouth Harbour.

Instow/Appledore (River Torridge)

This ferry service, an optional means of crossing the Torridge without passing through Bideford, has recently been revived after many years. It runs generally for 2 hours either side of high tide.

Website: www.appledoreinstowferry.com
Email: contact@appledoreinstowferry.com

The ferry will operate from early April 2014 until October.

Water taxi

A water taxi service operates between Rock and Padstow between 19:00 and midnight from Easter to end October, weather and tides permitting.

Tel: 01208 862815 (9am to 5pm)
Website: www.rock-watertaxi.co.uk
Email: info@rock-watertaxi.co.uk
Or contact the boat direct on 07778 105297.

Newquay/Crantock (River Gannel)

Fern Pit Café & Ferry, Fern Pit, Riverside Crescent, Newquay, Cornwall TR7 1PJ
Tel: 01637 873181
Website: www.fernpit.co.uk
Email: mail@fernpit.co.uk

Ferry operates as follows: Mid May to mid September continuous, 7 days a week, 10:00-18:00. Weather dependant.

Gillan Creek

Anthony Jenkin Tel: 01326 231357
Ferry operates April 1st to October 31st on demand during normal office hours. It runs approx 3 hours either side of high tide when the stepping stones are submerged.
Website: www.stanthony.co.uk
Email: info@stanthony.co.uk

Helford River

River Boats, Helford Passage, Falmouth, Cornwall TR1 5HP Tel: 01326 250770
Website: www.helford-river-boats.co.uk
Email: ian@helford-river-boats.co.uk

Ferry operates Good Friday/1st April to 31st October 09:30 to 17:00 daily on demand. July & August ferry may run into the evening. It is possible to use local taxi services if the ferry is not operating. Autocabs, tel: 01326 573773 or Cove Cars, tel: 07980 814058.

Falmouth/St Mawes (River Fal)

Cornwall Ferries
Tel: 01326 741194
Website: www.falriver.co.uk

Ferry operates all year. June-October 3 ferries per hour, fewer at other times. Ferries operate from Falmouth Prince of Wales Pier all year and Custom House Quay summer only.

St Mawes/Place (Percuil River)

Cornwall Ferries (see above)
Tel: 01872 741194
www.falriver.co.uk

1 June - 30 September from 09:00 - 17:00 running every ½ hour, subject to demand. Falmouth Water Taxi service also operates between Falmouth and St Mawes or Place, weather permitting, between March and October, 9am - 6pm (until 10.30pm May-Sept). If needed, it is advisable to telephone 2-3 days in advance in the Summer.

Tel: 07522 446659.
www.falmouthwatertaxi.co.uk

St Mawes Kayaks also offer a water taxi service: Telephone 07971 846786 or visit www.stmayeskayaks.co.uk

Fowey/Polruan (River Fowey)

Polruan Ferry Co Ltd, Toms Yard, East Street
Polruan-by-Fowey, Cornwall PL23 1PB
Tel: 01726 870232

Ferry operates all year at 5-10 min intervals.
07:00 to 23:00 1st May-30th September
(Saturdays 07:30 start, Sundays 09:00 start)
07:00 to 19:00 1st October-30th April (Saturdays
07:30 start, Sundays 10:00 to 17:00).

Website: ctomsandson.co.uk
enquiries@ctomsandson.co.uk

Cremyll/Plymouth

Cremyll Ferry, Cremyll Quay, Cremyll,
Torpoint, Cornwall PL10 1HX
Tel: 07746 199508
Website: www.cremyll-ferry.co.uk

The ferry operates depending on weather,
tides and other circumstances permitting.
All year round at 30 minute intervals.

**Summer Service from 1st April to 30th
September.**
From Mt Edgcumbe:
Weekdays 06:45 to 20:30, Saturdays 08:00 to
21:30, Sundays 09:00 to 21:00.

From Plymouth:
Weekdays 07:15 to 20:45. Saturdays 08:15 to
21:45, Sundays 09:15 to 21:15.

**Winter Service from 1st October
to 31st March.**
From Mt Edgcumbe:
Weekdays 06:45 to 18:30. Saturdays
08:00 to 18:30, Sundays 09:00 to 18:00.

From Plymouth:
Weekdays 07:15 to 18:45, Saturdays
08:15 to 18:45, Sundays 09:15 to 18:15.

Closed Christmas, Boxing & New Year's Days

We urge you to contact the ferry operator
direct if you are relying on this service,
particularly if you are anticipating a fairly
late finish and need to confirm the time of its
last run.

Sutton Harbour/Mount Batten

Mount Batten Ferry 0751 537 0000
www.mountbattenferry.com
mountbattenferry@gmail.com

All year round, every ½ hour.
Summer weekdays 07:45 to 23:00, Saturday
08:45 to 22:30 and Sunday 08:45 - 18:15
Winter weekdays 07:45 - 18:15, Saturday
08:45 - 23:00 and Sunday 08:45 - 18:15

We urge you to contact the ferry operator direct
if you are relying on this service, particularly if
you are anticipating a fairly late finish and need
to confirm the time of its last run.

Wembury (Warren Point)/Noss Mayo (River Yealm)

Bill Gregor, Mobile: 07817 132757

Ferry operates the Monday before Good Friday
until last Sunday in Sept, 10:00 to 16:00.
In bad weather, school term-time & weekdays,
ferry may be restricted to 10:00 - 12:00 &
15:00 - 16:00, BUT use the signal board to call
ferry if required.
Eco-Taxi based in Kingsbridge will carry
walkers between Plymouth and Dartmouth
and from all estuaries in South Devon.
Tel: 07811 385275.

Alternatively, Ivy Cabs may also carry walkers
round the South Hams estuaries.
Tel: 01752 696969

Bigbury/Bantham (River Avon)

Marsh Dawes, The Boathouse,
Bantham, Kingsbridge, Devon.
Tel: 01548 561196 Mobile: 07837 361306

Ferry operates May - September, daily except
Sundays, 10:00 to 11:00 and 15:00 to 16:00.

Eco-Taxi based in Kingsbridge will carry
walkers between Plymouth and Dartmouth and
from all estuaries in South Devon.
Tel: 07811 385275

Alternatively, Ivy Cabs may also carry walkers
round the South Hams estuaries.
Tel: 01752 696969

Salcombe to East Portlemouth Ferry

The Salcombe Ferry
Tel: 01548 842061/560558
Simon Shortman

All year round on the hour and half hourly
when busy. Please note that the ferry point
is Jubilee Pier in summer & Whitestrand
Pontoon in winter. We urge you to contact the
ferry operator direct if you are relying on this
service, particularly if you are anticipating a
fairly late finish and need to confirm the time
of its last run.

Dartmouth/Kingswear (River Dart)

Sat Nav Codes - Kingswear TQ6 0AA.
Dartmouth TQ6 9AP
Tel: 01803 752342
www.southhams.gov.uk/
DartmouthLowerFerry
Email pat.webb@southhams.gov.uk

Ferry operates all year on a continuous service
07:00 to 22:45, Sundays 08:00 to 22:45

Ferries & River Crossings

Dartmouth Passenger Ferry (River Dart)

Dartmouth Steam Railway & River Boat Co.
5 Lower Street, Dartmouth TQ6 9AJ
Tel: 01803 555872
www.dartmouthrailriver.co.uk

Ferry operates all year on a continuous service 07:30 to 23:10, Sundays 09:00 to 23:10.

Check web for specific times.

Shaldon/Teignmouth

Ferry operated by Greg Allen.
Tel: 07896 711822
www.teignmouthshaldonferry.co.uk
Email: captgreg28@yahoo.com

April – mid July	08:00 to 18:00
Mid July – end August	08:00 to 20:30
September – October	08:00 to 18:00
*November – January	08:00 to 16:30
February – March	08:00 to 17:00

*Closed Mon & Tues in December & January

If operating, the ferry runs from the beach opposite the Ferry Boat Inn.

Starcross/Exmouth (River Exe)

Exe to Sea Cruises, Mr Mark Rackley
Tel: 01626 774770 / 07974 022536 / 07974 772681 / 07779 157280

Ferry operates mid-April – end October, hourly, 7 days a week. From Starcross,on the hour from 10:10 until 16:10, until 17:10 (mid-May to mid September). From Exmouth, on the half hour from 10:40 until 16:40 (Easter and October), until 17:40 (mid-May and June-mid September).

Turf/Topsham (River Exe)

Steve Garrett Tel: 07778 370582
www.topshamtoturfferry.co.uk
Email: seadreamferry@btinternet.com

Ferry operates weekends Easter - end May. Daily June – August. Weekends in September, from Turf 11:45 to 15:00 and from Topsham 11:30 to 14:15.

Topsham Ferry (River Exe) (between Topsham Quay riverside and Topsham Lock canalside)

Exeter City Council
Canals and Rivers Department
Tel: 01392 274306 (office); 07801 203338 (ferryman).

This service is tide dependant, please check tide times. Ferry operates Easter-September daily except Tuesdays, 9:30 to 17:00; October-March Saturdays, Sundays and Bank Holidays 11:00 to 17:00 or sunset. Wave or phone for service. Between April and September the ferry may be available outside these hours, weather and tides permitting; phone for details.

Weymouth Harbour

Weymouth and Portland Borough Council, Harbour Master's Office,
13 Custom House Quay, Weymouth DT4 8BG
Tel: 01305 838423

From April, Ferries operate (rowing boats), but are weather dependant.
www.harbour.weymouth.gov.uk

South Haven Point to Sandbanks, Poole

See end of Walk 70, page 130.

South Haven Point/Sandbanks

Shell Bay/Sandbanks
(Mouth of Poole Harbour) Bournemouth - Swanage Motor Road & Ferry Company,
Shell Bay, Studland BH19 3BA
Tel: 01929 450203 Fax: 01929 450498
www.sandbanksferry.co.uk

All year round. Daily every 20 mins.

Sandbanks 07:00 to 23:00 hrs

Shell Bay 07:10 to 23:10 hrs

Christmas Day every half hour.

If you are relying on a ferry service we urge you to contact the ferry operator direct, particularly if you anticpate a fairly late finish and need to confirm the time of its last run.

Tide Times

The tide tables included in this edition refer to the times of low water at Devonport.

These tables will act as a guide for those wishing to paddle across the Gannel (Newquay) or the Erme. Please be sure to read the warnings given under the relevant section in the Guide. Coast Path walkers are advised not to try to wade any of the other estuaries around the route, but for tide times at such locations walkers should consult the local tide tables, which are usually easily available.

Those crossing the Gannel or Erme should note that there can be considerable differences in tide heights between springs and neaps; these are not shown on the accompanying tables, which should be used for general timing guidance only. Again, details are available in tide tables locally.

- Newquay (The Gannel) deduct 30 minutes
- River Erme as at Devonport

The tidal information for the port of Devonport is reproduced by permission of the Controller of Her Majesty's Stationery Office and the UK Hydrographic Office (www.ukho.gov.uk) © British Crown copyright. All rights reserved.

March 2015 LOW WATER From 29th March add 1 hour for BST			
1	Sun	0859	2125
2	Mon	0958	2218
3	Tue	1045	2302
4	Wed	1126	2341
5	Thu		1203
6	Fri	0016	1237
7	Sat	0047	1305
8	Sun	0113	1329
9	Mon	0137	1352
10	Tue	0201	1415
11	Wed	0226	1442
12	Thu	0257	1516
13	Fri	0338	1602
14	Sat	0436	1712
15	Sun	0612	1900
16	Mon	0750	2027
17	Tue	0906	2138
18	Wed	1010	2237
19	Thu	1105	2329
20	Fri	1155	
21	Sat	0017	1242
22	Sun	0101	1325
23	Mon	0143	1405
24	Tue	0222	1443
25	Wed	0259	1519
26	Thu	0337	1558
27	Fri	0421	1645
28	Sat	0515	1745
29	Sun	0628	1907
30	Mon	0819	2048
31	Tue	0927	2146

April 2015 LOW WATER Add 1 hour for BST			
1	Weds	1014	2231
2	Thurs	1055	2310
3	Fri	1132	2346
4	Sat		1205
5	Sun	0017	1235
6	Mon	0046	1301
7	Tue	0113	1328
8	Wed	0140	1354
9	Thu	0209	1424
10	Fri	0242	1500
11	Sat	0324	1547
12	Sun	0423	1656
13	Mon	0551	1834
14	Tue	0726	2004
15	Wed	0844	2115
16	Thu	0947	2215
17	Fri	1043	2307
18	Sat	1132	2355
19	Sun		1218
20	Mon	0039	1302
21	Tue	0121	1342
22	Wed	0201	1420
23	Thu	0238	1456
24	Fri	0316	1535
25	Sat	0358	1619
26	Sun	0448	1713
27	Mon	0551	1821
28	Tue	0706	1939
29	Wed	0828	2052
30	Thu	0926	2145

Tide Times

		May 2015 *LOW WATER* Add 1 hour for BST				June 2015 *LOW WATER* Add 1 hour for BST	
1	Fri	1011	2229	1	Mon	1049	2311
2	Sat	1051	2308	2	Tues	1131	2352
3	Sun	1127	2344	3	Weds		1211
4	Mon		1201	4	Thurs	0033	1252
5	Tue	0018	1235	5	Fri	0114	1331
6	Wed	0052	1307	6	Sat	0155	1412
7	Thu	0125	1340	7	Sun	0237	1456
8	Fri	0159	1415	8	Mon	0324	1544
9	Sat	0237	1455	9	Tues	0416	1640
10	Sun	0322	1545	10	Weds	0519	1748
11	Mon	0421	1650	11	Thurs	0631	1904
12	Tue	0536	1812	12	Fri	0746	2019
13	Wed	0700	1936	13	Sat	0854	2125
14	Thu	0817	2049	14	Sun	0954	2222
15	Fri	0922	2150	15	Mon	1048	2314
16	Sat	1018	2244	16	Tues	1136	
17	Sun	1109	2333	17	Weds	0000	1221
18	Mon	1156		18	Thurs	0044	1303
19	Tue	0018	1240	19	Fri	0125	1341
20	Wed	0101	1321	20	Sat	0202	1416
21	Thu	0141	1359	21	Sun	0237	1450
22	Fri	0219	1436	22	Mon	0311	1525
23	Sat	0257	1513	23	Tues	0347	1602
24	Sun	0335	1553	24	Weds	0427	1648
25	Mon	0419	1640	25	Thurs	0519	1746
26	Tue	0512	1737	26	Fri	0620	1852
27	Wed	0613	1841	27	Sat	0724	1955
28	Thu	0717	1946	28	Sun	0825	2055
29	Fri	0820	2047	29	Mon	0922	2150
30	Sat	0916	2140	30	Tues	1015	2242
31	Sun	1004	2227				

		July 2015 *LOW WATER* Add 1 hour for BST				August 2015 *LOW WATER* Add 1 hour for BST	
1	Weds	1105	2331	1	Sat	0004	1227
2	Thurs	1153		2	Sun	0052	1313
3	Fri	0018	1240	3	Mon	0138	1357
4	Sat	0104	1324	4	Tues	0221	1439
5	Sun	0149	1408	5	Weds	0303	1521
6	Mon	0233	1452	6	Thurs	0346	1604
7	Tues	0318	1536	7	Fri	0431	1653
8	Weds	0404	1625	8	Sat	0525	1756
9	Thurs	0456	1721	9	Sun	0635	1919
10	Fri	0558	1830	10	Mon	0804	2047
11	Sat	0711	1949	11	Tues	0920	2153
12	Sun	0828	2103	12	Weds	1017	2244
13	Mon	0935	2205	13	Thurs	1105	2330
14	Tues	1031	2259	14	Fri	1147	
15	Weds	1120	2346	15	Sat	0010	1227
16	Thurs		1205	16	Sun	0048	1301
17	Fri	0029	1246	17	Mon	0120	1331
18	Sat	0108	1323	18	Tues	0147	1357
19	Sun	0143	1355	19	Weds	0211	1419
20	Mon	0214	1425	20	Thurs	0232	1441
21	Tues	0243	1453	21	Fri	0254	1508
22	Weds	0309	1520	22	Sat	0325	1544
23	Thurs	0337	1551	23	Sun	0408	1640
24	Fri	0413	1636	24	Mon	0518	1821
25	Sat	0509	1749	25	Tues	0704	1948
26	Sun	0629	1909	26	Weds	0821	2057
27	Mon	0743	2018	27	Thurs	0927	2159
28	Tues	0848	2121	28	Fri	1026	2255
29	Weds	0949	2219	29	Sat	1120	2347
30	Thurs	1045	2313	30	Sun		1210
31	Fri	1137		31	Mon	0035	1256

Tide Times

September 2015 LOW WATER Add 1 hour for BST			
1	Tues	0120	1340
2	Weds	0203	1421
3	Thurs	0243	1501
4	Fri	0323	1541
5	Sat	0404	1627
6	Sun	0454	1725
7	Mon	0600	1850
8	Tues	0739	2032
9	Weds	0903	2136
10	Thurs	0958	2225
11	Fri	1044	2307
12	Sat	1124	2346
13	Sun		1201
14	Mon	0021	1235
15	Tues	0051	1303
16	Weds	0116	1327
17	Thurs	0138	1349
18	Fri	0159	1411
19	Sat	0223	1438
20	Sun	0253	1514
21	Mon	0334	1604
22	Tues	0435	1735
23	Weds	0627	1921
24	Thurs	0757	2036
25	Fri	0907	2139
26	Sat	1007	2235
27	Sun	1100	2326
28	Mon	1149	
29	Tues	0013	1236
30	Weds	0059	1319

October 2015 LOW WATER Add 1 hour until 25th October			
1	Thurs	0140	1400
2	Fri	0220	1440
3	Sat	0259	1519
4	Sun	0339	1603
5	Mon	0426	1658
6	Tues	0527	1814
7	Weds	0656	2001
8	Thurs	0832	2107
9	Fri	0929	2156
10	Sat	1014	2237
11	Sun	1054	2315
12	Mon	1131	2349
13	Tues		1203
14	Weds	0018	1232
15	Thurs	0045	1259
16	Fri	0110	1324
17	Sat	0134	1350
18	Sun	0201	1420
19	Mon	0234	1457
20	Tues	0315	1548
21	Weds	0414	1710
22	Thurs	0553	1853
23	Fri	0731	2011
24	Sat	0844	2116
25	Sun	0945	2212
26	Mon	1038	2303
27	Tues	1128	2351
28	Weds		1214
29	Thurs	0036	1258
30	Fri	0118	1340
31	Sat	0158	1420

November 2015 LOW WATER Add 1 hour for BST			
1	Sun	0237	1500
2	Mon	0317	1542
3	Tues	0401	1632
4	Weds	0455	1735
5	Thurs	0604	1856
6	Fri	0731	2019
7	Sat	0843	2114
8	Sun	0934	2158
9	Mon	1017	2237
10	Tues	1055	2313
11	Weds	1130	2345
12	Thurs		1203
13	Fri	0016	1235
14	Sat	0047	1306
15	Sun	0118	1338
16	Mon	0150	1413
17	Tues	0226	1453
18	Weds	0309	1544
19	Thurs	0406	1654
20	Fri	0525	1821
21	Sat	0658	1941
22	Sun	0815	2049
23	Mon	0920	2148
24	Tues	1016	2241
25	Weds	1107	2330
26	Thurs	1155	
27	Fri	0016	1240
28	Sat	0059	1323
29	Sun	0140	1403
30	Mon	0218	1442

December 2015 LOW WATER Add 1 hour for BST			
1	Tues	0257	1522
2	Weds	0336	1605
3	Thurs	0422	1655
4	Fri	0517	1754
5	Sat	0621	1902
6	Sun	0732	2009
7	Mon	0836	2105
8	Tues	0929	2153
9	Weds	1015	2235
10	Thurs	1057	2315
11	Fri	1137	2353
12	Sat		1216
13	Sun	0031	1254
14	Mon	0108	1333
15	Tues	0146	1412
16	Weds	0225	1454
17	Thurs	0309	1541
18	Fri	0359	1637
19	Sat	0501	1746
20	Sun	0618	1905
21	Mon	0741	2020
22	Tues	0854	2125
23	Weds	0956	2222
24	Thurs	1050	2313
25	Fri	1140	
26	Sat	0000	1226
27	Sun	0044	1309
28	Mon	0124	1349
29	Tues	0202	1425
30	Weds	0237	1500
31	Thurs	0311	1535

Easing the Load

Budleigh Salterton

On long trips it is a good idea to:

Send guides, maps etc. ahead to larger post offices Poste Restante.

The only snag is if you arrive on a Saturday evening.

Start out with a few map-sized envelopes and the smallest available roll of sellotape so that you can despatch finished guides, maps, books etc. home.

Kit Transfer

Coast Path walking can be arduous in places but some of the hard work can be eliminated. One of the harder tasks can be having to carry a heavy pack from one B&B to the next. There are, however, potential ways around this. For transfer of kit anywhere on the Coast Path, the Association has an agreement with Luggage Transfers Ltd.

Luggage Transfers South West

Luggage Transfers Ltd, started in 2008 by two SWCPA members, moves up to 10,000 bags a month for walkers on the Coast Path, and is the only comprehensive service covering the entire Path.

The large volume of deliveries means that they can combine and "daisy chain" transfers which has kept the cost of the service low at an average of £8 for each bag movement. The effect of volume delivery also saves an estimated 200 tons of carbon emissions each season.

In addition, Luggage Transfers encourages walkers to donate 25p per transfer to the Association in order to raise funds for the Path. It also encourages its accommodation providers to become Business Members of the Association, which brings us a membership fee to be used for Path improvements. In return, Business Members get an enhanced entry in the accommodation list of the Annual Guide and on the website. Try and use them if you can to repay their support for us.

To book your luggage transfers with them, go to their website at www.luggagetransfers.co.uk. Alternatively, click on the accommodation list at the Association's own website. For telephone enquiries, call 01326 567247. The office is open 9.00am to 7.00pm 7 days a week from March until October inclusive, and office hours November until February.

Walking Holiday Companies

For those who require a Coast Path walk without carrying rucksacks and have their accommodation fixed in advance there are several businesses that will arrange everything. All you have to do is let them know your requirements and pay them. Also there are some excellent organisations that run walking holidays with guides. The South West Coast Path Association realised that there are too many to be listed in this guide so we have now listed them on our web site at www.southwestcoastpath.org.uk

The Countryside Code

- Be safe - plan ahead and follow any signs
- Leave gates and property as you find them
- Protect plants and animals, and take your litter home
- Keep dogs under close control
- Consider other people

Because our Coast Path is so special and so popular, it is important to treat it with care and to use it in an environmentally sensitive way by employing the following principles:

- Use guidebooks and information
- Keep to the path to minimise erosion
- Report problems to the South West Coast Path Association
- Always consider the interests of landowners and other users
- Take special care where the Coast Path is routed onto roads

Supporting Local Businesses

- Use public transport to reach the path wherever possible
- Support local shops and services

Website News

Any news concerning the state of the Coast Path received after this book is printed will be published in newsletters and on our web site www.southwestcoastpath.org.uk

Coast Path Safety Advice

Your safety is your responsibility - please look after yourself and other members of your group. Keep to the path and stay away from cliff edges - please follow advisory signs and waymarks. Supervise children and dogs - please look out for your children and pets at all times. Be prepared and well equipped - wear suitable clothing and footwear and be ready for possible changes in the weather.

Stay within your capabilities - some sections of the Coast Path can be strenuous and/or remote. In an emergency dial 999 and ask for the coastguard.

Weather

The South West Coast Path is more exposed to wind than any other long distance trail, so please pay attention to gale forecasts as well as rain. Along some sections, strong winds can be dangerous, especially when rounding exposed headlands and crossing bridges; a high backpack can act like a sail.

Always use sun protection especially on bright cloudy or breezy days when the risk of sunburn seems lower.

Detailed local forecasts are available from the UK Meteorological Office on 0870 900 0100 (24 hours) or www.metoffice.gov.uk/weather/uk

Military Ranges

Two lengths of the Coast Path may be affected by the use or otherwise of military ranges. The use of one, at Tregantle in south east Cornwall, only means that a more inland and less pleasant route must be used for a length of some 1.25 miles/2km in Section 46, Portwrinkle-Cremyll (Plymouth Ferry). However, if there is military use of the other, east of Lulworth Cove in Dorset, this means the whole of Section 67 between Lulworth Cove and Kimmeridge Bay will be impossible. Generally the Lulworth ranges are closed to walkers Monday to Friday during school term time and also up to six times a year at weekends. Try to arrange your walk so as not to miss this superb but tough section.

Information details for the ranges are included in the relevant Section descriptions.

Safety & Other Advice

Telephones

Mobile phones sometimes will not work in remote places and it's reassuring to see a public telephone box just when you need it. However, many of these remote telephones have recently been converted to only take debit cards. You can use the following cards in these boxes - Switch; Maestro; Delta; Solo; Visa Debit but not Electron. There are still some telephone boxes which will accept BT Phonecards and all boxes will accept BT Chargecards (these are only available to BT landline customers). Mobile phones are always useful to have whilst on the Coast Path. However, do not rely on them as coverage is not always good in the South West. You may also have difficulty in obtaining top-up in some areas.

Banks

There are small Post Offices in most villages. Overseas visitors, we suggest, will find their cashpoint cards very useful. ATM machines are widely available along the Coast Path and can be sourced at www.link.co.uk/ atmlocator/Pages/ATMLocator.aspx

Dogs

1. Beaches

Most district councils and unitary authorities have implemented dog bans on beaches generally from 1st May to 31st October. Our Association and most of the general public regard this as a sensible measure.

There are several sections of the South West Coast Path that cross beaches and are officially marked as such. These beaches are Croyde Bay in Devon, Harlyn Bay, Constantine, Treyarnon, Perranporth and Penberth slipway in Cornwall, and Studland in Dorset. The routing of the Coast Path (with its designation as a National Trail) across these beaches means that they are public rights of way. A public right of way DOES carry precedence over seasonal regulations banning dogs, and ultimately any walker in the process of walking along, but not stopping on, these sections of the path may be accompanied by a dog under TOTAL control.

However we strongly recommend the following:

a) If an alternative route is provided and signposted, that you use it.

b) That residents near to dog ban beaches use other walks and do not use the beach path during the ban period.

c) Total control means that the dog should be on a short (not extendable) lead.

d) That your progress should be as unobtrusive as possible to other beach users. To aid this, close attention should be paid to the actual route marked on the map.

e) Lastly, but most importantly, should the worst happen, any dog mess MUST be removed from the beach.

2. Along the Coast Path

Many walk the Coast Path with their dogs and all have an enjoyable time and we receive many reports of dogs completing the whole path.

However we do urge caution because the Coast Path is very high along many sections, and it takes only an excited dog to go chasing after a rabbit, to cause much grief if it goes over the edge. If your dog is well-trained and you can trust it, then please enjoy your Coast Path walk with your four-legged friend. If it is not and you cannot, then do take care.

Many sections along the South West Coast Path will have farm livestock grazing.

Again, walkers should maintain proper control of their dogs.

Important - Please Note

Information included or available through the South West Coast Path Association (SWCPA) is given in good faith and is believed to be accurate and correct at the time of going to print – however it cannot be guaranteed not to include inaccuracies or typographical errors.

Advice received via the SWCPA should not be relied upon for personal decisions and you should take into account the weather and your own capabilities before following the walks set out in this Guide. It is for the individual concerned to weigh up the risks of each of the walks described in this book.

The SWCPA makes no representations about the suitability of walks to any one person and will accept no liability for any loss or damage suffered as a result of relying on this book; it should be used for guidance only.

In no event shall the SWCPA be liable for any personal injury or any loss suffered as a result of using this publication.

Week 1 (Seven days)			
Day	Distance		From - to
1	10mi	15km	Minehead - Porlock Weir
			Take National Rail main line to Taunton; bus Taunton - Minehead; or National Express coach to Minehead
2	12mi	20km	Porlock Weir - Lynton
3	13mi	21km	Lynton - Combe Martin
4	13mi	20km	Combe Martin - Woolacombe
5	16mi	27km	Woolacombe - Braunton
6	12mi	20km	Braunton - Instow
7	11mi	18km	Instow - Westward Ho!
Total	87mi	141km	*Take bus Westward Ho! - Barnstaple; train Barnstaple - Exeter; National Rail main line from Exeter; or National Express coach from Westward Ho!*

Week 2 (Seven days)			
Day	Distance		From - to
1	11mi	18km	Westward Ho! - Clovelly
			National Rail main line to Exeter; train Exeter - Barnstaple; bus Barnstaple - Westward Ho!; or National Express coach to Westward Ho!
2	10mi	16km	Clovelly - Hartland Quay
3	15mi	25km	Hartland Quay - Bude
4	10mi	16km	Bude - Crackington Haven
5	11mi	18km	Crackington Haven - Tintagel
6	9mi	15km	Tintagel - Port Isaac
7	12mi	19km	Port Isaac - Padstow
Total	78mi	127km	*Bus to Bodmin Parkway; National Rail main line from Bodmin Parkway.*

Week 3 (Six days)			
Day	Distance		From - to
1	14mi	22km	Padstow - Porthcothan
			National Rail main line to Bodmin Parkway; bus Bodmin Parkway - Padstow
2	11mi	18km	Porthcothan - Newquay
3	11mi	18km	Newquay - Perranporth
4	12mi	20km	Perranporth - Portreath
5	12mi	20km	Portreath - Hayle
6	6mi	9km	Hayle - St Ives
Total	66mi	107km	*Train St Ives-St Erth; National Rail main line from St Erth; or National Express coach from St Ives.*

Week 4 (Six days)			
Day	Distance		From - to
1	14mi	22km	St Ives - Pendeen Watch
			National Rail main line to St Erth; train St Erth - St Ives; or National Express coach to St Ives
2	9mi	15km	Pendeen Watch - Sennen Cove
3	12mi	19km	Sennen Cove - Lamorna Cove
4	9mi	15km	Lamorna Cove - Marazion
5	11mi	17km	Marazion - Porthleven
6	13mi	22km	Porthleven - Lizard
Total	68mi	110km	*Bus Lizard Town - Helston; bus Helston - Redruth; National Rail main line from Redruth*

It is possible to use one accommodation base in summer between St Ives and Marazion as summer bus service 300 travels in a circuit both ways around the Land's End peninsula. See page 15 Local Transport.

Suggested Itineraries

Week 5 (Six days)

Day	Distance		From - to
1	11mi	17km	Lizard - Coverack *National Rail main line to Redruth; bus Redruth-Helston; bus Helston - Lizard Town*
2	13mi	21km	Coverack - Helford
3	10mi	16km	Helford - Falmouth
4	14mi	22km	Falmouth - Portloe
5	12mi	20km	Portloe - Mevagissey
6	12mi	19km	Mevagissey - Par
Total	72mi	115km	*National Rail main line from Par*

Week 6 (Seven days)

Day	Distance		From - to
1	13mi	21km	Par - Polperro *National Rail main line to Par*
2	12mi	20km	Polperro - Portwrinkle
3	13mi	21km	Portwrinkle - Plymouth
4	15mi	24km	Plymouth - Wembury (ferry crossing)
5	14mi	22km	Wembury (ferry crossing) - Bigbury on Sea
6	14mi	22km	Bigbury on Sea - Salcombe
7	13mi	21km	Salcombe - Torcross
Total	94mi	151km	*Bus Torcross - Plymouth; National Rail main line or National Express coach from Plymouth*

Week 7 (Six days)

Day	Distance		From - to
1	10mi	16km	Torcross - Dartmouth *National rail main line or National Express coach to Plymouth; bus Plymouth - Torcross*
2	11mi	17km	Dartmouth - Brixham
3	11mi	17km	Brixham - Babbacombe
4	16mi	27km	Babbacombe - Exmouth
5	13mi	21km	Exmouth - Sidmouth
6	11mi	17km	Sidmouth - Seaton (Devon)
Total	72mi	115km	*Bus Seaton - Exeter; National Rail main line or National Express Coach from Exeter*

Week 8 (Seven days)

Day	Distance		From - to
1	14mi	23km	Seaton (Devon) - Seatown (Dorset) *National Rail main line or National Express coach to Exeter; bus Exeter - Seaton.*
2	12mi	19km	Seatown (Dorset) - Abbotsbury
3	11mi	17km	Abbotsbury - Ferry Bridge (Wyke Regis)
4	13mi	21km	Isle of Portland
5	14mi	23km	Ferry Bridge (Wyke Regis) - Lulworth Cove
6	14mi	23km	Lulworth Cove - Worth Matravers
7	14mi	22km	Worth Matravers - South Haven Point (Poole Harbour)
Total	92	148km	*Ferry South Haven Point-Sandbanks; bus Sandbanks-Poole or Bournemouth; National Rail main line or National Express coach from Poole or Bournemouth.*

www.southwestcoastpath.org.uk

Other breakdowns are obviously possible, although the above is probably the best one for individual full weeks. A good alternative to use with direct nationwide public transport access at both ends of each stage would be:-

- **Stage 1:** Minehead to Barnstaple (68 miles/110km)
- **Stage 2:** Barnstaple to Bude (56 miles/90km)
- **Stage 3:** Bude to St Ives (108 miles/174km)
- **Stage 4:** St Ives to Falmouth (103 miles/165km)
- **Stage 5:** Falmouth to Plymouth (81 miles/131km)
- **Stage 6:** Plymouth to Exmouth (98 miles/158km)
- **Stage 7:** Exmouth to Weymouth (60 miles/97km)
- **Stage 8:** Weymouth to Poole (via Portland) (56 miles/90km)

Those interested in devising their own lengths might wish to know the locations of train access points on the Coast Path. On the national network, these are at Barnstaple (branch line from Exeter), Newquay (branch line from Par), St Ives (branch line from St Erth), Penzance, Falmouth (branch line from Truro), Par, Looe (branch line from Liskeard), Plymouth, Paignton, Torquay, Teignmouth, Dawlish, Exmouth (branch line from Exeter), Weymouth and Poole (for access to South Haven Point). Other locations are served during the summer by private railways, usually with steam-powered trains – Minehead (West Somerset Railway), Kingswear and Paignton (Dartmouth Steam Railway) and Swanage (Swanage Railway).

Reporting Problems on the Path

Be our Eyes and Ears on the Ground

With 630 miles of path to cover, it is impossible for the path wardens and rangers or the Association's local representatives to keep up with everything on the path at all times. So, if you encounter any problems, be they broken or missing signposts or waymarks, broken stiles or gates, real difficulties with the path surface, or anything else you think we should know about, contact us at our office address or phone number on page 3, or e-mail us. We will get in touch with the relevant path ranger with your concerns.

Wembury Bay looking to Plymouth

Around the South West Coast Path

Background

The South West Coast Path is one of the "family" of National Trails. It is generally well signposted and waymarked, using the National Trail symbol of the acorn. In some parts of the Coast Path waymarking relates to the local environment, for example the use of granite waymarks in parts of West Cornwall and Purbeck stone signs in Dorset. Be sure when walking the route to follow any such directions on the ground rather than relying on literature - things change over time, even including the route of the South West Coast Path, literature can become out-of-date.

Those who set out to walk all or any of this beautiful trail should remember that much of it is a cliff-top path - in places a very high cliff top. Those who manage the Coast Path want to keep it safe, but walkers should be reminded that it is unwise to leave the path at any point on the seaward side. Sometimes the edges of cliff tops away from the path can be unstable and unsafe.

Now and again the descriptions suggest an alternative path away from the officially designated route. These alternatives will themselves follow rights of way or, occasionally, "permitted routes" maintained by the landowner for use by the public. They are suggested for a more scenic and enjoyable experience than the formal route.

Once again, the Association stresses that ANYONE USING THE PATH SHOULD NOT WANDER OFF IT, ESPECIALLY ON THE SEAWARD SIDE. TO DO SO WOULD BE PUTTING YOURSELF AND POSSIBLY OTHERS IN DANGER OF SEVERE PERSONAL INJURY, OR EVEN DEATH.

 Always follow the National Trail Waymark.

That said, the South West Coast Path is a wonderful environment enjoyed by millions. Choose a length, long or short, and undertake one of the greatest walking experiences the country has to offer.

The Environment of the South West Coast Path

The South West Coast Path is one of the country's National Trails; it is, indeed, the longest of them at 630 miles/1,105km. In common with all National Trails, the Coast Path passes through an outstanding environment. In the Coast Path's case, this outstanding environment is recognised by the large number of formal designations throughout its length. These include both international and national designations.

International Designations

i. North Devon Biosphere Reserve

Biosphere Reserves are places with world-class environments designated by UNESCO to promote and demonstrate a balanced relationship between nature and people. They are places where conservation and sustainable development go hand in hand. North Devon is a UNESCO Biosphere Reserve because of its blend of special landscapes and wildlife areas, rich cultural heritage and communities that care about it and want to sustain it into the future. The core area of the Biosphere Reserve is at Braunton Burrows (Section 7 of the Trail Descriptions following), but including the outer areas the Reserve covers the Coast Path between Lynmouth and Marsland Mouth (Sections 3-13).

ii. Cornwall and West Devon Mining Landscape World Heritage Site

World Heritage Sites are designated by UNESCO for their "Outstanding Universal Value". This World Heritage Site is defined by the mining landscape which was formed by the cultural tradition of non-ferrous hard-rock mining. It contributed to developing the Industrial Revolution in Britain and pioneered its transfer overseas. The designation covers ten distinct areas, of which five relate to the Coast Path. These are the St Agnes Mining District (Section 24), the Port of Hayle (Sections 25 and 26), the St Just Mining District (Sections 27 and 28), the Tregonning and Gwinear Mining District with Trewavas (Section 32) and the Luxulyan Valley and Charlestown (Section 41).

iii. Jurassic Coast World Heritage Site

This was England's first World Heritage Site designated for its natural properties. Is it designated as it clearly depicts a geological "walk through time" of 185 million years of Earth's history in 95 miles/152km. Geological history of the Triassic, Jurassic and Cretaceous periods are successively exposed and are accessible over the length of the Site, which stretches between Exmouth and Swanage (Sections 58-70).

Around the South West Coast Path

National Designations

Most of the South West Coast Path is covered by the national landscape designations of National Park or Area of Outstanding Natural Beauty (AONB). In landscape terms these designations are regarded as equal, representing the country's finest landscapes.

i. **Exmoor National Park**
   Minehead - Combe Martin (Sections 1-3).

ii. **North Devon AONB**
   Combe Martin - Marsland Mouth, excluding Ilfracombe, the Taw-Torridge Estuary and Westward Ho! (Sections 4-8, 11-13).

iii. **Cornwall AONB**
   The entire coast of Cornwall, excluding Bude and its environs, Polzeath and Rock, Carnewas - Newquay, Gwithian - St Ives, Newlyn - Marazion, Charlestown - Par and Looe - Rame Head (Sections 13-25, 27-44, 46).

iv. **South Devon AONB**
   Plymouth - Brixham (Sections 48-54).

v. **East Devon AONB**
   Exmouth - Lyme Regis, excluding Sidmouth and Beer - Seaton (Sections 58-61).

vi. **Dorset AONB**
   The entire coast of Dorset, excluding Weymouth - Portland (Sections 62-64, 66-70). The South Dorset Ridgeway (Section 71) also falls within this designation.

The Landscape of the South West Coast Path

The wealth of landscape and environmental designations outlined above gives some idea of the quality of the landscape through which the South West Coast Path passes. However, this hides the fact there is a wide range of landscape types to be experienced. For those not over-familiar with the South West, we have divided the Coast Path into seven areas, shown on the map on page 2, and noted on each of the Section descriptions. This will help to pinpoint geographically the various path Sections, but can also be used to describe the path's landscapes.

The various areas are identified by using a colour coding system as shown on the map on page 2 and set out in the Contents page 5. The colour code is used on the corner tabs of the Walk Sections, the title information and the page numbers.

i. Exmoor

Minehead - Combe Martin (Sections 1-3)

The Exmoor length is characterised by two main landscape types. The first is the meeting of the rolling expanse of high moorland and the sea. The coastline itself is one of high cliffs, some of them among the highest sea cliffs in England, but this height is sometimes disguised by the cliffs' convex shape, usually referred to as "hog's back". Views are often extensive inland, over the undulating moorland, while seaward in good visibility the coast of Wales may be seen across the Bristol Channel. In contrast, substantial lengths of the Exmoor coast comprise deep and steep valleys cutting across the high land. These valleys, locally known as "combes", are typically wooded, often with ancient oak woodland. Often this woodland spreads along the adjacent cliff faces, also convex in shape. Views from the Coast Path here are inevitably less extensive, and sometimes quite limited by the woodland, but the nature of the ancient woodland makes for an environment of considerable ecological interest. The combes and the height of the cliffs in this length result in some notable gradients in places.

ii. North Devon

Combe Martin - Marsland Mouth (Sections 4-13)

Most of the North Devon coast faces north over the Bristol Channel. Much of this length comprises cliffs of moderate height with, in the east, some prominent headlands like Morte Point and Baggy Point which offer fine coastal vistas. In the centre of this length is the large joint estuary of the Taw and Torridge Rivers, flanked by areas of sand dunes and marshland. Adjacent to the estuary and just east of it are extensive sandy beaches, popular with surfers and families. Seascapes typically have the coast of Wales beyond the Bristol Channel as the backdrop in the east of this length. In the centre and west the offshore island of Lundy, at the "mouth" of the Bristol Channel, is the focal point. At the west end of this length is Hartland Point, one of the Coast Path's major headlands (referred to as the Point of Hercules in a Roman geography). It marks an abrupt change in direction from the east-west typical of most of North Devon (and Exmoor) to the north-south length beyond. This north-south length is very dramatic, with high cliffs fronted by jagged fingers of rock stretching into the Atlantic. Deep and steep valleys cut into this coastline, but there are no bays or harbours – an historic attempt to make a harbour at Hartland Quay was foiled by the elements. This is a section of great atmosphere.

iii. North Cornwall

Marsland Mouth – Portreath (Sections 13-24)

This section of coast trends either north-south or north east-south west. As such, it faces the prevailing Atlantic westerlies, making for a sometimes exposed landscape. This is exacerbated by the fact that much of the length comprises high cliffs, often quite sheer, with prominent headlands giving excellent coastal vistas. In places the feet of these cliffs are fronted by extensive sandy beaches, as north of Bude or at Watergate and Perran Beaches, north and south of Newquay. The cliff line is also punctuated by numerous sandy coves. There are also two main breaches in the cliff where river estuaries reach the sea, the Camel at Padstow and the Gannel at Newquay. These estuaries are also flanked by extensive sandy beaches. The uncompromising nature of the cliffs means there are few ports or harbours. Padstow, sheltered within the Camel estuary, is an ancient port and Newquay has a medieval origin, sheltered behind the promontory of Towan Head. Newquay has now, of course, expanded into a major holiday centre. Smaller 19th century harbours at the north-east end at Bude, originally largely based on its canal, and at the south-west end at Portreath, originally based on exporting mineral ores, have also expanded into tourism centres. These are very much exceptional settlements on this coast.

iv. West Cornwall

Portreath - Falmouth (Sections 25-37)

Most of this part of the coast is occupied by the two great peninsulas of Penwith, the westernmost part of England, and the Lizard, the southernmost. Both are composed of hard, resistant rocks making for a rugged cliff coastline, but their characters differ. Penwith is largely granite and inland of its impressive cliffs, frequently marked by rock pinnacles and solid jointed slabs, is a rough semi-moorland landscape. The Lizard has a much smoother profile, with its inland landscape an unusual flat-topped plateau.

The exposed locations of these two peninsulas result in harsh, weather-beaten coastlines with a lack of large-scale tree cover, though both are magnificently dramatic. Only on the eastern, lee side of the Lizard does the coastline become a little more lush. Flanking these two peninsulas are lower, more sheltered lengths – St Ives Bay on the north-east side of Penwith, Mount's Bay between Penwith and the Lizard and the Helford and Fal estuaries east of the Lizard. It is in these sheltered areas the only ports and harbours of any size are found, principally Penzance and Falmouth.

v. South Cornwall

Falmouth - the Tamar (Sections 38-46)

The South Cornwall stretch of coast is relatively sheltered being either south-east or south-facing and being largely in the lee of the large peninsula of the Lizard. Cliffs of moderate height are found along most of the length, and there are numerous intimate little bays and some quite prominent headlands. In the eastern half of the length the coast is cut by wooded river valleys, at Fowey, Looe and Seaton. In the centre is the major feature of St Austell Bay, the only part that lacks the otherwise ubiquitous cliffs. This bay also has the only major length of coastal development in South Cornwall, based on the town of St Austell and its extensions. Elsewhere, small ancient fishing ports such as Mevagissey, Fowey and Looe are scattered along the coast, all of them very picturesque. Major estuaries, of the Fal and Tamar, mark the two ends, each of them of great historic maritime importance.

vi. South Devon

Plymouth - Lyme Regis (Sections 47-61)

This section of coast may be conveniently subdivided into three landscape types. In the west, between the Rivers Tamar and Dart, is an area of largely slate cliffs, sometimes quite rugged, these being cut by the drowned mouths of wooded river valleys. This area is usually referred to as the South Hams and extends south to the major headland of Prawle Point, west of this headland being relatively exposed and the east of it much more sheltered. To the east, between the Dart and the Exe, is an area of low, mostly red sandstone cliffs. This length, the "Riviera", is largely occupied by towns based on tourism such as Paignton, Torquay, Teignmouth and

Dawlish, and being east-facing is mainly sheltered. Much of this length presents an almost continuously developed coastline. Further east still, between the Exe and the Dorset border at Lyme Regis, the cliffs rise again. This section, East Devon, has a slightly different character to the rest of the south coast of Devon. The red sandstone cliffs continue across the Exe for a while. Then, halfway along the East Devon coast, chalk and greensand make for a change in the landscape, to a mixture of white cliffs and extensive undercliffs and landslips. South Devon has many holiday resorts, some of the earliest in the country such as Exmouth and Teignmouth, some famed for their elegance such as Torquay, and some based on historic towns and villages such as Dartmouth and Beer. The biggest urban area of all on the South West Coast Path is Plymouth. Its historic importance is, of course, largely based on the Royal Navy.

vii. Dorset

Lyme Regis - South Haven Point (Poole Harbour) (Sections 62-70)

South Dorset Ridgeway (Section 71)

Geology is both the curse and the boon of the Dorset part of the South West Coast Path. As a curse, the geology means the Dorset cliffs are vulnerable to slippage, especially at the western end. This has meant that several diversions, necessary but hardly ideal, have had to be put in place for the Coast Path. The Marine and Coastal Access Act 2010 may help resolve some of these issues. Under its provisions, work is proceeding along the entire English coast to identify an appropriate coastal path and associated access room. In the South West, only the area between Portland and Lulworth has been addressed so far under this programme but work has now started on the remainder of Dorset. It is hoped that replacement and alternative routes will be established as a result of this work where cliff falls have severed the Coast Path. Initial proposals are expected during 2015. However, as a boon, Dorset's exposed and accessible layers of geological history have made it a textbook example for a wide range of coastal features. These features are also landscape highlights – the great shingle bar of Chesil Beach backed by the semi-freshwater lagoon of the Fleet; the fortress-like monolith of the Isle of Portland, jutting into the English Channel; the textbook arch of Durdle Door; the erosion of soft rock once the harder limestone has been broken through forming hollowed-out bays, as at Lulworth Cove; the offshore Purbeck stone stacks at Handfast Point. Inland, the rolling green hills evoke the spirit and landscape of Thomas Hardy, a worthy addition to the range of South West Coast Path landscapes.

Combe Martin

Section by Section

Key to Walk Descriptions

Based on the Suggested Itinerary on page 27, the South West Coast Path has been divided into 70 Sections. Each Section represents a day's or half-day's walk of the Itinerary. However, it must be emphasised that these Sections should not be confined to use by those walking long stretches of the Coast Path. Each Section is designed to be used on its own as a one-off if so wished, as well as by those planning long walks of several days. The Sections are arranged in anti-clockwise order, from Minehead to Poole, with an additional Section 71 for the alternative inland South Dorset Ridgeway.

Each Section entry follows in the following format:

Distance – length of the Section in miles and kilometres;

Cumulative distance – total length of the Coast Path from Minehead to the end of the Section in miles and kilometres;

Ascent – height climbed during the Section in feet and metres;

Cumulative ascent – total height climbed on the Coast Path from Minehead to the end of the Section in feet and metres;

Grading – each Section is graded as Easy, Moderate, Strenuous or Severe. Inevitably, such grading is subjective to an extent, and not all of any Section will be identical throughout, but the grading will give an idea of the effort required;

Timing – this is an estimated fair average for completing the Section. Times will vary depending on weather, number in party, gear carried, number of refreshment or photograph stops. The estimate should be an aide in planning.

OS Maps – the reference numbers of the OS Maps needed to walk the Section are given. Both Landranger (1:50,000) and Explorer (1:25,000) maps are given;

Area – for those not geographically acquainted with the South West, the Coast Path has been sub-divided into seven areas for ease of identification of each Section's location; see map on page 2 and area descriptions on pages 31-33.

Path Description booklet – the Association has published a series of Path Description booklets which give detailed walking directions as well as pointing out items of interest along the route; see page 10. The relevant Path Description booklet title for the Section is given.

There is then an overview of each Section. This covers the landscape, its general character and some of its highlights.

Next, there is a short description of how the Section can be undertaken as a day or part-day walk with public transport or a local circular walk. For more details about local public transport see pages 15-21.

Finally, the main body of the Section description contains simplified instructions for walking in a Minehead – Poole direction, generally only highlighting those locations where it is possible to go astray.

Remember, as a National Trail, the South West Coast Path is usually well signed and waymarked throughout its length, using the National Trail acorn symbol. Bear in mind that things change over the years, including the actual route of the Coast Path, so using out-of-date literature can be misleading. If in doubt, follow the signs and waymarks on the ground.

The various areas are identified by using a colour coding system as shown on the map on page 2 and set out in the Contents page 5. The colour code is used on the corner tabs of the Walk Sections, the title information and the page numbers.

Week 1 - Day 1

OS Maps: Landranger 181; Explorer OL9

	This Walk	Cumulative	This Walk	Cumulative	Grading	Timing
Ascent	1,824ft	1,824ft	556m	556m	Official: Moderate	4.5 hours
Distance	9.5mi	9.5mi	15.3km	15.3km	Alternative: Strenuous	

For detailed directions see our Minehead to Porlock Weir Path description booklet.

This is a classic example of where moorland meets the sea. Inland, the high expanse of Exmoor rolls away, broken by deep wooded valleys; where it meets the Bristol Channel there are high, convex cliffs, cut by deep and narrow "coombes". This is a lonely, remote length, away from main roads and settlements, with often the only evidence of modern life being development far away on the opposite shore of the Bristol Channel on the South Wales coast. At the western end is the contrasting landscape of Porlock Vale, a flat-floored area of farmland and marshland behind its shingle ridge, quite different in character from the rest of this Section.

Directions

Minehead and Porlock Weir are connected by a year-round bus service. However, there are no "staging posts" along this length although there are possible circular walks based on Minehead or Porlock via Selworthy Beacon, on the inland "official route".

The South West Coast Path starts from the celebratory marker on the sea front, approximately 100 yards/91m beyond the Quay Inn. The current route, which may not be shown on older maps, proceeds along the sea front, past the quay. Just before Greenaleigh Farm it turns left on ascending zigzags to North Hill.

At the summit of North Hill follow the acorn sign towards Selworthy and Bossington. At the next Coast Path sign there is a fork, the route to the right being marked "Rugged Cliff Top Path", and either option can be taken. Do not be put off by the description of the seaward path as "rugged" – it is a splendid alternative and not difficult, and gives much better sea views than the inland "official" path. It is well waymarked, and dogs are permitted but must be under very close control. There is likely to be cattle grazing.

On the "rugged" path, at the stile, take the left fork towards a bench, then continue downhill to take the lower path by a "Rugged Path" signpost. From Grexy Combe (GR 937 481) take the well-defined diagonal path up the hill to a wall, which is then followed first towards the sea then parallel to it to Western Brockholes. Here it turns inland to re-join the inland "official" path behind Hurlstone Point. (This seaward path will add about an hour to the estimated time.)

The inland route, meanwhile, follows good tracks parallel to the sea. Joining the "rugged" path on Bossington Hill, the now-combined route descends Hurlstone Combe. There is an optional diversion out to Hurlstone Point which gives a superb view. From Hurlstone, take care not to follow the obvious path to the left which contours round Bossington Hill.

The path descends and goes inland to Bossington village and then just past the car park out towards the sea again. The route now crosses the marsh to Porlock Weir, easy to follow the whole way. At high spring tides it can become impassable, and signs to Porlock village should be followed. (For tidal information consult Minehead TIC - see page 179.) If the diversion via Porlock village is taken, leave the village on the Toll Road then bear right on a footpath that goes behind West Porlock to Porlock Weir.

Week 1 - Day 2

OS Maps: Landranger 181 (eastern half); Landranger 180 (western half); Explorer OL9

	This Walk	Cumulative	This Walk	Cumulative	Grading	Timing
Ascent	3,156ft	4,980ft	962m	1,518m	Moderate, strenuous in parts	5.5 hours
Distance	12.3mi	21.8mi	19.8km	35.1km		

For detailed directions see our Porlock Weir to Lynmouth Path Description booklet.

This is a Section of two halves. In the east, approximately between Porlock Weir and the Devon/Somerset border, Exmoor meets the sea at a run of high, convex but well-wooded cliffs. The Coast Path here is a woodland walk with frequent glimpses of the sea, quiet and remote in character. To the west the cliffs become more open and steeper and the area around The Foreland and Countisbury is a spectacular viewpoint with panoramas over the double-decker towns of Lynton and Lynmouth.

Directions

Lynmouth view

The bus service which linked Porlock Weir and Lynton ended in September 2014 after the bus company which operated it ceased trading. At the time of writing, it is not yet known if another company will fill this gap in bus provision. For up to date details, it is recommended you visit www.travelinesw.com, or telephone 0871 200 2233

The official route is signposted left of the Anchor Hotel at Porlock Weir but it is possible to go in front of the hotel, past the shops then left signposted to Culbone.

Reaching Culbone turn right to visit the charming tiny church, which is recommended. From the church retrace steps and turn right uphill on the Coast Path. After about 300 yards/275m bear right into Culbone, Embelle and Yenworthy Woods. This route may not be shown on some older maps. Unfortunately, recent land slippages towards the end of Yenworthy Wood have forced an inland diversion via Yenworthy Combe.

Continue to Sister's Fountain, where the access path to the bus route at County Gate on the A39 leaves the Coast Path. Go uphill through a pair of wild boar head gateposts, then take care not to miss the narrow signposted path 300 yards/275m past the cottage as the drive bears left. An alternative waymarked route may be taken between Culbone and Yenworthy Wood. Although slightly more inland, it offers better views than the mainly woodland more coastal route.

At Coddow Combe, the route is signposted left off the lighthouse track "Countisbury 1.5 miles". From Countisbury the now spectacular path continues down the seaward side of the A39 road. Lower down it joins the road for a short way before descending on zigzags to the foreshore. Walk into Lynmouth, crossing the footbridge, then turn right to the sea front. Lynton is vertically above Lynmouth and is reached by turning left up the steps before the cliff railway (which can be taken as an interesting alternative). A new route is also available past the Esplanade car park at the end of the sea front, where a pleasant path, signposted to Lynton, goes left up the steep wooded hillside to emerge on the Coast Path west of Lynton. Both Lynmouth and Lynton have all facilities.

It is interesting to know that from Lynmouth it is possible to walk Devon's Coast to Coast route using the Two Moors Way and its southern extension to the south coast at Wembury. Guide books are available from Lynton TIC.

Week 1 - Day 3

OS Maps: Landranger 180; Explorer OL9

	This Walk	Cumulative	This Walk	Cumulative	Grading	Timing
Ascent	3,766ft	8,746ft	1,148m	2,666m	Strenuous	7 hours
Distance	13.3mi	35.1mi	21.4km	56.5km		

For detailed directions, see our Lynmouth to Ilfracombe Path Description booklet.

This generally quiet and remote Section passes through a series of spectacular coastal landscapes: the Valley of Rocks with its rocky crags and pinnacles; the steep wooded cliffs at Woody Bay; the breathtaking scenery of the deep and steep crevice carved through the cliffs at Heddon's Mouth; the wide open spaces of Holdstone Down; and the heights of the Great Hangman, the highest point on the entire Coast Path and one of the highest coastal locations in the country.

Directions

Lynton and Combe Martin are connected by a summer bus service (year-round at weekends). Heddon's Mouth (6.5 miles/10.5km from Lynton) makes a good break in this length (though not on the bus route). It has refreshment facilities at Hunter's Inn and as there is a parallel higher path between here and Woody Bay there is scope for a scenic circular walk.

The Coast Path out of Lynton is on North Walk, and this path leads to Castle Rock in the Valley of Rocks. The next section follows a minor but sometimes busy road, but a diversion to the right from the turning circle at the end of the Valley avoids its first length. Continue past the Toll House and up the hill. A permissive path on the right to Crock Point then avoids another length, and also gives stunning views.

The Coast Path leaves the road just before the Woody Bay Hotel opposite the Red House. Arriving at another road turn left uphill. Follow the next Coast Path sign ahead. When this superb stretch reaches the dramatic Heddon's Mouth valley follow it down to the valley floor. On reaching the stone bridge over the Heddon River turn right, over the river, and at the next path turn hard left. Continue for 100 yards/91m to the signpost on the right to Combe Martin. (Inland on either side of the river the path leads to the pub and shop at Hunter's Inn.)

Climb steeply away from the valley floor, keeping right at the top where the path levels off. Continue round the headland (take care in windy conditions) then the path heads inland to reach a stone wall; this is followed parallel to the sea. The wall ends and the signed path continues across the heathland of Holdstone Down. At Sherrycombe the route follows the grass track along the top of the combe to the inland end and then down. Ascending Great Hangman from Sherrycombe bear away from the wall on the left and ignore the many paths going to the right, meeting the wall higher up. From Great Hangman the path is obvious to Little Hangman and beyond to Combe Martin.

Goats near Lynton

Week 1 - Day 4 (half day)

OS Maps: Landranger 180; Explorer 139 or OL9

	This Walk	Cumulative	This Walk	Cumulative	Grading	Timing
Ascent	1,280ft	10,026ft	390m	3,056m	Moderate, strenuous in parts	2.5 hours
Distance	5.3mi	40.4mi	8.6km	65.1km		

For detailed directions see our Lynmouth to Ilfracombe Path description booklet.

This is a Section of rocky inlets, one of which, Watermouth, is spacious enough for boats to be moored. These bays are divided by rugged headlands. The cliffs here are grey and slatey, making for a forbidding looking coastline, notwithstanding the little bays. At the western end the site of a prehistoric hill fort gives a panoramic view over Ilfracombe. This Section is never far from the A399 coast road and various tourist facilities, so despite the impressive cliffs it is not a lonely length.

Ilfracombe

Looking Back from Hagginton Point Picnic Spot

Directions

Combe Martin and Ilfracombe are linked by a regular bus service, allowing a bus-walk to be easily undertaken on this Section.

The Coast Path leaves the Lime Kiln car park in Combe Martin, passing the TIC, then forks right to join the A399 road. Turn right (Seaside Hill Road) above the beach. Turn right onto a narrow tarmac lane which climbs steeply to re-join the A399 road. Walk on the slightly raised path along the roadside through two gates. Go along a path beside a field to a flight of steps, then turn left up the slip road back to the main road and on to the brow, passing the bus shelter. Turn right to follow the road down to the old main road, with a bus shelter, now used as an Information Point, over to the right. Here turn left beside the entrance to the Sandy Cove Hotel to follow a track towards Watermouth Cove.

At Watermouth it is possible to cross the foreshore for some 110 yards/100m to a flight of steps at most states of the tide; take care, as the rocks can be slippery. However, if the tide is high, use the route running parallel to the main road. (Check the Watermouth tide timings by contacting Ilfracombe or Combe Martin TICs - see page 179.)

This roadside path is a great improvement as it avoids the need to walk in the road carriageway. It was completed in late 2013 following the Association's offer of £50,000 from our reserves towards its cost, because of our safety concerns. The offer enabled the remainder of the funding to be secured from the Rural Development Fund for England and Devon County Council, a successful conclusion to a decade of pressure.

The next pleasant section of path passes the western side of Watermouth Cove and on around Widmouth Head and then Rillage Point. There is then a roadside section into Hele. Turn right here then climb some steps on the far left of the beach. The path zigzags up past Beacon Point to the top of Hillsborough. Follow the waymarks down the hill to Ilfracombe Harbour.

Week 1 - Day 4 (half day)

OS Maps: Landranger 180; Explorer 139

	This Walk	Cumulative	This Walk	Cumulative	Grading	Timing
Ascent	2,037ft	12,063ft	621m	3,677m	Easy to moderate; strenuous west of Lee Bay	3.5 hours
Distance	7.3mi	47.7mi	11.7km	76.8km		

For detailed directions see our Ilfracombe to Croyde Bay Path Description booklet.

Most of this Section is characterised by grass-topped cliffs fronting numerous small coves and a foreshore of rock ledges. Half-way along is the focal point of Bull Point lighthouse. At Morte Point the character of the coastline changes abruptly as the enormous beach of Woolacombe Sands in its vast bay comes into view, often dotted with surfers. The dark jagged rocks of Morte Point give this headland a superb brooding atmosphere.

Directions

Ilfracombe and Woolacombe are linked by a regular bus service, allowing a bus-walk to be easily undertaken on this Section.

From Ilfracombe Harbour pass the Sandpiper Inn into Capstone Road. After some 170 yards/150m turn right to pass around Capstone Point. At the far end take a flight of steps that goes up behind the back of the Landmark Theatre. Follow this path to the top of the gardens and through a gate by a shelter. Bear right along Granville Road then right again onto an unmetalled road which leads to the Torrs Walk on the right; the Torrs Walk is well waymarked.

At the top of the Torrs Walk bear right and follow the path down the field to the stile in the corner. Continue ahead around the hill to another stile then cross the field to meet the old coach road ahead. Bear right on this track, which later becomes a minor road into Lee Bay. Refreshments are available year-round at the Grampus Inn in Lee village, a short way inland.

The next length from Lee Bay is quite strenuous. Proceed up the road from Lee, turning right at the top of the hill through a brick-pillared gate. Two steep valleys are crossed before Bull Point and its lighthouse are reached. The path continues on and out around Morte Point, a spectacular jagged slate ridge like a dinosaur's back emerging from the sea. The path leaves Morte Point and continues beneath the cliffs past small sandy bays to arrive at Woolacombe.

Signpost south of Morte Point

Week 1 - Day 5 (half day)

OS Maps: Landranger 180; Explorer 139

	This Walk	Cumulative	This Walk	Cumulative	Grading	Timing
Ascent	725ft	12,788ft	221m	3,898m	Moderate	3 hours
Distance	6.3mi	54.0mi	10.2km	87.0km		

For detailed directions see our Ilfracombe to Croyde Bay Path Description booklet.

The main feature of this Section is the vast sandy beach of Woolacombe Sands, backed by a substantial line of dunes. Busy with families and surfers close to the town, it becomes surprisingly empty away from the facilities. Beyond the beach is the superb headland of Baggy Point, a contrast to the beach with its steep cliffs and broad, grassy top. Rounding the headland another, smaller sandy bay comes into view, Croyde Bay, with the wider vista of Bideford Bay beyond.

Directions

Croyde Bay is an excellent centre for a circular walk using the Coast Path, around Baggy Point to Putsborough, giving views over Woolacombe Sands while experiencing the superb character of the headland.

At Woolacombe the Coast Path leaves the Watersmeet Hotel parallel to the Esplanade road, then turns up Challacombe Road. It leaves this road on the right at approximately the National Trust sign – there may be no waymark here. The path continues through the enormous dunes of Woolacombe Warren – the waymarking means that going astray is unlikely. An alternative is to follow Marine Drive and the track beyond, which gives better views. If the tide is low many walk the length of Woolacombe Sands but this should not be attempted on a high or rising tide.

The official path leaves the Warren by a set of steep steps, joining the extension to Marine Drive and the alternative route. It continues along the track then a road, leaving it to the right after the caravan site. As an alternative, take the earlier path on the right to the car park at Putsborough, where there are seasonal refreshments and toilets (the beach route joins here). Go left of the caravan site to a stile and up the cliff slope to re-join the official path.

The excellent high level path continues to the end of Baggy Point, giving superb views. At the end of the headland, bear right to join the lower path towards Croyde. Follow the road, partly on a parallel path. Do not leave the road at the first slipway. The official path leaves the road a little further on to cross the beach, but many will continue on to visit Croyde and its facilities.

Woolacombe Warren

Week 1 - Day 5 (half day)

OS Maps: Landranger 181 (eastern half); Landranger 180 (western half); Explorer OL9

	This Walk	Cumulative	This Walk	Cumulative	Grading	Timing
Ascent	506ft	13,294ft	154m	4,052m	Easy	3.25 hours
Distance	8.8mi	62.8mi	14.0km	101.0km		

For detailed description see our Croyde Bay to Barnstaple Path Description booklet.

The length immediately adjacent to Croyde Bay follows a low cliff and gives stunning views over the truly enormous length of Saunton Sands with the dune complex of Braunton Burrows behind. Beyond is the sweep of Bideford Bay, with the possibility of seeing as far as Hartland Point lighthouse, many miles away. Offshore on the horizon is the isle of Lundy. The remainder of this Section is low and level, through a huge range of dunes (the official route) or along the seemingly endless Saunton Sands. Then comes the twin estuary of the Rivers Taw and Torridge, with mudbanks and reclaimed marshes making for a birdwatcher's delight. This is a length displaying a relatively rare aspect of the South West coast.

Directions

Croyde Bay and Braunton are linked by a regular year-round bus service, making this a good bus-walk possibility.

The Coast Path leaves Croyde Bay via the beach (no dogs May-September) and on to the low cliffs at Down End. Turn left at the old coastguard lookout to the B3231 road. Cross the road with care here, turn left then climb some stone steps. The path now contours round Saunton Down, parallel to and above the road. This ends opposite the large white building of the Saunton Sands Hotel.

From here there are optional routes. The first option is to cross the road and pass around the hotel to the Saunton Sands car park, where there are toilets and seasonal refreshments. Leave the car park by the entrance road and after 55 yards/50m bear right along a stony lane to the B3231. Continue carefully along the road for some 400 yards/365m, past the Golf Club driveway, turning right at a red brick partially rendered house.

If there is no need for the toilets or refreshments, a better option is to turn left uphill opposite the hotel, away from the road. Follow the path as it bears round to the right until it arrives at the B3231 opposite the red brick house described above. Cross the road to continue on the same route as above.

This route now enters the Braunton Burrows nature reserve, designated a UNESCO Biosphere Reserve for its nature conservation importance. The route through the Burrows is well waymarked; first follow a clear track through patchy woodland along the edge of the golf course with the military training area on the right. After the Sandy Lane car park follow the signing for nearly two miles along a rough, traffic-free, military dirt road known as the American Road to arrive at Broad Sands car park by the estuary of the Taw and Torridge rivers. Follow another dirt road, approximately eastwards, to arrive at the White House, a well-known local landmark.

Many walkers prefer to miss the Burrows and walk from Saunton Sands car park the length of the beach, for some 3.5 miles/5.5km. Near the end of the beach, just after a wooden groyne, look out for a slatted wooden catwalk entering the dunes to the left. Follow this to arrive at the Broad Sands car park. This beach route keeps the sea in sight, not the case with the Burrows route.

From the White House follow the estuary side on top of the Great Sea Bank. This is followed, between estuary and reclaimed marshes, to the old quay at Velator on the edge of Braunton. To visit Braunton and its facilities, turn left at Velator along the footpath and cycleway, following the former railway track.

Local taxi firm, Saunton Taxis, are happy to do bag transfer as well as walkers. They have a 6 seater taxi and their web site is at www.sauntontaxis.co.uk

Boardwalk from Airy Point

Week 2 - Day 2

OS Maps: Landranger 190; Explorer 126

	This Walk	Cumulative	This Walk	Cumulative	Grading	Timing
Ascent	2,382ft	19,248ft	726m	5,867m	Moderate to strenuous	5 hours
Distance	10.3mi	109.0mi	16.6km	175.4km		

For detailed directions see our Clovelly to Hartland Quay Path Description booklet.

There is a great contrast in this Section between east and west.
In the east the landscape is one of parkland, the domesticated and partly
ornamental landscape of the grounds of Clovelly Court. After leaving the
parkland a run of high cliffs culminates at Hartland Point, one of the great
defining headlands of the Coast Path. Here the coast turns from east-west
to north-south and its character changes into one of the Coast Path's most
breathtaking stretches, with dark brooding cliffs behind jagged fingers
of rock stretching into the Atlantic Ocean. Experiencing its magnificent
scenery is well worth the effort of crossing the spectacular deep valleys
which cut the coast. The Section ends at the pub and hotel at Hartland
Quay, which has a wonderful remote atmosphere.

Blackchurch Rock

Directions

Hartland Quay has no public transport. However, there are numerous walking links from the Coast Path to Hartland village, 2.5 miles/4km inland, which is on the bus route to Clovelly.

If using Clovelly as a base, it is requested that walkers use the main car park. If you are only walking the Path and not visiting the village, car parking is £7.50. If you are on your own however, it is cheaper to pay for the village visit which is £6.75. Enquire at the Visitor Centre.

From the main car park walk out of the entrance and turn right down the road for some 220 yards/200m to a black gate on the left. Go through and follow the track first right and through a gap in the wall, then leave the track and follow the marked path down to the right. After a while go through a kissing-gate then follow the fence on the right to another gate into shrubbery. Continue through the shrubbery through more gates. Turn right at a T-junction and right again at the next fork. Soon the path arrives at an unusual seat known as the "Angel's Wings". At the track, turn hard right – not along the track. After passing a superb viewpoint the path descends steeply into a valley to another track. Go right here. The signed detour to the viewpoint is well worth the effort.

The Coast Path goes down the valley to the shore at Mouth Mill. Cross the stream then follow the grass track inland past the lime kiln. At times of storm, high water or heavy rain the stepping stones across the stream do get washed away, making it difficult to cross. A bridge is planned to help with this problem.

Shortly, turn right and climb the valley side. Half-way up, follow the steps to the right. On reaching the top pass through fields to a stile on the right leading to some descending zigzags. Cross the bridge at the bottom, turn left then take the first right.

After the prehistoric earthwork of Windbury Castle the path continues on the cliff-top to Shipload Bay and then on to Hartland Point, where there are seasonal refreshments. The Coast Path turns sharp left off the lighthouse track towards the coastguard lookout before the lighthouse gate. A short diversion gives a good view of a wreck on the rocks below.

At Hartland Point, there is a café open from April to October and some days in winter too. From Hartland Point the path descends into an unusual valley, almost parallel to the coast, at Smoothlands, before climbing again. Descending then to the valley at the Abbey River the path goes inland to cross at a stone bridge. At the next cliff top, past an old folly tower, the path arrives at a road by the old Rocket House. Bear right to follow the path downhill to Hartland Quay, a lonely outpost with car park, toilets and refreshments, as well as a hotel.

Week 2 - Day 3

OS Maps: Landranger 190; Explorer 126 (most of length); Explorer 111 (Bude)

	This Walk	Cumulative	This Walk	Cumulative	Grading	Timing
Ascent	4,170ft	23,418ft	1,271m	7,138m	Severe	8.5 hours
Distance	15.4mi	124.4mi	24.8km	200.2km		

For detailed directions see our Hartland Quay to Bude Path Description booklet.

This is an awe-inspiring and dramatic coastline. Great jagged ridges of rock stretch out into the Atlantic Ocean, backed by high, surf-fringed cliffs. The coast is punctuated by jutting headlands and tiny, often inaccessible beaches. In the south, towards Bude, the coast softens a little and, at low tide, long sandy beaches appear. This is a spectacular Section.

Directions

Hartland Quay has no public transport connections. There is, however, an infrequent bus service between Bude and Morwenstow, half-way along, which could be used for a bus-walk on the southern half of this Section.

Note that this is probably the most arduous of all the days in the suggested itinerary. It is necessary to cross ten river valleys to complete the length, all of them steep and deep. Because of this, many may prefer to split the length at Morwenstow.

From Hartland Quay a track then a grassy path passes behind St Catherine's Tor. There is a climb then the cliff path reaches the dramatic waterfall at Speke's Mill Mouth. Keep to the eastern side of the stream here for some 150 yards/135m then cross by the wooden footbridge. Follow the signs up the valley inland of Swansford Hill. Take care at Sandhole Cliff, after joining the metalled road, to look out for the signpost after about 0.3 mile/0.5km indicating the turn right back to the coast. (It is hoped this length of road may be eliminated in the near future.) After Welcombe Mouth, Marsland Mouth marks the Cornish border, indicated by a wooden sign. The ascents and descents continue, and a diversion to Morwenstow might be worth considering. The church is picturesque and interesting and there are seasonal refreshments nearby. At the radio dishes do not miss the sign directing right towards the cliff edge. Descending to Duckpool, cross the stream by a footbridge. There are toilets here.

Continue on to Sandy Mouth where there are more toilets and seasonal refreshments. The going now eases at last and after passing over the open cliffs at Maer Down the path arrives at Crooklets Beach at Bude. Follow the path along the low cliffs behind the beaches into the town, which has all facilities.

Stanbury Mouth

Week 2 - Day 4

OS Maps: Landranger 190; Explorer 111

	This Walk	Cumulative	This Walk	Cumulative	Grading	Timing
Ascent	2,494ft	25,912ft	760m	7,898m	Easy then strenuous	4.75 hours
Distance	10.2mi	134.6mi	16.4km	216.6km		

For detailed directions see our Bude to Crackington Haven Path Description booklet.

Low grassy cliffs and surfing beaches south of Bude give way to an ever higher and more rugged coastline fronted by rough rock ledges and cut by deep and steep valleys. There are some superb viewpoints along this later quiet and remote-feeling length which reward the effort. Crackington Haven is a pleasant spot and on the cliffs above, St Gennys Church is a superb spot for contemplation.

Directions

A regular bus service links Bude with Crackington Haven, and also serves Widemouth Bay, about 3 miles/7km from Bude, thus offering a number of bus-walk options.

The path south from Bude starts at the sea lock on the historic Bude Canal, then climbs to the cliff top at Compass Point and on to Efford Beacon. There are excellent views from here. The path over Efford Down to Upton and on to Widemouth Bay is easy to follow. Widemouth has toilets and refreshments, the last before Crackington Haven. (There are further refreshment facilities a little inland at Whalesborough, reached by a scenic footpath from Widemouth.)

South of Widemouth the path follows the low cliff for a short distance then diverts inland slightly at Wanson Mouth to join the coast road in the stream valley. Turn right and follow the road as it climbs steeply to Penhalt Cliff. There are more magnificent views from the cliff-top car park.

From the southern end of the car park the Coast Path crosses a field and descends steeply to Millook Haven. Now follow the steep road uphill for a short distance then turn right onto the cliff top at Raven's Beak. From here the path climbs steadily past the stunted oak woodland at Dizzard Point and on to Chipman Point. Two further deep and steep valleys are crossed, then a ridge walk leads to Castle Point, which gives tremendous views. Another steep valley crossing leads on to Pencannow Point and views over Crackington Haven. The path descends easily into the cove, where there are toilets, refreshments, buses and accommodation.

South of Bude

Week 2 - Day 5 (half day)

OS Maps: Landranger 190; Explorer 111

	This Walk	Cumulative	This Walk	Cumulative	Grading	Timing
Ascent	2,264ft	28,176ft	690m	8,588m	Strenuous	3.75 hours
Distance	6.8mi	141.4mi	10.9km	227.5km		

For detailed directions see our Crackington Haven to Tintagel Path Description booklet.

This is a Section of high cliffs, the highest, indeed in Cornwall. Not only are they high, but they also present an appearance of bulk, of being literally massive, and the walker will often feel dwarfed by them, especially on a climb or descent or perhaps on a headland. Much of this Section is also quite lonely, and this combination makes this a coast with an imposing character.

Directions

Crackington Haven and Boscastle are linked by a regular bus service, making this an option for a bus-walk.

There are toilets and seasonal shops, cafes and a pub at Crackington Haven. Leave behind the beach near the toilets and head out for the headland of Cambeak. Rounding the headland, keep away from its high and sheer cliff edges. Beyond Cambeak the path is relatively level, passing above the landslip zone at Strangles Beach. Ahead looms High Cliff, the appropriately-named highest cliff in Cornwall. There is a steady ascent but the descent on the south side is very steep. The path then climbs through a landfall at Rusey Cliff, twisting and turning to the top. A cliff top section through fields follows to the sheer black cliff at Buckator. The path then dips slightly before continuing at high level to Fire Beacon Point. Here the descent is steep, but helped by attractive slate steps. The path then follows the cliff face into the inlet of Pentargon, with its impressive waterfall. This is best seen from the southern side – do not be tempted to leave the path for a better view.

Shortly afterwards the path passes refreshment facilities at Boscastle Farm Shop (call 01840 250827 for details).

The now easy path continues on to Boscastle. Aim for the white mast on Penally Hill, then follow the path alongside the beautiful harbour inlet into Boscastle, now happily restored after its 2004 experiences.

Boscastle

Week 2 - Day 5 (half day)

OS Maps: Landranger 190 (eastern half); Landranger 200 (western half); Explorer 111

	This Walk	Cumulative	This Walk	Cumulative	Grading	Timing
Ascent	1,230ft	29,406ft	375m	8,963m	Moderate	2.25 hours
Distance	4.6mi	146.0mi	7.4km	234.9km		

For detailed directions see our Crackington Haven to Tintagel Path Description booklet.

This fairly short Section is a great local favourite, as it combines all the best of the Coast Path – headlands, sandy bays, historic features and, yes, steep valleys, all in a manageable but picturesque length which is not too taxing. In addition, although popular, it never seems crowded and is, indeed, a "real" walk. With all this and its convenient bus links it is a perfect Coast Path taster.

Directions

Boscastle and Tintagel are linked by a regular bus service. It also serves Rocky Valley, half-way between the two, enabling a variety of bus-walks to be undertaken.

Boscastle has been attractively rebuilt after the floods of 2004, and has all facilities.

The Coast Path leaves the south side of the harbour over the new stone bridge and climbs towards the headland of Willapark, with its prominent white watch tower. The path cuts across the neck of the headland, but a diversion to the end is worthwhile.

After a steep descent and climb at Grower Gut the path continues easily, turning seaward of the Manor House at Trevalga. The headland beyond gives views over the rocky offshore islands important for breeding seabirds. The path continues past Firebeacon Hill – look out for the Ladies Window rock arch in the gully to the right – then passes seaward of a cliff-top caravan and camping site. There is then a descent into the exquisite Rocky Valley. There is a path up the valley to a bus stop on the coast road, passing prehistoric carvings in the cliff wall.

From the footbridge in the valley the path climbs again, round the edge of the grassy Bossiney Common and above the sandy bay at Bossiney Haven. Another climb then leads to another headland also, confusingly, called Willapark. Again the Coast Path cuts across the neck of the headland and, again, a diversion to the end is worthwhile.

The path now continues to Barras Nose headland, from where it descends to Tintagel Haven below the castle ruins. Here are toilets, cafe and English Heritage gift shop. A good but steep path leads inland to the village.

Path down to Tintagel Haven

Week 2 - Day 6

OS Maps: Landranger 200; Explorer 111 (eastern half); Explorer 106 (western half)

	This Walk	Cumulative	This Walk	Cumulative	Grading	Timing
Ascent	2,589ft	31,995ft	789m	9,752m	Severe	4.75 hours
Distance	9.1mi	155.1mi	14.7km	249.6km		

For detailed directions see our Tintagel to Port Isaac Path Description booklet.

Both ends of this Section are relatively popular and accessible. At Tintagel the Coast Path passes the remains of the medieval castle perched on its isolated headland then the atmospherically located cliff-top church and the now picturesque evidence of coastal slate quarrying. At the other end is the beautifully quaint village of Port Isaac in its scenic bay. The long central length, though, comprises high cliffs cut by sometimes precipitously steep valleys. It is remote, lonely and often tough, and will be especially appreciated by those who relish an empty, arduous and dramatic coastline.

Trebarwith Strand

Directions

There is a regular bus service between Tintagel and Port Isaac; occasionally a change at Camelford is needed. A bus-walk is therefore possible on this Section.

Tintagel has all necessary facilities. Surprisingly, however, little in the village is very old other than the Old Post Office, once a local manor house.

From the village walk down the path to Tintagel Haven. From here the Coast Path climbs past the entrance to the Castle and gives excellent views over the headland which forms the castle site. A good path continues seaward of the church and on beyond past the Youth Hostel in its former quarry building and round Penhallic Point with its superb views.

The path drops steeply to Trebarwith Strand, where there are toilets, refreshments and pub, the last facilities before Port Isaac. The next part is particularly tough as it climbs steeply out of the Trebarwith valley then almost immediately drops down to sea level and up again at Backways Cove. There follows a level stretch of about a mile/1.5km to the stream valley behind Tregardock Beach. Descend on the inland side of the detached piece of cliff known as The Mountain, then climb again to Tregardock Cliff. Another level length follows, before the deepest and steepest valley yet at Jacket's Point. At the top yet another deep valley almost immediately follows. Then comes a further valley, at Barrett's Zawn. This is an area of massive rock falls. The next valley follows, this one with exceptionally steep and stony sides.

At last the path levels out again through cliff-top meadows, with just a small valley to cross at St Illickswell Gug. Eventually, the path reaches the road at Cartway Cove. Take the path on the right and round the headland to Port Gaverne, a charming spot. Follow the road uphill to the car park at the edge of Port Isaac. Go through this and follow the well-signed path above the attractive harbour inlet into the village.

Port Isaac is a very picturesque village clustered round the little harbour at the head of a sheltered bay. It has all facilities.

Looking back along coast from Port Isaac

Week 2 - Day 7

OS Maps: Landranger 200; Explorer 106

	This Walk	Cumulative	This Walk	Cumulative	Grading	Timing
Ascent	2,923ft	34,918ft	891m	10,643m	Strenuous then easy	5.5 hours
Distance	11.7mi	166.8mi	18.9km	268.5km		

For detailed directions see our Port Isaac to Padstow Path Description booklet.

This Section can be divided into three distinct characters. From Port Isaac to Port Quin is a rollercoaster of a path, closely following the ups and downs and ins and outs of the quiet, scenic but energy-sapping coast. From Port Quin to Polzeath the character becomes rather more open, if still very scenic, including the broad headland of The Rumps and Pentire Point, a wonderful airy lookout. From Polzeath to the Padstow ferry the landscape is tamer, more domesticated, often with housing or tourist development and more estuarine than maritime as it reaches the mouth of the River Camel.

Directions

There is a regular bus service between Port Isaac and Rock, the ferry point for Padstow. This service also passes through Polzeath at the mouth of the Camel estuary, giving several scenic bus-walk options, including an almost level estuary-side one. There is a popular circuit using the Coast Path between Port Isaac and Port Quin and others from Polzeath around Pentire Point.

Port Isaac has all necessary facilities, and is a scenic gem. To leave the village, take the road to the right behind the fish market. Climbing, it bears right and becomes a cliff path, soon dropping into Pine Haven. From here to Port Quin the path is magnificent and clear, but tough as it follows the cliff edge next to a prominent fence line. There is an optional diversion to the end of Varley Head.

The path enters the beautiful Port Quin inlet, descending to what was once a busy pilchard port, though there are no facilities here now. Follow the road westbound up the steep hill and a little way up the Coast Path leaves to the right, towards Doyden Point. The path follows above the cove, keeping seaward of and below the large house. Head to a prominent stone cairn, then continue ahead on a grassy path and past some old mineshafts. From the cairn a diversion to the right goes to the folly of Doyden Castle and to Doyden Point, where there is a superb view back to Port Quin.

Looking West to Kellan Head

St Enodoc Church

There is a sharp descent to Epphaven Cove then the path passes through a delightful little wooded valley before climbing past the impressive Lundy Hole. The clear cliff path now heads for the Iron Age fortress on The Rumps headland. A detour to the end is well worthwhile.

From The Rumps the path climbs through a little former quarry area then continues at high level round Pentire Point, giving spectacular views. An easy descent follows to Polzeath, all well marked. Polzeath has all necessary facilities, including now an all-year café, "Tubestation", open Wednesday-Saturday during the winter. The path follows the road past the beach car park then goes right by the cottages, where the road bends sharp left on the steep hill. It now follows a low cliff to Daymer Bay, where there are toilets and a seasonal cafe, then down steps to the beach. At the far end of the beach it leaves through dunes and over a footbridge below Brea Hill. It is possible to detour to visit the little St Enodoc Church from here.

To continue on the Coast Path follow the path clinging to the side of Brea Hill, though it is possible to go over the top or, at low tide, along the beach. On the far, south, side of Brea Hill the well-signed path continues through dunes to arrive at Rock car park. The ferry to Padstow is in the estuary just below. However, be warned that at exceptionally low tides the ferry may sail from some way downstream, in front of the dunes.

For ferry details see page 18.

A water taxi service operates between Rock and Padstow between 19:00 and midnight from Easter to 31st October, weather and tides permitting. For further details see page 18.

Note that it is possible to walk Coast to Coast across Cornwall between Padstow and Fowey on the south coast, using the Saints' Way. A guidebook is available from Padstow TIC.

Week 3 - Day 1 (half day)

OS Maps: Landranger 200: Explorer 106

	This Walk	Cumulative	This Walk	Cumulative	Grading	Timing
Ascent	744ft	35,662ft	227m	10,870m	Easy	2.5 hours
Distance	5.7mi	172.5mi	9.1km	277.6km		

For detailed directions see our Padstow to Porthcothan Path Description booklet.

The length from Padstow to Stepper Point, at the mouth of the Camel, is a scenic length of ever-changing estuarine views with sandy stretches, especially at low tide. Beyond, the coast is an easy but picturesque length of cliffs, which include occasional views right across the headland at the mouth of the estuary and up the Camel as well as west to Trevose Head. The two elements of this Section combine to form a popular local walk.

Directions

A regular bus service links Padstow with the inland end of Trevone, about one mile/1.5 km from the Coast Path. This allows for a possible bus-walk. There are also a number of possible circular walks from Padstow using the Coast Path which take in the Stepper Point headland.

Padstow is a charming and bustling little harbour town a short way up the Camel Estuary. If arriving from Rock, notice that normally this arrives in Padstow at the harbour, but at low tide it lands a short distance downstream at St Saviour's Point. In either event, it is well worthwhile taking time to explore the town.

The Coast Path leaves the north end of the harbour past the TIC and proceeds on low cliffs alongside the estuary. After passing a wooded little stream valley at St George's Cove the path heads inland of a marshy area before going back to the cliffs and on to Hawker's Cove. Refreshments (including gluten free teas) are available at Hawker's Cove at the "Rest a While" tea garden. The cafe is normally open 10.30am to 4.30pm, 1st April until late October, weather permitting. Only outside seating is available and it may be best to telephone 01841 532919 to check opening times. Pass behind the old pilots' houses here then fork right to climb to Stepper Point, with its Daymark tower. From here there are remarkable views, inland to Bodmin Moor as well as along the coast.

The path is now on the exposed Atlantic coast. Go round the precipitous inlet of Butter Hole Cove, looking out for the small Pepper Hole to the right of the path just before. An easy length to Gunver Head follows, with excellent sea views. Approaching Trevone the path skirts the impressive Round Hole collapsed cave – approach this with caution as the sides are sheer. Follow the cliffs round into the bay at Trevone, which has toilets, cafe and pub, as well as a car park.

Stile at Padstow

Week 3 - Day 1 (half day)

OS Maps: Landranger 200; Explorer 106

	This Walk	Cumulative	This Walk	Cumulative	Grading	Timing
Ascent	817ft	36,479ft	249m	11,119m	Easy	3.5 hours
Distance	7.9mi	180.4mi	12.7km	290.3km		

For detailed directions see our Padstow to Porthcothan Path description booklet.

This is a popular Section, never far from a variety of holiday accommodation. It is perhaps most associated with a range of scenic sandy surfing beaches, some of them quite extensive. As a contrast, around the middle of the length is the great landmark of Trevose Head and its lighthouse, visible from great swathes of the North Cornwall coast and an atmospheric location.

Directions

A regular bus service passes the inland end of Trevone, about one mile/1.6km from the Coast Path, and links to Porthcothan. The same route serves Constantine Bay, about two-thirds of the way along the coast from Trevone, giving a potential for a variety of bus-walks.

Trevone has all necessary facilities. The path crosses the rear of the beach and leaves behind the little headland on the south-west side of the bay, following the cliff edge round rocky Newtrain Bay. Reaching Harlyn there are refreshments and toilets. Cross the stream on the road bridge then follow the beach below the low cliff for some 330 yards/300m before climbing left onto the cliff and then continuing to the headland at Cataclews Point.

The path passes inland of Padstow's lifeboat station, accessible by a cul-de-sac path, and then goes on to Trevose Head, passing the lighthouse. On a clear day the coastal views are incredibly extensive, ranging from the satellite dishes north of Bude to the granite hills of West Penwith behind St Ives. This is an atmospheric headland.

After an old quarry the path passes a Round Hole collapsed cave and descends to the partly rocky Booby's Bay. Continue on to the rear of Constantine Bay, a very attractive and extensive beach at low tide. Walk the length of the beach. There are toilets and seasonal refreshments at the far end and a bus stop a little way inland. Beyond the dunes the path rounds Treyarnon Head to cross another attractive beach at Treyarnon Bay, with seasonal toilets and refreshments.

An unusually indented coastline follows, with sheer-sided headlands and impressive coves. Near Pepper Cove the ramparts of an Iron Age cliff fort may be seen, and the whole coastline is quite spectacular. The path then turns into another sandy cove, at Porthcothan Bay, which has toilets and refreshments and also has a pub, the Tredrea Inn, about 500 yards/458m inland up the road.

Porth Meor Beach

Week 3 - Day 2

OS Maps: Landranger 200; Explorer 106

		Cumulative	This Walk	Cumulative	Grading	Timing
Ascent	1,447ft	37,926ft	441m	11,560m	Moderate	5 hours
Distance	11.1mi	191.5mi	17.9km	308.2km		

For detailed directions see our Porthcothan to Newquay Path Description booklet.

This is a relatively well-walked Section, particularly around Newquay. It shows the interplay of high cliffs and sandy beaches particularly well. Almost the whole length is characterised by high, flat-topped cliffs, sometimes with prominent headlands, which for long stretches form the back of extensive attractive sandy beaches, many of them popular with surfers. While never a lonely Section, its cliffs and bays make it one well worth exploring, helped by the relatively easy terrain.

Directions

Porthcothan and Newquay are linked by a regular bus service. This route follows a road parallel and close to the coast, meaning that there are a number of possible links to the Coast Path from this bus, allowing for quite a range of possible bus-walks.

Porthcothan has all facilities that may be needed. The Coast Path leaves past the shop and keeps in front of the houses and on around the headland. After a short steep descent and climb, an easy level walk leads to Park Head, an excellent viewpoint. There have been numerous landslips here so keep to the path inland of the white posts. The whole headland is worth wandering over and exploring. Ahead now is the National Trust's Carnewas property, with its spectacular beach. The Trust's cafe and Information Centre are open through the summer. On the beach below are the massive stacks forming Bedruthan Steps.

The Bedruthan Steps area can be busy, but the steps to the beach are closed in the winter months. A quieter length follows to Trenance Point and into the sandy bay of Mawgan Porth, where there are toilets, refreshments and a pub as well as a bus stop. Surprisingly, this was once the site of an unfinished canal project.

Cross the stream using the road then leave it to the right on the sharp bend on the hill out of Mawgan Porth. There then follows a long high level length to Watergate Bay on airy flat-topped cliffs, cut by a couple of minor descents. The path passes Iron Age remains here while inland is the contrast of Newquay Airport. The path continues on the cliff top behind the magnificent Watergate Beach, much used for surfing and other activities. The path then descends to the road by the Watergate Bay Hotel, and here there are toilets, refreshments and another bus stop.

Cross the stream at the road then turn right by the car park and climb back to the cliffs, which are now followed to the outskirts of Newquay. The coastal view ahead to the town and its headlands is excellent. The Coast Path leaves the road to pass round the headland of Trevelgue Head, an important prehistoric location. Although the path bypasses the island at the very end, this can be visited via the footbridge, and is worth the diversion for the views. The path returns to the road by Porth

Bethruthan Steps

Beach before leaving it at steps down on the left, to pass underneath the main road and cross the next little headland to emerge above Lusty Glaze beach – look for the information board here relating to the canal previously encountered at Mawgan Porth.

The path continues into the park at Barrowfields, skirting its seaward side, to reach the main road into Newquay town centre. Follow this just past the railway station then take the old tramway road on the right. Follow the waymarked route along the footpath above Towan Beach.

At the corner go down the steps on the right then from the car park cross Beach Road and follow the tarmac path ahead. At the end follow the steps on the left to pass a bowling green and public toilets to Fore Street. Turn right here as far as the Red Lion and here turn right again to the harbour down North Quay Hill.

As well as all facilities, Newquay has a branch line railway station linking to the main line to Penzance and is the centre of a network of local bus routes.

Week 3 - Day 3 (half day)

OS Maps: Landranger 200; Explorer 104

	This Walk	Cumulative	This Walk	Cumulative	Grading	Timing
Ascent	1,145ft	39,071ft	349m	11,909m	Moderate	3.5 hours
Distance	6.3mi	197.8mi	10.2km	318.4km		

For detailed directions see our Newquay to Perranporth Path Description booklet.

This Section includes some superb viewpoints from headlands in and around Newquay, the panoramas quite unspoiled by the proximity of the large town. Beyond Newquay a range of landscapes is experienced, from wide sandy beaches to exposed cliff tops to small sandy bays to dune systems. In addition, unexpectedly, the wooded estuary valley of the river known as The Gannel is crossed at the edge of Newquay. This variety, and the proximity to a range of facilities and accommodation, make this a popular, well-used length.

Directions

A regular bus service links Newquay with Holywell Bay, and also serves Crantock, between the two. This gives a number of bus-walk possibilities.

Newquay is the biggest town on Cornwall's north coast. Although usually busy, being especially popular with surfers and also with groups of young holidaymakers, it is in a very attractive setting of beaches and headlands. All the facilities are here, and there is a branch railway linking to the main line to Penzance.

From Newquay Harbour the Coast Path climbs past the old Huer's Hut to Towan Head. This is a good lookout spot, and is excellent for seabird watching. From Towan Head the path then follows the back of Fistral Beach. This is probably the country's most popular surfing beach and international competitions are held here. The path climbs to the cliffs at the southern end and then crosses the road to go along Pentire Crescent which leads into Penmere Drive. The path then arrives above the Gannel Estuary. However, this misses the major headland of Pentire Point East, which is well worth the diversion to the end. (If following the diversion round the headland, on returning from the end aim for the far bottom of the car park at the neck of the headland. From here head along the suburban road parallel to the Gannel. Follow this to the Fern Pit Cafe.)

There are four options from here for crossing the Gannel, depending on the tide and time of year.

OPTION 1: FERN PIT FERRY (deduct 2 miles/3km from total mileage)

The first option is to use the Fern Pit Ferry from behind the cafe. The cafe is approximately 0.7 mile/1.1km west of Penmere Drive. The ferry operates continuously, 7 days a week, 10.00-18.00 mid May until mid September weather dependent – telephone 01637 873181. For further details see page 18.

OPTION 2: PENPOL CROSSING (official route)

Go along Penmere Drive then turn right into Trevean Way. Follow the waymarks right and go downhill across a grassy area. At the foot of the grass bank turn right along the footpath then take the steps on the left down to the tidal Penpol Footbridge across the Gannel Estuary. This can be used 3-4 hours either side of low water. Cross the Gannel here. (If coming from the headland circuit, continue past the Fern Pit Cafe and on along Riverside Avenue, then ahead and right. At a junction where there is a footpath to the right keep ahead, ignoring the footpath. Bear right into Penmere Drive, again ignoring another footpath on the right. Go along Penmere Drive and re-join the route detailed in Option 1.)

OPTION 3: TRENANCE FOOTBRIDGE (add 3 miles/4.8km to total mileage)

This route is usable at most states of the tide. From the Newquay side of the Penpol crossing continue upstream on the path parallel to the river until it arrives at the A392 Gannel Road. There is a footbridge on the right just before the junction with the A3058 Trevemper Road. Cross the bridge and continue ahead. Do not follow the creekside path to Penpol but instead take the bridleway on the left towards Trevemper. Turn right just before reaching the tarmac and follow the footpath through Treringey to arrive at the south side of the Penpol tidal footbridge.

OPTION 4: MAIN ROAD ROUTE (add 4.5 miles/7.2km to total mileage)

Continue past the Trenance footbridge and along the A392 Trevemper Road from the roundabout. At the next roundabout turn right and after about 100 yards/90m take the little unsigned lane on the right. This leads to Trevemper, going forward and right as the lane goes left. After the gate turn left on the route described under Option 3 through Treringey.

Options 2, 3 and 4 come together at Penpol. Follow the lane then take the signed path on the right above the estuary. After passing the ferry landing for Option 1 this path leads to Crantock Beach car park. Crantock village with its facilities and bus stop is a little way inland. Cross the car park to the dunes; bear left at the junction of grassy paths on entering the dune area and follow this inland of the main dune area to re-emerge at a coastal path which leads to the cliffs of Pentire Point West where the Bowgie Inn provides meals and refreshments. The path goes round Porth Joke (known locally as Polly Joke), then on around Kelsey Head to Holywell Bay, descending across more dunes either into the village or to cross the river on a seaward footbridge. There are facilities, some seasonal, here.

The Islands, Newquay

Week 3 - Day 3 (half day)

OS Maps: Landranger 200; Explorer 104

	This Walk	Cumulative	This Walk	Cumulative	Grading	Timing
Ascent	755ft	39,826ft	230m	12,139m	Moderate	2 hours
Distance	4.5mi	202.3mi	7.3km	325.7km		

For detailed directions see our Newquay to Perranporth Path Description booklet.

The theme of this Section is sand, in the form of both dunes and beaches, although it begins by rounding headlands at Penhale and Ligger Points. However, even at Penhale the inland vista is dominated by dunes, although the adjacent Army camp is also prominent. For the bulk of this Section sand is everywhere around, on the seemingly endless length of Perran Beach and the dunes which back it. Both ends, Holywell and Perranporth, are busy holiday settlements but the more remote areas of Perran Beach can be surprisingly quiet.

Directions

Holywell Bay and Perranporth are linked by a regular bus service, making a bus-walk a feasible option here.

Holywell Bay has all facilities, some seasonal.

From Holywell Bay the path rounds Penhale Point, skirting the seaward edge of the somewhat unattractive Penhale army camp. It then goes on out to Ligger Point, where there is a panoramic view of the length of Perran Beach. The path heads towards the dunes then descends behind the cliff quarry to the beach. It now follows the back of the beach for some 1.5 miles/2.5km. This is possible even at high tide, and usually on firm sand. At Cotty's Point the tide often makes it necessary to climb the steps leading to Perran Sands holiday park. At the top of the steps turn right following the slate Coast Path waymarks. The path descends back to the beach on the south side and then crosses the stream by the footbridge when nearly at Perranporth, where there are again all needed facilities.

Looking back to Penhale Point

Week 3 - Day 4

OS Maps: Landranger 200 (Perranporth); Landranger 203 (remainder); Explorer 104

	This Walk	Cumulative	This Walk	Cumulative	Grading	Timing
Ascent	2,250ft	42,076ft	686m	12,825m	Moderate then strenuous	5.75 hours
Distance	12.2mi	214.5mi	19.7km	345.4km		

For detailed directions see our Perranporth to Portreath Path Description booklet.

This Section is one in which Cornwall's coastal mining heritage is paramount. There is much evidence of former mining activity, this including somewhat stark areas of spoil and sometimes slightly sad building relics, but also some grand and imposing engine houses and chimneys. In some locations, the large-scale level of the activity is difficult to imagine now. Nevertheless, the scale and grandeur of the cliffs, the beaches and the surf mean that nature always re-asserts itself.

Directions

A regular bus service links Perranporth to St Agnes. A skeletal summer service links Perranporth to Portreath, also passing St Agnes and Porthtowan along the way, giving numerous bus-walk options.

Perranporth is a busy holiday centre with all facilities. The Coast Path goes west from the main car park and follows the hill up Cliff Road. Keep left of the castellated building then along Tregundy Lane. Go half left at the entrance to the Youth Hostel and on to the cliffs, the path clinging to the cliff face out to Cligga Head. Here the path enters quarry and mine workings, but is well signposted. There is then a level stretch alongside Perranporth Aerodrome before the steep descent to Trevellas Porth, a valley marked by many relics of the mining industry. Go upstream to cross at the road bridge, then back to the cliffs and back down again into Trevaunance Cove, where there are toilets and refreshments. The bus stop at St Agnes is a little way inland.

On reaching the road at Trevaunance Cove go straight across passing the Driftwood Spars car park and a large tall house on the right. Follow the waymarked footpath immediately right along a metalled lane then fork right along a footpath. Soon the path climbs steeply to the cliff top. A long and scenic high-level path now goes around St Agnes Head, giving superb views ahead, then past the iconic engine house at Towanroath before descending to Chapel Porth, a small and attractive cove with toilets and seasonal refreshments. Refreshments are available at the Chapel Porth Beach Cafe daily from 1st April until the end of October and weather permitting at weekends during the winter. Phone 01872 552487 to check opening times. The toilets here are only unlocked when the cafe is open. Follow the stream inland for 200 yards/185m then turn right and up to the cliffs, before it is back down again into Porthtowan. Again there are toilets and refreshments and a magnificent beach. There is a bus stop a little inland.

Follow the road inland then turn right up West Beach Road, then left up the narrow road to the cliff top. More mine workings are passed, then the path runs alongside a prominent fence next to MOD land before reaching a road which descends into Portreath. This former industrial harbour town has all facilities.

Cligga Head

Week 3 - Day 5

OS Maps: Landranger 203; Explorer 104 (eastern half); Explorer 102 (western half)

	This Walk	Cumulative	This Walk	Cumulative	Grading	Timing
Ascent	1,362ft	43,438ft	415m	13,240m	Moderate/ easy	5.5 hours
Distance	12.4mi	226.9mi	19.9km	365.3km		

For detailed directions see our Portreath to Hayle Path Description booklet.

There are two distinct characters to the coast of this Section. Between Portreath and Godrevy it is one of high, level cliffs, the sea far below. In contrast, between Godrevy and Hayle the walk focuses on sand, either dunes or beach, on the focal view of Godrevy lighthouse and on the great colourful sweep of St Ives Bay. This is never a lonely or remote length, but it is a scenic, fascinating and rewarding one.

Directions

A skeletal summer bus service links Portreath and Hayle, and also passes Godrevy, half-way between the two. This allows for bus-walk options over the whole Section or over either of the two distinct character lengths.

Portreath has all facilities and a nice beach. Leave the town crossing the bridge next to the car park then right, up Battery Hill. Continue ahead, meandering between properties at the end, turning right just beyond them up steps to the top of Western Hill, with its excellent views. After a couple of noticeable valleys the path then embarks on a long easy cliff-top walk along Reskajeague Downs, eventually arriving at Hell's Mouth, where there is a seasonal cafe. The path then narrows and turns right at an obvious T-junction. Cross a stile next to a gate and cross the seaward side of a field before continuing easily round Navax and Godrevy Points, the lighthouse becoming a focal point offshore. Keep seaward of the car park and access road and follow the signs along the low cliffs and over the dunes to another car park, at the Godrevy Cafe. Follow the boardwalk from the car park to cross the Red River. Turn left for 30 yards/29m then go right, following the large slate waymarks through the former quarry, now a nature reserve.

Keep ahead through the dunes, following the signposts. Note it is often possible to walk along the beach here but beware the incoming tide which can mean being cut off below the cliffs. If the tide is right, leave the beach at the lifeguard hut near the foot of Black Cliff. If coming through the dunes, keep ahead above the hut. Then, with either option, turn left up some steps just before two chalets. Turn right towards a house, leaving it on the right, and walk along a line of chalets on the left. The path is slightly overgrown but then opens out at a car park. Follow the access track ahead then bear right onto the raised walkway parallel to the harbour and continue ahead on this level. Descend the steps at the far end and follow the pavement ahead then cross the old swing bridge to the road. Turn right to reach the railway viaduct in the centre of Hayle.

Gwithian

Week 3 - Day 6

OS Maps: Landranger 203; Explorer 102

	This Walk	Cumulative	This Walk	Cumulative	Grading	Timing
Ascent	617ft	44,055ft	188m	13,428m	Easy	2.5 hours
Distance	5.6mi	232.5mi	9.0km	374.3km		

For detailed directions see our Hayle to Pendeen Watch Path Description booklet.

This Section is never far from roads and houses, so often has a suburban air. However, this is outweighed by the views over the River Hayle estuary and, particularly, by the vistas over the great sweep of St Ives Bay with its vast sandy beaches and dunes, the iconic offshore Godrevy Lighthouse as a focal point and the fabulous sea colours, turquoises, greens and blues, whenever the sun shines on this length.

Directions

A regular bus service links Hayle and St Ives, giving a bus-walk option. In addition, a branch-line railway plies between Lelant and St Ives, and this gives marvellous sea views. This makes for an unusual and especially scenic train-walk option.

Towards St Ives

Hayle has all facilities, including a railway station on the main line to Penzance. Walk to the viaduct and turn right on the path immediately before it. Go ahead to Carnsew Road and continue on the pavement, turning right on a narrow path at the end of a stone building, by the pedestrian traffic lights. A short way down this path turn left next to a fence to arrive alongside a large lagoon. Keep on to the end then bear left to the road. Continue as the road passes alongside the River Hayle estuary on The Causeway, a birdwatchers' delight. Cross to the far side of the road then back to the riverside again before forking right at the Old Quay House - take care on the road here. Under the bridge turn right, signed to St Ives Park and Ride. At the car park attendant's kiosk turn left to a lane, then turn right here. Follow the lane next to the railway and estuary all the way to Lelant Church. Go along the path next to the church to pass under the railway. Just before the beach turn left along the seaward side of the railway through dunes. (NB this is also the route of the St Michael's Way, a cross-peninsula path from Lelant to Marazion - a guide leaflet is available at St Ives TIC.)

Follow the clear path parallel to the magnificent Porthkidney Beach. Approaching the headland of Carrack Gladden the path forks - keep right then continue ahead. Descend the road to Carbis Bay, where there are toilets and seasonal refreshments, walking inland of the cafe but seaward of the hotel. Climb over a railway bridge then continue as the path becomes a minor road. Pass the path taking St Michael's Way inland then at a little cross-roads go straight ahead, steeply downhill. (Turning right shortly after the St Michael's Way turning down a private, pedestrians only path gives a more scenic alternative to the official route, re-joining at the little cross-roads.) Cross the railway bridge and double back right then left to arrive at Porthminster Beach, just below St Ives railway station.

Week 4 - Day 1

OS Maps: Landranger 203; Explorer 102

	This Walk	Cumulative	This Walk	Cumulative	Grading	Timing
Ascent	3,428ft	47,483ft	1,045m	14,473m	Severe	7 hours
Distance	13.9mi	246.4mi	22.3km	396.6km		

For detailed directions see our Hayle to Pendeen Watch Path Description booklet.

There are no settlements on this Section and the character is lonely and remote. It is also tough going, with rocky scrambles and boggy lengths. But it can only be described as a magnificent length. Stark cliffs, rock pinnacles, tiny scenic coves with translucent water, rugged exposed headlands - all are here. Inland the view is often of empty moorland. This is the Coast Path at its most awe-inspiring. Prepare for its rigours, then enjoy the wonderful experience.

Directions

A regular summer bus service links St Ives and Pendeen village, a little inland of the Coast Path. It also passes through other inland settlements linked by footpath to the Coast Path, principally Zennor, Treen (Gurnard's Head) and Morvah, allowing for various bus-walks options.

A warning:- this is a tough and deserted length of the Coast Path. There are no settlements or refreshment facilities, though there are some path links inland to small settlements. The terrain is often rough and rocky and in places can be boggy. But a compensation:- this is a length of wonderfully dramatic coastal scenery.

From the path below St Ives railway station keep along as close as possible to the sea and harbour. The official route goes round the green St Ives Head, usually known as The Island. This is reached by following signs to the museum from the far end of

Towards Gurnard's Head

the harbour and on through a small car park. From The Island go through the old "Downlong" quarter to Porthmeor Beach and the Tate. There are also short cuts direct to here – follow signs to the Tate.

Go along the rear of Porthmeor Beach then bear off right along the path next to the putting green. The Coast Path now leads out to the rugged Clodgy Point and then on round Hor Point to Pen Enys Point, where it cuts across the neck of the headland. Pass the trig point on Carn Naun, where there are extensive views forward and back, then descend to cross the stream at River Cove. Just beyond the path passes the offshore Carracks, where seals are regularly seen. Approaching Zennor Head the path forks – keep right to follow the seaward path round the headland. From Zennor Head the path heads inland – look out for the signed Coast Path descending steeply to the right. If in need of refreshments, or for the bus, continue along the path inland to Zennor, where there is a pub and seasonal cafe.

On the Coast Path, more ups and downs lead to the distinctive headland of Gurnard's Head. The path cuts across its neck, but a diversion onto the headland, an Iron Age fortified site, is worth the effort. There are also diversions inland here to Treen, where refreshments are available at the Gurnard's Head Inn and there is a bus stop.

The Coast Path continues, generally easy to follow if not always an easy walk. Approaching Bosigran, another Iron Age fortification, head for the high point of the ridge, following Coast Path signs and keeping on the landward side of a low wall. At the crest of the ridge head inland and downhill aiming for a stream and building. Cross the stream on a small bridge near a ruined building then follow the path uphill, just seaward of an obvious stone wall. There is a diversion path inland here to a bus stop at Rosemergy. After heavy rain the path round here can be boggy.

Further on the Coast Path, look out for a path inland to Morvah for another bus stop if needed. Otherwise keep on the obvious Coast Path round the back of Portheras Cove and on to the lighthouse at Pendeen Watch. Pendeen village, with its pubs, cafe, shop, toilets and bus stop, is about 1 mile/1.5km inland.

Week 4 - Day 2

OS Maps: Landranger 203; Explorer 102

	This Walk	Cumulative	This Walk	Cumulative	Grading	Timing
Ascent	1,683ft	49,166ft	513m	14,986m	Moderate	4.25 hours
Distance	9.0mi	255.4mi	14.6km	411.2km		

For detailed directions see our Pendeen Watch to Porthcurno Path Description booklet.

This Section offers a wide range of walking experiences. Between Pendeen Watch and Botallack the overriding experience is of Cornwall's coastal mining heritage. This ranges from unattractive early 20th century industrial relics to romantic stone-built cliff-face engine houses, all this next to sheer cliffs and often wild seas. Beyond Botallack is a superb length of scenic exposed cliffs, highlighted by the magnificent headland of Cape Cornwall. This Section has all that is best on the Cornish coast - rugged cliffs, mining relics, translucent water, turquoise coves, purple heather, rocky scrambles, the view of a lighthouse. Then, approaching Sennen Cove, there is a sweep of broad sandy beaches backed by dunes, and the length ends with a scenic harbour and a lifeboat station. A wonderful length.

Crowns engine houses, Botallack

Directions

A regular summer bus service links Pendeen village, a little inland of the Coast Path, with Sennen Cove. It also serves St Just, inland of Cape Cornwall, which is used as the centre of various Coast Path-based circular walks. Bus-walks are also possible from Geevor and Botallack, reached by footpath from the coast.

Sennen

From Pendeen Watch the path goes along the road to the end of the row of cottages, then turns right at a granite marker. (The road continues into Pendeen village, with its range of facilities.) The Coast Path is clear and leads to the old mining area at Geevor. A diversion inland leads to refreshments and toilets at the mining museum, which is itself well worth a visit if possible. Follow the signed track beyond Geevor to the National Trust's Levant Beam Engine House, open for steaming at certain times. From here the official path follows the clear track parallel to the coast, but a narrower path to seaward with better views leads from the far end of the car park. The two options come together as more mines are passed at Botallack. Look to seaward to see the famous Crowns Mine engine houses perched improbably on the cliff.

Beyond Botallack, as the mines give way, look for the signed path to the right which leads to the headland at Kenidjack Castle. A lot of the waymarking in this area uses granite stones, perfect for the landscape setting. From the old building on the headland descend left to a track, go left then bear right on a path down to another track. Go left here then turn right to cross the floor of the Kenidjack Valley. Climb to the top and turn right. Ahead now is the distinctive shape of Cape Cornwall, surmounted by its chimney. Turn right immediately before the road and then bear right across a field past the ruins of a chapel to a stone stile. Cross this, turn left and then climb right to reach the top of the headland. Savour the views, then join the path which descends over the seaward side of the Cape by zigzags and steps to reach the National Coastwatch Institution watchhouse. This recent addition to the Coast Path provides a superb experience. Go to the left of the watchhouse then down the steps and along a path past some stone buildings and through a gate to reach another set of granite steps descending to the right. In the nearby car park are seasonal refreshments and toilets. St Just is about 1 mile/1.5km up the road.

At the bottom of the steps go left then climb right on the track to a road at the top. Bear off right at the sign and follow the clear path into the Cot Valley. A new route has been established down the valley. For this, turn left at the road and almost immediately right, over a footbridge and past old mine workings, climbing to reach a path which heads to the cove at Porth Nanven. Just before reaching the cove climb left onto the cliffs. There is a good clear cliff-face path to the beach at Gwynver, although with one rocky climb. From Gwynver the path continues through the dunes behind the sandy beaches, which can be walked at low tide, to the car park at Sennen Cove. This is a popular family and surfing spot with all facilities.

Week 4 - Day 3 (half day)

OS Maps: Landranger 203; Explorer 102

	This Walk	Cumulative	This Walk	Cumulative	Grading	Timing
Ascent	1,542ft	50,708ft	470m	15,456m	Moderate	3.25 hours
Distance	6.6mi	262.0mi	10.6km	421.8km		

For detailed directions see our Pendeen Watch to Porthcurno Path description booklet.

This is the most westerly length of coast in England. Much of it has the character of moorland meeting the sea, with great granite headlands and massive rock outcrops interspersed with isolated coves with exquisite sea colours. Towards Porthcurno the moorland is replaced by a more pastoral landscape, but the cliffs and coves continue. Much of this Section has a quiet character, interrupted only by the visitor mecca of Land's End.

Directions

Sennen Cove and Porthcurno are linked by a regular bus service, which also goes to Land's End. This allows for a choice of bus-walks and there are also numerous circuits possible based on the Land's End area.

Land's End islands

Sennen Cove has all facilities. Leave the village passing the Round House gallery into the car park. Turn left up steps then right, towards the lookout. From here a range of parallel paths all lead to Land's End. Bear right to the First and Last House, at England's most westerly point, then keep seaward of the main complex to the outpost at Greeb Cottage. The complex has toilets and refreshments if needed. The path goes behind Greeb Cottage; then again a choice of paths all lead towards the beautiful bay of Nanjizal. At the far end of the bay head inland up the track then turn right steeply uphill on a stepped path. After passing through a gate look out for the official, unsigned, path leaving the main track to go seaward over a little rocky scramble. The path descends then climbs to the Coastwatch station on Gwennap Head. The main track also leads here, but less scenically.

The official path is clear from Gwennap Head down into Porthgwarra. An alternative, in good conditions only and for the sure-footed only, is to leave the main path to the right some 150 yards/140m after the Coastwatch station, then pass the hole of Tol-Pedn-Penwith ("the holed headland of Penwith") before bearing left to re-join the main path.

Porthgwarra is a charming little hamlet with toilets and seasonal refreshments and unusual passages through the cliffs. Leave along a track next to some cottages, climbing again to the cliffs. The clear path descends to Porth Chapel, passing St Levan's Holy Well. Continue straight ahead over the bridge, climbing again to arrive at the car park of the unique cliff-face Minack Theatre. Leave by the path next to the theatre entrance. The path drops very steeply, with deep steps, to Porthcurno Beach. If in doubt, because of the conditions or possible vertigo, follow the road. At the bottom of the steps keep left above the beach to Porthcurno's facilities.

Week 4 - Day 3 (half day)

OS Maps: Landranger 203; Explorer 102

	This Walk	Cumulative	This Walk	Cumulative	Grading	Timing
Ascent	1,381ft	52,089ft	421m	15,877m	Strenuous	3.25 hours
Distance	5.5mi	267.5mi	8.8km	430.6km		

For detailed directions see our Porthcurno to Penzance Path Description booklet.

This is a quiet, remote and very scenic Section of cliffs and headlands, punctuated by some picturesque coves and a lighthouse. The larger coves, at each end, Porthcurno and Lamorna, are particularly attractive and are the only access points for cars, so are more popular, Otherwise, the sound of the sea and seabirds are likely to be the only disturbances in this beautiful length.

Directions

A regular bus service goes to Porthcurno and passes about 1 mile/1.5km inland of Lamorna Cove, making a bus-walk feasible. Many undertake one of a variety of circular walks between Porthcurno and Treen using the Coast Path.

Porthcurno has all facilities in summer. The Coast Path leaves at the back of the beach, climbing a steep track to Percella Point before turning to run parallel to the sea. A seaward loop gives a good view of the beautiful Pednvounder Beach, but requires a little scramble to return to the official route. The path then reaches the neck of Treen Head, or Treryn Dinas, the site of an Iron Age fortification. A cul-de-sac diversion heads for the end and the Logan Rock.

Continue on the clear path over the cliff to descend into Penberth Cove, a superb little fishing hamlet with an old capstan. There are toilets but no refreshments.

After climbing away from Penberth the path continues along the cliff top, with one steep descent and climb at Porthguarnon, then starts to head inland. After passing a seaward house look out for the signed path to the right which descends into the wooded valley of St Loy and on to the boulder beach. Keep along the top of the beach for 55 yards/50m before leaving up the path. This climbs to pass above the lighthouse of Tater-du. Approaching Lamorna Point the path crosses a length of tumbled rocks, making for slow going, until it suddenly descends to the car park at Lamorna Cove. Here are toilets and seasonal refreshments.

Penberth Cove

Week 4 - Day 4

OS Maps: Landranger 203; Explorer 102

	This Walk	Cumulative	This Walk	Cumulative	Grading	Timing
Ascent	725ft	52,814ft	221m	16,098m	Strenuous then easy	3.5 hours
Distance	9.4mi	276.9mi	15.1km	445.7km		

For detailed directions see our Porthcurno to Penzance and Penzance to Porthleven Path Description booklets.

West of Mousehole this Section is one of lushly vegetated cliffs, but most of it is urban or semi-urban in character as it passes through Newlyn and Penzance. However, it is really defined by its views over the magnificent Mount's Bay, dominated by the iconic sight of St Michael's Mount and its castle, which give this coast a magical character.

Directions

A regular bus service passes about 1 mile/1.5km inland of Lamorna Cove and also serves Newlyn, Penzance and Marazion, giving a variety of possible bus-walk options.

Lamorna Cove has a seasonal cafe, toilets and, a little way inland, a pub. The Coast Path leaves the cove behind the harbour, bearing right to the cliffs. The well-marked path eventually leads to a road which descends into Mousehole. The road leads to the harbour; however, the official route turns right opposite "Lowena" then continues towards the sea, turning left along a terrace to a car park. It briefly passes along the harbour before turning left then right to reach the main harbour-side road. Mousehole has all facilities and is very picturesque.

At the far end of the harbour go through the car park, on along a concrete walkway then up some steps. Turn right along the road, then along a seaward track to arrive at Newlyn. Follow the road round the harbour and past the fish market, turning right just after the Seamen's Mission to cross a bridge. Bear right past the Tolcarne Inn then follow the promenade to Penzance. Pass the harbour then go right through the large car park to where a walkway leaves from its far right-hand end. Penzance has all facilities, is the end stop of the main-line railway and is the hub of local bus services. The train and bus stations are next to the car park.

The walkway follows the sea wall to the edge of Marazion. At the end of the walkway and cycle route either cross over and follow the road or cross the dunes to a large car park, cross this and continue behind the sea wall into Marazion.

Marazion is the centre for access to St Michael's Mount and is the southern end of the cross-peninsula St Michael's Way from Lelant. The little town of Marazion has all facilities.

Newlyn Harbour

Week 4 - Day 5

OS Maps: Landranger 203; Explorer 103 (Porthleven); Explorer 102 (remainder)

	This Walk	Cumulative	This Walk	Cumulative	Grading	Timing
Ascent	1,916ft	54,730ft	584m	16,682m	Moderate then strenuous	4.75 hours
Distance	10.6mi	287.5mi	17.1km	462.8km		

For detailed directions see our Penzance to Porthleven Path Description booklet.

Between Marazion and Cudden Point this Section is dominated by the sweep of Mount's Bay and its iconic focal point of St Michael's Mount. It is a charming length of low cliffs and small fields. East of Cudden Point the Mount is lost but the local landscape is bolder, with craggy headlands, long sandy beaches, inaccessible coves and picturesque cliff-top engine houses.

Directions

There are regular bus services which link Marazion and Porthleven and also serve Perranuthnoe and Praa Sands between the two, making a variety of bus-walks possible, Marazion is a pleasant little town with all facilities and the causeway to St Michael's Mount.

St Michael's Mount

The Coast Path leaves along the main road, following it for some way to the speed restriction sign. Turn right before the cemetery, then bear left on a concrete path down steps and follow the path to the beach. Cross the top of the beach to some metal steps, climb them and continue ahead. Just after Trenow Cove the path turns inland. Look out for the signed right turn after 275 yards/250m, which goes back to the low cliffs and on to Perranuthnoe. There are toilets and seasonal refreshments here.

Take the lane on the seaward side of the car park, bearing right and then left into a field. The well-marked path leads to Cudden Point, with magnificent views over Mount's Bay. It descends past Little Cudden to Bessy's Cove, where it joins a track. Go ahead, bearing right at some granite gate posts, then through Prussia Cove on a lane between large stone buildings. Keep ahead on the path which passes above Kenneggy Sand and then descends to Praa Sands, where there are toilets and seasonal refreshments. Go down the slipway to the beach then along in front of the shop, taking the steps up beside the cafe. Keep along the top of the grassy dunes, turning left when signed at the end then right into a housing estate. At the end bear right and climb to the cliffs. The path skirts behind Rinsey Head then through a car park and down to a restored engine house. It continues to Trewavas Head, inland of more restored engine houses. Beyond there have been numerous cliff falls – be sure to follow the signed path. This then enters Porthleven on a lane – fork right entering the town to pass alongside the harbour to its head. Porthleven has all facilities.

Week 4 - Day 6 (half day)

OS Maps: Landranger 203; Explorer 103

	This Walk	Cumulative	This Walk	Cumulative	Grading	Timing
Ascent	1,109ft	55,839ft	338m	17,020m	Moderate	3.25 hours
Distance	7.1mi	294.6mi	11.4km	474.2km		

For detailed directions see our Porthleven to The Lizard Path Description booklet.

This is a Section mostly of low cliffs with cliff-face paths, long stretches being above extensive beaches. It harbours a couple of unexpected features, firstly in the shape of Loe Bar, a large strip of shingle barring the freshwater Loe Pool from the sea, and secondly in the unusual position of Gunwalloe Church, hidden away in the corner of a sandy cove. Add a cliff-top monument to Marconi, a couple of picturesque coves and the rocky and atmospheric harbour at Mullion Cove and it makes for a fascinating length.

Directions

Porthleven and Mullion village, which is some 0.5 mile/1km from the Coast Path, are both served by regular but separate bus routes, which meet at Helston. The Mullion bus also serves Poldhu Cove, 1.5 miles/2.5km along the coast from Mullion Cove, allowing various bus-walks.

Porthleven has all facilities. The Coast Path goes alongside the harbour towards the clock-tower at the end near the pier. Follow the road past this building, going right at the fork and keep on out of the town to a car park. Climb the steps and continue ahead on the track to Loe Bar. Cross the bar to the far side, forking right, downhill, shortly after the memorial. After passing a renovated fishery building the path arrives at Gunwalloe Fishing Cove. Go ahead onto the National Trust's Baulk Head, then above Halzephron Cove to a road. Bear right to a small car park then go right again, away from the road, on the cliffs down to Gunwalloe Church Cove. There are toilets and seasonal refreshments here. The picturesque church is tucked away at the right-hand end of the cove.

Skirt the beach to a road, then take the signed path over a footbridge and over the rear of the beach to the path rising away. Immediately after the car park at the top turn right along the cliff top before returning to the road and dropping into Poldhu Cove, where there is a bus stop, toilets and refreshments. Cross the stream on the road and turn right up the driveway signed to the Marconi Centre, leaving this after 110 yards/100m for a path to the right.

This passes the Marconi monument on the cliffs then drops into Polurrian Cove. Climb away past the Polurrian Hotel and along the slightly suburban path to the Mullion Cove Hotel.

Keep to seaward and drop down to the harbour, where there are seasonal refreshments. There are toilets 110 yards/100m up the road.

Towards Loe Bar

Week 4 - Day 6 (half day)

OS Maps: Landranger 203; Explorer 103

	This Walk	Cumulative	This Walk	Cumulative	Grading	Timing
Ascent	1,303ft	57,142ft	397m	17,417m	Moderate	3.25 hours
Distance	6.8mi	301.4mi	10.9km	485.1km		

For detailed directions see our Porthleven to The Lizard Path Description booklet.

This is an exposed Section of high, flat-topped cliffs and spectacular coves and bays. The coastal landscape is superb throughout, but punctuated by some real scenic gems, of which Kynance Cove is probably the pick. The combination of steep cliffs, unusual geology and flora, beautiful sea colours and long stretches of easy walking make this a rewarding length. And watch out for choughs, Cornwall's iconic bird now returned to re-colonise this coast.

Directions

A regular bus service links Mullion village with Lizard Town, each settlement about 0.5 mile/1km inland from its respective end, thus giving a possible bus-walk. In addition, there are many easy local circuits based on the Coast Path in the Lizard-Kynance area.

Mullion Cove has seasonal refreshments and there are toilets a little way inland. The Coast Path leaves the quay slightly inland to the right, up the hill just after the cafe. Climb to the cliffs, keeping to the right to hug the coastline. There is an information board on the unique flora and fauna of the area here.

The easy and clear path rounds Parc Bean Cove and Lower Predannack Cliff. Approaching Vellan Head, be sure to keep close to the coast for the official route – the more obvious track misses the views. After the deep valley at Gew Graze the path rounds Rill Point and descends to Kynance Cove. The steep descent leads to a footbridge by the seasonal cafe. There are also toilets here. If the sun is shining the sea is brilliant turquoise.

From the cafe either follow the main track up towards the car park or cross the little beach (at low tide) and climb a partly stepped path to the cliffs, leaving this at a sign pointing right. This passes adjacent to the car park, where the main track arrives, and the Coast Path then continues clearly and easily above Pentreath Beach at Caerthillian and round Old Lizard Head, and on to Lizard Point, England's most southerly point, where there are cafes, gift shops and toilets. The nearby lighthouse is open to visitors at certain times. A path leads inland to Lizard Town, which has all facilities including regular bus services.

Kynance Cove

Week 5 - Day 1

OS Maps: Landranger 203 (Lizard); Landranger 204 (remainder); Explorer 103

	This Walk	Cumulative	This Walk	Cumulative	Grading	Timing
Ascent	2,293ft	59,435ft	699m	18,116m	Moderate, strenuous in places	5.75 hours
Distance	10.6mi	312.0mi	17.1km	502.2km		

For detailed directions see our The Lizard to Coverack Path Description booklet.

This is a Section of cliffs and coves, punctuated by headlands giving excellent views along the coastline. Here and there are areas of sandy beach at the foot of the cliffs, but only at Kennack are they very extensive. This coast is largely sheltered from the worst of the prevailing south-westerly winds, and consequently has a lush, well-vegetated character. This being a relatively unfrequented stretch, substantial lengths are quiet and remote.

Lloyd's Signal Station

Directions

Lizard Town, about 0.5 mile/1km inland of the Coast Path, has a bus service which also passes a little inland of Cadgwith, about half-way along this length, which presents a bus-walk possibility. In addition, there are numerous easy circuits based on The Lizard using the Coast Path which are popular and attractive.

Lizard Point has cafes and toilets, while Lizard Town, inland, has all necessary facilities. Lizard Point has the distinction of being England's most southerly point and is a fine location. The Coast Path leaves the Point alongside the car parking area and on in front of the lighthouse. There is a Heritage Centre at the lighthouse and both lighthouse and Heritage Centre are open to the public at certain times (www.lizardlighthouse.co.uk). After passing the lighthouse descend to cross a footbridge then climb, passing in front of the Housel Bay Hotel and on past the Lloyds Signal Station, bearing right here. The route passes Bass Point National Coastwatch Institution lookout, the first in the country to be established. At Kilcobben Cove the path goes behind The Lizard lifeboat station with its new boathouse which was completed in 2011. It then arrives at Church Cove. Go left for a short distance then take the path through the gate on the right. There are some ups and downs to a path junction just after a stone stile at Polgwidden Cove; keep right here. A little further on the path skirts the dramatic collapsed cave of the Devil's Frying Pan. Follow the signed path past the cottages and down into the picturesque little fishing hamlet of Cadgwith.

Cadgwith has a pub, shop, refreshments and toilets. There is a superb little beach here where the fishing boats are hauled up. This is overlooked by a convenient grassy knoll with seats known as The Todn (Cornish for lawn). Walk through Cadgwith and up the hill, turning right on the signed path a little way up. The Path then descends to Poltesco, crossing a footbridge. There is a diversion to the right leading to the attractive and interesting cove, complete with old serpentine works, where the local colourful rock was made into useful items. Climbing out of Poltesco, the path then joins a road which leads to the beach at Kennack Sands. There are toilets here and seasonal refreshments.

Follow the path behind the beaches and on to the cliffs to reach the neck of the long promontory of Carrick Luz, the site of an Iron Age cliff fort. The path cuts across the neck and then negotiates the steep valley at Downas Cove. Another, shallower valley crossing leads to the end of Black Head and its lookout hut. The path now descends over the cliffs towards Chynhalls Point going amongst the natural rock outcrops which can be slippery in wet weather. Beyond the Point the path soon reaches Coverack.

An alternative inland path avoids the slippery Chynhalls Cliff. At the top of the Coast Path descent, the wide alternative path goes through gorse and passes a Sculpture Park, then the edge of a caravan park before arriving at a bungalow on a tarmac road. Turn right towards the hotel and then almost immediately bear left down a narrower path to rejoin the Coast Path at Chynhalls Point.

Reaching the road at Coverack, the path soon veers off right down some steps to arrive at a car park at the end of the village. Follow the road past the harbour. Coverack, a pretty place, has all facilities, including a regular bus service into Helston.

Week 5 - Day 2

OS Maps: Landranger 204; Explorer 103

	This Walk	Cumulative	This Walk	Cumulative	Grading	Timing
Ascent	2,192ft	61,627ft	668m	18,784m	Moderate	5.75 hours
Distance	13.1mi	325.1mi	21.1km	523.3km		

For detailed directions, see our Coverack to Helford Path Description booklet.

This is a sheltered Section of the Coast Path. It includes low cliffs facing away from the prevailing winds, but also lengths of pleasant rural field paths, a little inland, necessary to avoid inaccessible coastal working and former quarries. In addition this Section has substantial lengths which fringe a tidal creek and on wooded estuary-side paths passing pretty beaches where the Coast Path reaches the Helford River. While not as dramatic as some Sections, it is an attractive stretch with a quiet charm of its own.

Directions

Separate bus routes from Helston serve Coverack and Helford Passage, across the river via ferry (Good Friday or 1st April to October) from Helford, allowing a bus-walk based on Helston. There is an attractive local circuit using the Coast Path between Helford and Gillan Creek.

There are all necessary facilities at Coverack. The Coast Path follows the road away from the pub and past the harbour, continuing straight ahead on a narrow lane when the road goes left. Look out for the sign pointing right, just before the end of the lane. The path goes over sometimes boggy ground next to the coast to arrive at Lowland Point. Next, the old workings at Dean Quarry are passed on their seaward side. The well-signed path then arrives at the open area at Godrevy Cove. The next length of coast is inaccessible due to operating quarries, so the Coast Path heads across the open area inland to pick up a signed path going uphill between fields. This leads to the little hamlet of Rosenithon. At the T-junction, turn right on the lane, uphill, turning left into a field just after the right-hand bend. Cross three fields in the same direction, stone stiles between them, to emerge on a lane. Go left then, at a junction, right, which leads to Porthoustock, a coastal hamlet with public toilets.

The route of the next stretch, to another coastal hamlet, Porthallow, is also a rural inland walk. It leaves Porthoustock past the telephone box and up the hill. Where the road bears right go straight ahead on a narrower lane. Go past a row of thatched cottages and over a little grassy bank at the end next to a greenhouse to a kissing-gate. Just past the gate there is a fork in the path. Bear right and follow the path climbing to the far top corner of the field to cross a lifting-bar stile and a Cornish stile (a sort of stone cattle grid) into another field. Turn right in this field alongside the hedge, then bear away left at the top to cross another Cornish stile to a road. At the road go left, passing through the tiny hamlet of Trenance. Here the route follows the road round to the right to a T-junction. At the junction go slightly right and immediately left onto an enclosed path which leads to a track between buildings. Here is the charming Fat Apples Cafe, open all year though winter hours are limited. At the road turn right to arrive at Porthallow.

Porthallow has a pub, toilets and seasonal refreshments. Fat Apples Cafe is open all year with winter opening hours between October and March. The staff at Fat Apples Cafe are happy to fill up flasks and dry clothes. They will help with lifts if they are free to do so. Look out for the marker indicating the half-way point of the Coast Path, equidistant (at 315 miles) from Minehead and Poole. Leave Porthallow along the back of the beach and up the steps. The path now follows the coastline, keeping close to the edge round Nare Point and then past a couple of pretty beaches. Moving into the mouth of the Helford River the path continues alongside its tidal tributary, Gillan Creek.

Looking back to Porthallow

From Easter/1st April to 31st October use the signal board to request the ferry. Telephone 01326 231357 or see page 19 for ferry details.

Otherwise, the route goes left from the creekside up the hill to a sharp left-hand bend. Here go straight ahead along the field edge, then bear right over two further fields to a road. Turn right to Carne, at the head of the creek, then right again along the north side of the creek to St Anthony Church. Past the church turn left uphill then shortly right on a farm track which leads into a field. Cross diagonally left to the top of the field to a kissing-gate.

For a short, direct route from here go through the gate and turn left. However, the Coast Path includes an optional extra of a circuit of Dennis Head. For this circuit do not pass through the gate but turn right then almost immediately left over a stile. At the next junction continue straight ahead to reach the end of the headland. The path circles around the headland, re-joining the outward route to the stile and then the kissing-gate.

Go through the gate and continue along the top of the field. The route now heads up the estuary side of the Helford River through woods and past coves. Towards the end the path reaches a track – follow to the road and go right here then quickly left. The path then emerges next to the main car park at Helford. Go down the hill into the village. Helford has a pub and shop and there are toilets and a seasonal cafe at the car park. The cafe will take telephone orders to be ready on arrival, so it is possible to phone from St Anthony and have your order ready when you reach Helford – call 01326 231893.

Porthallow Coast Path Halfway Marker

Week 5 - Day 3

OS Maps: Landranger 204; Explorer 103

	This Walk	Cumulative	This Walk	Cumulative	Grading	Timing
Ascent	1,397ft	63,024ft	426m	19,210m	Moderate	4.5 hours
Distance	10.0mi	335.1mi	16.1km	539.4km		

For detailed directions see our Helford to Falmouth Path Description booklet.

There are two contrasting parts to this Section. Between Helford and Rosemullion Head it is a sheltered walk alongside the mouth of the beautiful Helford River, with undulating, relatively low cliffs alternating with charming little beaches. Between Rosemullion Head and Falmouth the walk flanks the sweep of Falmouth Bay, with rather larger coves overlooked by the great headland of Pendennis Point at the Falmouth end, crowned by its castle. Over the bay is St Anthony Head lighthouse. None of this is a lonely or remote walk, and the Falmouth end is decidedly urban, but it is never uninteresting and always very scenic.

Directions

Helford Passage and Falmouth are linked by a regular bus service, which also serves two of the beach coves along the route, at Maenporth and Swanpool, giving numerous bus-walk options. The short circular walk round Pendennis Head in Falmouth is a great local favourite.

Helford has pub, shop and toilets; Helford Passage, over the river, has a pub and seasonal refreshments. There is a seasonal ferry link.

For ferry details see page 19.

It is possible to use local taxi services if the ferry is not operating – Autocabs, tel: 01326 573773 or Cove Cars tel. 07980 814058. Alternatively Sailaway St Anthony Ltd, tel: 01326 231357 may be able to help.

Walk around Helford River

If the ferry is not operating, a 13 mile/21km walk around the Helford River is possible. This will add another day to the itinerary. For this route, from Helford take the path up the hill in front of the Shipwright Arms to arrive at Penarvon Cove. Go round the back of the cove and turn inland up a track to a road. Turn right then left on a track to the permissive path along the atmospheric Frenchman's Creek. At the end take the path on the right signed to Withan past Frenchman's Pill Cottage, crossing a footbridge. Follow the path through the woods and aim for the far left corner of the field, taking the stile on the left. Follow the boundary on the left past Withan Farm, then head west over the fields to a lane. Here turn left to a crossroads, turning right here towards Mawgan. The lane joins a larger road; turn right past Gear then down and up into Mawgan-in-Meneage village. Turn right just after the church on the path towards Gwarth-an-drea then left behind a bungalow to a road. Turn right and at the junction bear right and continue downhill to the bridge at Gweek. There is a shop and pub here. Take the road opposite the Gweek Inn and at

Tolvan Cross turn right along a bridleway to a road junction. Go straight ahead, towards Porth Navas. After crossing the stream take the footpath on the left along the field edge to the road. Follow the road ahead to Nancenoy and Polwheveral. At the crossroads after Polwheveral turn right then after 140 yards/128m take the path on the left along the field edge then across the field corner to a road junction. Take the Porth Navas road opposite through

Pendennis Castle

the village to Trenarth Bridge, then turn right towards Falmouth. At the junction at Trebah turn right, then right again into Bar Road. At the end turn left on a footpath which leads to the Helford River, turning left to the Ferryboat Inn at Helford Passage, the landing place for the ferry from Helford.

Ferry users start from here

Coast Path, Helford Passage - Falmouth

From the Ferryboat Inn, facing the pub, turn right along the river and up to a grassy hill. Keep on to a concrete track and follow this, passing behind Trebah Beach at Polgwidden Cove. Continue on the riverside to Durgan, turning sharp right to enter the little village. Go up the road, ignoring one path to the right, until the road turns left and the path continues straight ahead. Follow this path, arriving at Porth Saxon Beach behind a building and then through a field to Porthallack Beach. The path then climbs round Toll Point to arrive at a wooded area. At the fork keep right and follow the path onward to Rosemullion Head, leaving the Helford River behind.

Keep seaward round the headland then descend to go through a small wood and then on, the path becoming suburban now, to reach Maenporth where there are toilets and refreshments and a bus stop. Turn right behind the cafe and continue to Swanpool, with more toilets and refreshments and another bus stop. Take the path from the far end of the beach to arrive at Gyllyngvase, then keep along Falmouth's promenade to the far end. The official path goes around the magnificent Pendennis Point – keep to the seaward road all the way to the end then at the car park descend on the signed path up the river, parallel to the road above. The path emerges from woods and passes the Leisure Centre, descending above the docks to a T-junction. Turn right then go ahead under the railway bridge, passing the Maritime Museum and along Falmouth's main shopping street to arrive at the Prince of Wales Pier at the far end. Falmouth, of course, has all facilities, including a rail link to the main line at Truro.

Week 5 - Day 4 (half day)

OS Maps: Landranger 204; Explorer 105

	This Walk	Cumulative	This Walk	Cumulative	Grading	Timing
Ascent	974ft	63,998ft	297m	19,507m	Easy	2.75 hours
Distance	6.2mi	341.3mi	10.0km	549.4km		

For detailed directions see our St Mawes to Portscatho Path Description Booklet.

This Section includes a trip on the ferry across the mouth of the River Fal, a treat of scenery and interest in its own right. Beyond, the walk round St Anthony Head is one of superb estuarine and coastal views, followed by an easy but charming path on low cliffs, sheltered from the westerlies, while passing some fine sandy beaches and giving excellent views up the South Cornwall coast.

Directions

A regular bus route serves Portscatho and St Mawes from Truro, which is also linked to Falmouth by bus and train. There is also a very popular circular walk using the Coast Path in the St Anthony Head area and another from Portscatho.

Two ferries are required to cross between Falmouth and the Coast Path at Place, east of the large estuary. The first goes between Falmouth and St Mawes, across the mouth of the main Fal Estuary, sometimes referred to as Carrick Roads.

The ferry operates all year from Prince of Wales Pier (year round) and Custom House Quay (summer only). Tel: 01326 741194.

For ferry details see page 19.

The second leg of the crossing is the ferry between St Mawes and Place, crossing the mouth of the Fal's tributary, the Percuil River. This ferry operates 1 June – 30 September from 09:00 – 17:00 every half hour, subject to demand. Tel: 01326 741194. In winter an alternative may be offered by a water taxi service, tel: 07971 846786. For details visit www.stmaweskayaks.co.uk .

For ferry details see page 19.

There is also Falmouth Water Taxi service which operates between Falmouth and St Mawes or Place, weather permitting between March and October 0900 to 1800 (2230 May to September). If needed, it is advisable to telephone 2-3 days in advance in the Summer. Tel: 07522 446659, www.falmouthwatertaxi.co.uk.

Information is also available from the Fal River Visitor Information Centre at Prince of Wales Pier, or visit www.falriver.co.uk.

If arriving at St Mawes and wishing to proceed to Place when the Place ferry is not operating it is possible to take the regular bus service from St Mawes to Gerrans, walking from here to Place (2.5 miles/4km). For this option, go to Gerrans Church and pick up the walking route described below. In addition, a local taxi company, Roseland Taxis, will carry walkers around here and throughout the Roseland Peninsula – tel: 01872 501001, M: 07817 447667, website www.roselandtaxis.co.uk

St Mawes Ferry

Portscatho

Walk between St Mawes and Place

A walking route also exists between St Mawes and Place, via Gerrans. This adds 9 miles/14km to the overall route, effectively an extra day to the itinerary. Leaving the ferry point in St Mawes, turn left along the road. Approaching the castle, take the minor lane left, which leads to a footpath at the end. This becomes a scenic path alongside the Carrick Roads – the Fal Estuary. At a minor road go right then bear left in front of the boatyard and then on a bank above the shore. This leads to the churchyard of St Just in Roseland, a beautiful spot. Pass the church and keep to the path next to the shore. Follow the path as it bears right up the hill, signed St Just Lane, to emerge on a road. Turn left, ignoring the first footpath on the right, but take the second a little afterwards. Follow the path alongside field boundaries, first to the right, then to the left, then to the right again. Go down to the road at the end of the fourth field and turn right to the A3078 at Trethem Mill. Turn left and immediately right after the bridge up some steps and through a small wood. Out of the wood, cross the field diagonally right (bearing 110) then in the next field bear diagonally right again (bearing 140), leaving it by a wooded track. Cross the stile at the top and bear diagonally right again (bearing 137) to meet a hedge, which is followed to a road. Turn right on the road. At the next junction follow the road curving to the right past Polhendra Cottage then turn left through the second gate. Descend towards the bottom of the hedge visible on the opposite side of the valley (bearing 123). Cross the bridge and climb as close as possible with the hedge to the left. Cross the stone steps behind the gorse at the top and bear slightly left across the next two fields (bearing 125) to emerge on a road. Turn right to arrive at Gerrans Church. (Those who have taken the bus from St Mawes will join here – see above.)

At the church fork left into Treloan Lane, keeping ahead past the buildings. Go through the gate at the end of the lane, crossing an open field ahead into another enclosed track, which leads to Porth Farm. At the road turn right then go left at the sign indicating "Footpath to Place by Percuil River". Follow this very scenic path which leads to the ferry landing point then on to Place itself.

Coast Path, Place - Portscatho

At Place, walk up the lane past the gates to the grand house. Turn right into the churchyard of St Anthony Church, passing behind the church and up into a wooded area. Turn right at the track then at the creek look for the sign on the left taking the path alongside the plantation. The path now gives superb views over Carrick Roads to Falmouth. Approaching St Anthony Head keep to the coastal path to the right until passing through the gate towards the lighthouse. Just after the gate climb the steps to the left to the car parking area. There are also toilets here. Leave the car park next to the coast and the superb and easy path then leads to Portscatho, which has a shop, toilets and pubs, as well as a bus service to St Mawes and Truro.

Week 5 - Day 4 (half day)

OS Maps: Landranger 204: Explorer 105

	This Walk	Cumulative	This Walk	Cumulative	Grading	Timing
Ascent	1,674ft	65,672ft	510m	20,017m	Strenuous	3.75 hours
Distance	7.5mi	348.8mi	12.0km	561.4km		

For detailed directions see our Portscatho to Portloe Path Description Booklet.

This is a very quiet Section for the most part. Cliffs are relatively low at first, but increase in height as the great promontory of Nare Head, with its superb views, is approached. The long sandy beaches below the cliffs passed west of Nare Head are replaced by tiny isolated and inaccessible coves east of the headland. This length has a wonderfully remote atmosphere.

Directions

Portscatho and Portloe are both served by regular, but different, bus services, both linking with Truro. There are some local circular walks using the Coast Path around Nare Head, based on the inland village of Veryan.

Portscatho has a shop, pubs, toilets and bus service. The Coast Path leaves past the Harbour Club; keep right just after leaving the village at the footpath junction. The path goes round the back of Porthcurnick Beach, then up the road on the far side, turning right along the coastal edge. The path continues to undulate along the coast until it turns inland to reach a road. Turn right, past Pendower Court and down the road to its end at Pendower Beach. Cross the rear of the beach and head for the public toilets, going up the hill and turning right. The path soon diverts around the rear of the Nare Hotel to a road, descending to Carne Beach. Follow the road round the bend and up the hill for a short way, turning right to return to the cliffs. The path now heads for Nare Head, via a steep descent and ascent at Tregagle's Hole and past an old fisherman's cottage. A short diversion at the top of Nare Head reveals some stunning coastal views.

The path now goes round the seaward edge of Rosen Cliff and over the valley behind Kiberick Cove to Blouth Point. At the point enter a field and keep left for a short way before bearing right, downhill, towards some trees. The path zigzags upward to pass Broom Parc and then goes through a field to round Manare Point. After this it is downhill going over a short uneven section before joining a tarmac path which descends into Portloe. The village is very picturesque and has pubs and toilets as well as a bus service.

Portloe

Week 5 - Day 5

OS Maps: Landranger 204; Explorer 105

	This Walk	Cumulative	This Walk	Cumulative	Grading	Timing
Ascent	2,841ft	68,513ft	866m	20,883m	Strenuous then easy	5.75 hours
Distance	12.3mi	361.1mi	19.8km	581.2km		

For detailed directions see our Portloe to Mevagissey Path Description booklet.

This is a quiet Section of mostly high cliffs, often covered in lush vegetation. Towards Gorran Haven these cliffs reduce in height. The Section includes the great headland of Dodman Point, from where there are views to the Lizard in one direction and Devon in the other on a clear day. Below the cliffs are some sandy beaches, often all but inaccessible. This is a coastline for those preferring remoteness.

Directions

There are some excellent circular walks using the Coast Path at Dodman Point and linking to Gorran Haven, giving a variety of options here.

Gorran Haven

The scenic little harbour village of Portloe has toilets, pubs and a bus service. The Coast Path leaves behind the Lugger Hotel, leaving the road to reach a prominent converted chapel. Pass this then climb steeply to the cliffs. After a quite strenuous length the path arrives at West Portholland. Follow the road above the shore to a junction, then turn right to East Portholland. There are toilets here and a seasonal cafe and shop. Pass the cottages at the far end and climb behind them on a clear path to a field, turning right down the field edge. The path leads to a road which descends to Porthluney Cove. Here are toilets and seasonal refreshments and the picturesque setting is enhanced by the presence of Caerhayes Castle just inland. Walk behind the beach and turn right into parkland. Climb behind the field-edge trees then go to the right and follow the field edge to the woods. After crossing the rocky ridge at Greeb Point the path descends to a road behind Hemmick Beach. Cross the bridge and go right, climbing to the headland of Dodman Point ("The Dodman"), with its memorial cross and superb views. The path stays clear above the lovely sands of Bow or Vault Beach, then rounds the headland of Pen-a-maen to enter Gorran Haven. This little harbour village has a shop, pub and toilets. There is a Gorran community bus which runs 4 days a week www.gorranbus.org which walkers have recommended to us and can be hailed anywhere along its route.

Leave Gorran Haven up Church Street, turning right into Cliff Road. Turn right near the top of the hill and a stile on the left leads to the cliffs. The clear path leads to Chapel Point, where it crosses the tarmac access road to follow the path along the coast into Portmellon. Follow the road uphill and go down through the park on the right on entering Mevagissey. Steps descend to the harbour. Mevagissey is the archetypal Cornish fishing village and has all facilities.

Week 5 - Day 6

OS Maps: Landranger 204; Explorer 105 (western half); Explorer 107 (eastern half)

	This Walk	Cumulative	This Walk	Cumulative	Grading	Timing
Ascent	2,434ft	70,947ft	742m	21,625m	Strenuous then easy	5 hours
Distance	10.5mi	371.6mi	17.1km	598.3km		

For detailed directions see our Mevagissey to Charlestown and Charlestown to Fowey Path Description booklets.

The western half of this Section has a relatively remote feel, enhanced by some quite strenuous climbs and some attractive cliffs and headlands. To the east the coastline is more urbanised but with beaches and the lovely Georgian docks of Charlestown found among the houses, golf courses and clay industry. The cliff-top path between Porthpean and Charlestown was reinstated in late 2011, avoiding two miles of road diversion.

Directions

There are bus routes from St Austell to Mevagissey, Charlestown and Par, one of these routes serving both the latter two locations, so that a range of bus-walks is possible.

The attractive fishing village of Mevagissey has all facilities. The Coast Path goes along the back of the harbour and then turns right along its eastern side before forking left steeply uphill. After crossing some playing fields, pass seaward of the houses then continue along the undulating cliffs to descend behind the ruined fish cellars at Portgiskey Cove. Continue uphill along the seaward and far field boundaries to a fenced path at the top. Turn right here, parallel to the road. At the entrance to Pentewan Sands Holiday Park follow the B3273 road pavement and turn first right before the petrol station, signposted to Pentewan. There are a few shops, toilets and a pub in the village. The official route then follows the road through Pentewan and up the hill for about 100 yards/90m, taking the first turn sharp right along The Terrace and along a narrow path at the end to arrive at the cliffs. A more interesting alternative turns right, away from the road into the harbour area just after the public toilets then, immediately after the last cottage, goes left steeply uphill, through gardens, to arrive at the official route on the cliffs.

After some 1.25 miles/2km the path descends through a wood and reaches a track. Turn right here to arrive at another track just behind the remote Hallane Mill Beach. Turn left here then quickly right, climbing back up the cliffs to arrive at Black Head. A diversion from the memorial stone goes to the tip of this atmospheric location. Continuing from Black Head the path enters Ropehaven Woods with some confusing paths – it is important to follow the waymarking. Entering the wood turn right down a rocky and sometimes slippery path, then left. Go left again onto a walled path, ignoring descending paths on the right, to arrive beside a cottage and emerge onto a track. Go right here then leave the road to the right just after a parking area and follow the cliff-top path down, up and down again to Porthpean. Walk along the promenade to the far end and climb the steps to rejoin the newly reinstated cliff-top path all the way to Charlestown.

Charlestown has a fascinating Georgian harbour, the home of a group of tall ships, and has refreshments, toilets, pubs and buses. Note that the official Coast Path does not cross the dock gate at the mouth of the harbour, though many people use that route. On the east side climb past the public toilets and on to reach a suburban road for a short way, soon forking off right over a long grassy area. Arriving at a large car park above Carlyon Bay Beach keep to seaward then cross the beach access road where a new

Mevagissey Harbour

resort is being developed and continue ahead on the low cliffs. Keep seaward of the golf course to approach the old china clay works at Par Docks. At the little beach at Spit Point turn inland and follow the narrow path past the works and then alongside a railway line to emerge on a road. Turn right along the pavement past the docks entrance and under a railway bridge. Turn right at the junction, signposted to Fowey, over a level crossing and then under another railway bridge before forking right on the road, Par Green.

To continue beyond Par on the Coast Path, walk along Par Green, looking for house no. 52 and follow the path signed on the right.

Par has all facilities, including a mainline railway station; for the station turn left at the far end of Par Green along Eastcliffe Road.

Charlestown

Week 6 - Day 1 (half day)

OS Maps: Landranger 200 or 204; Explorer 107

	This Walk	Cumulative	This Walk	Cumulative	Grading	Timing
Ascent	1,132ft	72,079ft	345m	21,970m	Moderate	3 hours
Distance	7.0mi	378.6mi	11.1km	609.4km		

For detailed directions see our Charlestown to Fowey Path Description booklet.

This Section goes out to the prominent Gribbin Head. The west side of the headland is relatively exposed, mostly on high cliffs, with views west over St Austell Bay. The east side is more indented and sheltered, the cliffs lower, and the path passes numerous scenic little sandy coves. At its eastern end the path enters the lovely part-wooded estuary of the River Fowey, culminating in the atmospheric little town of Fowey.

Directions

Par and Fowey are linked by a bus service, making this a bus-walk option.
In addition, a popular local circular walk from Fowey takes in most of Gribbin Head, using the waymarked Saints' Way path with the Coast Path.

Par has all facilities, including a mainline railway station. For the Coast Path walk along the road called Par Green and follow the path which leaves the road next to no.52. After crossing the private clay haul road, fork right along a grassy path immediately before the chalet park. Follow this path before turning left then quickly right along the road to a small car park at the western end of the sands of Par Beach. Walk along the back of the beach to another car park at the far, eastern end. This is Polmear; a pub and buses are to be found on the road outside the car park.

The Coast Path crosses the car park to a footbridge and then up the cliffs and continues on to the little harbour village of Polkerris. Here are a pub, toilets and restaurant. The path continues from the back of the beach, up a ramp to join a zigzag path through woods to the top. The path now continues to the Daymark on Gribbin Head (or "The Gribbin"). The tower is open to visitors on some summer Sundays. From the Daymark follow the path downhill to the scenic cove at Polridmouth ("Pridmouth"), said to have inspired the setting for Daphne du Maurier's "Rebecca". Cross behind the beach and go up into the woods, then on over cliff-top fields and past a couple of small coves to arrive at another woodland. Look out for the path on the right, which goes past St Catherine's Castle and gives superb views upriver to Fowey. Now follow the path down a rocky track and behind Readymoney Cove before following the lane into Fowey.

Towards Gribbin Head

Note that it is possible to walk Coast to Coast across Cornwall between Fowey and Padstow on the north coast using the Saints' Way. A guidebook is available from Fowey TIC.

Week 6 - Day 1 (half day)

OS Maps: Landranger 200 or 204 (Fowey); Landranger 201 (remainder); Explorer 107

	This Walk	Cumulative	This Walk	Cumulative	Grading	Timing
Ascent	1,939ft	74,018ft	591m	22,561m	Strenuous	3.5 hours
Distance	7.1mi	385.7mi	11.5km	620.9km		

For detailed directions see our Fowey to Polperro Path Description booklet.

This is a connoisseur's Section – it is quiet and remote; it is scenic, with beautiful large sandy bays and smaller coves plus impressive headlands; it is started and finished at superbly picturesque locations, the Fowey estuary at one end and Polperro at the other; and it is quite hard work, emphasising that nothing this good should come too easily.

Directions

Polruan and Polperro are linked by a bus service, giving a bus-walk option, though unfortunately it does not operate at weekends. There is a popular scenic circular walk taking in Fowey and Polruan and using two ferries, an estuary tributary valley and the Coast Path.

Polruan looking up River Fowey

Fowey is a charming little town, well worth exploring, with all facilities.

The crossing of the river to Polruan on the opposite bank is by foot ferry. In summer it usually operates from Whitehouse Quay, along the Esplanade, and in winter from the Town Quay.

The ferry operates all year except Christmas Day at 5-10 minute intervals, telephone 01726 870232.

For ferry details see page 19.

At Polruan, a picturesque little place, go up the steps next to The Lugger. Turn right at the top in West Street then turn left up Battery Lane. At the grassy area keep left by the wall then through the car park parallel to the coast to a signed path on the right. After around 2 miles/3km the path passes above and behind the impressive Lantic Bay, climbing steeply at the far end. There is a higher path here, going to the top of the hill and turning right, or a lower one, turning off right 30 yards/28m before the top, dropping then climbing again to meet the higher path (ignore beach turnings to the right). The path goes out around Pencarrow Head then behind an old watch house to descend and pass behind two charming and remote coves at Lansallos West and East Coombes. After climbing past a marker warning shipping of an offshore rock more ups and downs follow until the path approaches the almost hidden inlet of Polperro. Follow the waymarked path to arrive at a rocky outlook point – go left here then fork right to descend to the harbour. Polperro, an impossibly picturesque harbour village, figures justifiably in most picture books and calendars of Cornwall. It has all facilities.

Week 6 - Day 4 (half day)

OS Maps: Landranger 201; Explorer OL20

	This Walk	Cumulative	This Walk	Cumulative	Grading	Timing
Ascent	1,260ft	80,649ft	384m	24,582m	Easy	3 hours
Distance	7.3mi	426.4mi	11.8km	686.3km		

For detailed directions see our Mount Batten to Warren Point Path Description Booklet.

This is a Section of low cliffs, much of it overlooking Plymouth Sound. Below the cliffs are extensive areas of rock platform and offshore the Great Mew Stone becomes a focal point. Caravan and chalet sites and suburban villages are never far away and this is never a lonely Section. Towards its eastern end, as the cliffs rise somewhat, is the picturesque mouth of the River Yealm, forming a dramatic wooded gap in the cliffs.

Directions

Separate bus routes serve Mount Batten and Wembury village, and also Heybrook Bay, midway along this section, all from Plymouth city centre, allowing bus-walk options. There is a popular circular walk using the Coast Path between Wembury and Warren Point and a longer, full-day circular using the waymarked Erme-Plym Trail between Wembury and Mount Batten plus the Coast Path.

Mount Batten has toilets and refreshments, as well as a direct ferry link to and from Plymouth's Sutton Harbour. From Mount Batten the Coast Path heads over the little hill and past the old fort tower to the grassy area at Jennycliff, where there are more toilets and refreshments. Keep close above the shore and at the end of the grass, from the doormat to Plymouth use the renovated steps down and stairs up again to access woodland. The path then undulates and emerges above Fort Bovisand. Descend steeply to a road and turn left; there are seasonal refreshments here. Follow round to the right and up to pass seaward of the chalets, past a cafe and toilets and on round the point and so to Heybrook Bay. There is a pub a little way up the road here, as well as a bus stop. Keep right and follow the path above the shore around Wembury Point and on to Wembury Beach. Yet more toilets and refreshments await here and the bus stop, together with pub and shop, are in the village a little way inland.

From Wembury Beach a Coast-to-Coast walk goes to Lynmouth on the north coast, following the Erme-Plym Trail and the Two Moors Way. Guidebooks are available from Ivybridge TIC.

Continuing on the Coast Path, climb seaward of the church and along the now higher cliffs to a junction of paths at the Rocket House. The path going inland from here leads to Wembury village and its facilities. For the Coast Path, bear right, downhill, to reach the ferry point. Note that operating times on this ferry can be limited – see page 19 and Walk 49.

Bovisand during Great South West Walks 2014

Week 6 - Day 5

OS Maps: Landranger 201 (western end); Landranger 202 (remainder); Explorer OL20

	This Walk	Cumulative	This Walk	Cumulative	Grading	Timing
Ascent	2,450ft	83,099ft	747m	25,329m	Easy then strenuous	5.75 hours
Distance	13.5mi	439.9mi	21.8km	708.1km		

For detailed directions see our Noss Mayo to Mothecombe and Mothecombe to Thurlestone Path Description Booklet.

This is a fine Section of high-level coastal cliffs, cut mid-way by the substantial and extremely picturesque estuary of the River Erme. The western end is a particularly good length, since the superb cliff coastline is easily accessed by a scenic former carriage route. Beyond that a series of descents and ascents, some quite steep, accentuate the dramatic landscape of the coastline. At the eastern extremity is the tidally insular Burgh Island, a focal point on this part of the coast. Because of its remoteness and strenuous nature, much of this section has a quiet character which will specially appeal to those in search of a lonely coastline.

Directions

This remote length of coast only has public transport at its western end, so no bus-walks are feasible. There is a very popular local walk using the Coast Path on the carriage drive from Noss Mayo.

The ferry at Wembury's Warren Point operates three ways over the River Yealm and its tributary Newton Creek. Warren Point is thus linked with both Newton Ferrers and Noss Mayo, and these two points with each other. For the Coast Path the link between Warren Point and Noss Mayo is needed. The ferry operates seasonally and at limited times – telephone 01752 880079.

For ferry details see page 19.

There is a signal board to summon the ferryman by the steps at Warren Point or the slipway at Noss Mayo. Alternatively, telephone beforehand.

Because of the somewhat limited nature of the ferry it may be necessary to make alternative arrangements to reach Noss Mayo. Both Wembury and Noss Mayo have a regular bus service to and from Plymouth, so it is possible to use these services as a link, perhaps combining with an overnight stop in Plymouth. Alternatively, local taxi companies are available:-

Eco-Taxi, based in Kingsbridge, will carry walkers between Plymouth and Dartmouth and from all estuaries in South Devon; telephone 01548 856347 or 07811 385275. Ivy Cabs, telephone 01752 895555, will also carry walkers round the South Devon estuaries as will John Pitcher at Wembury Cabs, details page 103.

It is also possible to walk round the Yealm Estuary from ferry point to ferry point. This is a distance of some 9 miles 14.5km, effectively adding an extra day or half day to the itinerary.

Walk around the Yealm Estuary

Walk uphill inland from the ferry steps to the house at the top, the Rocket House. Continue inland along the track, which in turn becomes a road. Where the road bears sharp right go ahead along a public footpath into a field, then keep ahead alongside a high wall. At the end of the wall, after two gates, bear left (bearing 330) across fields, then go down a few steps. The now enclosed path goes left then right to arrive at a road. This is Knighton, on the outskirts of Wembury. The bus stop for Plymouth is a little way to the left, just before the pub.

To continue the walking route around the estuary cross the road at Knighton to a minor lane, following it left to another junction. Turn right here and continue until the road meets another, more major, road. Cross this road, going ahead and left for a short way then turn right on a signed footpath. This is part of a waymarked route, the Erme-Plym Trail, and is shown on the OS Explorer OL20 map. Follow the waymarked route across fields, over Cofflete Creek, next to a lane and on to the village of Brixton. Turn right and follow the road through the village to Brixton Church then back on the Erme-Plym Trail up Old Road, along a suburban road, over fields, along a minor lane then over more fields to arrive at another village, Yealmpton. On reaching the A379 road at Yealmpton the Erme-Plym Trail is now abandoned. Here, turn right along the A379 then quickly left, into Stray Park. At the bottom bear right along a tarmac path then, when it arrives at a road, turn left along a stony track. At the footpath sign continue ahead, eventually emerging at a road by a car park. Turn left along the road to cross Puslinch Bridge then follow the road up the hill. Take the footpath on the right near the top of the hill, crossing a couple of fields to a road. Turn right and continue to meet a more major road, which is followed ahead to Newton Ferrers. At the edge of the village turn left down the road signed to Bridgend and Noss Mayo, and at the junction at the head of the creek keep to the right. Follow the riverside road, forking right into Noss Mayo. Keep on the road round Noss Creek and continue on the creekside road out of the village until this becomes a track. A signed path on the right leaves the track for the ferry point.

Coast Path, Noss Mayo-River Erme

From the ferry point, follow the path westward through the woods as it climbs to meet a track, an old carriage drive. The drive continues through woods, past a row of former coastguard cottages, into more woods, then on a superb cliff-face shelf round Mouthstone Point. Further on keep right where the more obvious path bears left inland to a car park, the drive continuing round Stoke Point and on to Beacon Hill. A series of ups and downs now ensues as the path approaches the estuary of the River Erme, which has been fairly described as England's most unspoiled river estuary, and is possibly the most attractive. The path crosses the top of a small beach then passes through a short woodland stretch to arrive at Mothecombe slipway on the Erme. There are seasonal refreshments a little way inland.

There is no ferry at the River Erme. It is usually possible to wade the river 1 hour either side of low water along the old ford and, under normal conditions, at low tide the water is about knee deep and the river bed is of sand with pebbles. The crossing is between grid references 614 476 and 620 478, ie the road by the row of coastguard cottages at Mothecombe and the end of the inland road to Wonwell Beach. However, great care should be taken as heavy rains or high seas can make conditions dangerous. Low water is approximately at the same time as at Devonport; see tide tables on pages 21-23.

If timing makes wading impossible there are local taxi companies Eco-Taxi telephone 01548 856347 or 07811 385275, or Ivy Cabs, telephone 01752 895555.

Alternatively, it is possible to walk round the estuary. There are no riverside rights of way and for the most part minor roads must be used. The distance is approximately 8 miles/13km, adding an extra half day to the itinerary.

Walk round the Erme Estuary

From the slipway follow the road inland, following signs to Holbeton. Go through the village and leave on the minor lane to Ford and then Hole Farm. At the sharp bend after this farm follow the waymarked Erme-Plym Trail to the A379 and across the River Erme at Sequer's Bridge. Then leave the waymarked trail, continuing very carefully along the A379 for a couple of hundred yards/metres, before turning right on the lane signed to Orcheton. Follow this for about 2 miles/3km then turn right, following signs for Wonwell Beach. Follow the lane downhill to arrive at the estuary.

Coast Path, River Erme-Bigbury-on-Sea

Just inland of the Wonwell slipway a path leaves the lane into the woods then continues above the shore, emerging on cliffs which rollercoaster up and down to the holiday park at Challaborough. Here are toilets and seasonal refreshments, and the path then soon reaches Bigbury-on-Sea. Here also are toilets and seasonal refreshments; the Bay View Cafe and Bistro will also supply packed lunches. On Burgh Island offshore, reached by walking across the sands or by unusual sea tractor, is a pub.

Week 6 - Day 6 (half day)

OS Maps: Landranger 202; Explorer OL20

	This Walk	Cumulative	This Walk	Cumulative	Grading	Timing
Ascent	876ft	83,975ft	267m	25,596m	Moderate	2.75 hours
Distance	5.7mi	445.6mi	9.2km	717.3km		

For detailed directions see our Mothercombe to Thurlestone and Thurlestone to Salcombe Path Description Booklet.

This is a well-used and popular Section, never far from residential and holiday accommodation. It is a length of low cliffs and sandy beaches, the coastline providing some interesting seascapes. These include views of the tidal Burgh Island, the estuary of the River Avon, the distinctive holed Thurlestone Rock and the headland of Bolt Tail. At the end of the Section, Hope Cove is a charming little settlement with a picturesque harbour and an old centre of historic cottages.

Directions

A regular, if infrequent, bus service links Thurlestone and Hope Cove, making a bus-walk option possible. There is a popular short circular walk using the Coast Path between Bantham and Thurlestone.

From the main facilities at Bigbury-on-Sea the Coast Path goes along the road, turning right immediately after the car park entrance to follow a short cliff-top length which re-joins the road further up. Cross the road and follow the path along the field edge next to the road. Leave the field where signed and cross the road, passing through Folly Farm and down the cliffs to the flat open area of Cockleridge Ham. At the edge is the ferry point for the crossing of the mouth of the River Avon.

The ferry is seasonal and operates at limited times – telephone 01548 561196. For ferry details see page 20.

The ferryman is alerted by waving. It must be noted that if the ferry is not operating on arrival the river should NOT be forded, despite its sometimes benign appearance. There are local taxi services, ie: Eco-Taxi, telephone 07811 385275; or Ivy Cabs, telephone 01752 895555.

Alternatively, there is a waymarked walk round the estuary between Bigbury-on-Sea and Bantham on the opposite bank. This route, the Avon Estuary Walk, is signed with blue waymarks and adds about 8 miles/13km to the route, or another half day to the itinerary. The route is shown on OS Explorer map OL20.

Avon Estuary Walk

The route is accessed by continuing up the road, without turning into Folly Farm, for a further 60 yards/55m and then turning right. The path reaches the golf course, turning left on a track then off this to the right, down another track past Hexdown Farm. Follow this track to the bottom then go left along a drive which eventually arrives at a road. There is a permissive path alongside the road and at the end of this a path goes right over a field, through the top of a wood then downhill over another field to a road alongside the estuary. This tidal road is then followed to Aveton Gifford on the A379. At high tide there is a waymarked diversion which crosses the

Burgh Island

tidal road on arriving at it and re-joins it next to the village. From Aveton Gifford cross the Avon on the A379 then take the first lane on the right, which becomes a track and continues to Stadbury Farm. Bear left approaching the farm onto a footpath, following field edges towards the valley bottom to cross Stiddicombe Creek. Enter the wood on the right and climb to leave at the far top corner. Follow the top edge of fields then cross a farm track and a stream to a junction of paths. Turn right and continue to Bantham village, where there is a pub, shop, toilets and seasonal refreshments as well as the ferry point.

Coast Path, Bantham-Hope Cove

From the ferry point go through the car park and round the edge of the dunes of Bantham Ham. Follow the shore, leaving the dunes and climbing past the edge of Thurlestone Golf Club to descend to Thurlestone Sands. Cross a long footbridge at an inland lagoon (South Milton Ley), pass public toilets and seasonal refreshments then join a road for a short stretch before turning back to the shoreline and over low cliffs to Outer Hope, where there are all facilities in season. Follow the path behind the little harbour and down to the old lifeboat station at Inner Hope, where the bus stop is situated. Buses to Kingsbridge leave from here. A little inland is the old village centre of Inner Hope, at The Square, a picture-postcard location worth seeing before leaving.

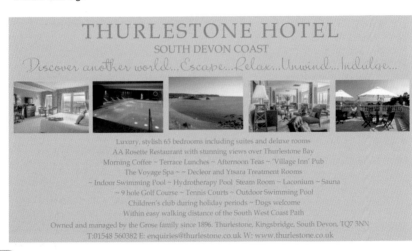

Week 6 - Day 6 (half day)

OS Maps: Landranger 202; Explorer OL20

	This Walk	Cumulative	This Walk	Cumulative	Grading	Timing
Ascent	1,506ft	85,481ft	459m	26,055m	Strenuous	4 hours
Distance	8.0mi	453.6mi	12.9km	730.2km		

For detailed directions see our Thurlestone to Salcombe Path Description Booklet.

This is a very scenic Section of the coast, largely comprising quite spectacular high cliffs soaring above tiny, mostly inaccessible coves. Near both ends are dramatic headlands, Bolt Tail in the west and Bolt Head in the east, offering superb coastal views in their respective directions. At the eastern end this Section turns into the mouth of the estuary of Salcombe Harbour, and there is the contrast of softer, sandy bays. This is a length which is never really remote, but never really busy.

Directions

Separate bus routes serve Hope Cove and Salcombe from Kingsbridge, a few miles inland, making a bus-walk feasible from there. However, there are numerous popular local circuits using the Coast Path which are based on Hope Cove and Salcombe.

Leave Hope Cove from the old lifeboat station at Inner Hope up the signed Coast Path and out to the magnificent viewpoint of Bolt Tail, where the ramparts of an Iron Age cliff fort are crossed to reach the end. The path doubles back along the cliff top over Bolberry Down and then down to the splendid little Soar Mill Cove. Climbing from the cove a long level stretch of easy walking follows. Keep along the cliff top and as the path approaches Bolt Head pass through a couple of gates, staying on the closest path to the cliff top as possible. A steep descent will then lead to the headland, where a sharp turn leads to the cliff-face path round Starehole Bay and then on to the Courtenay Walk below rocky pinnacles. Passing into woodland at the National Trust's Overbecks property the path joins a road which is followed past South Sands and North Sands – toilets and seasonal refreshments at both – and then on into Salcombe town centre. For a variation, there is a summer ferry service between South Sands and Salcombe. The town is a renowned yachting centre and has all facilities.

Hope Cove

Week 6 - Day 7

OS Maps: Landranger 202; Explorer OL20

	This Walk	Cumulative	This Walk	Cumulative	Grading	Timing
Ascent	2,251ft	87,732ft	686m	26,741m	Strenuous	6.75 hours
Distance	12.9mi	466.5mi	20.8km	751.0km		

For detailed directions see our Salcombe to Torcross Path Description booklet.

This is a superb Section of walking. Part of it is on exposed cliff faces, the sometimes stark cliffs contrasting with numerous tiny sandy coves below. A significant length in the middle is on an old "raised beach", a low shelf a little above the sea giving an easy passage here. In the east the path crosses the rocky spine of Start Point, behind its lighthouse, a dramatic stretch, before following a lush, sheltered length into Torcross.

Directions

Salcombe and Torcross are both on regular bus routes to and from Kingsbridge, a little inland, making a bus-walk possible from that town. There is also a popular local circuit using the Coast Path from the Salcombe Ferry.

Salcombe has all necessary facilities. The ferry across the estuary leaves from steps next to the Ferry Hotel, a little way downstream from the town centre.

The ferry operates all year; telephone 01548 842061 or 01548 560558.

For ferry details see page 20.

From the ferry point on the eastern side, where there are toilets and refreshments, the Coast Path follows the road down the estuary side then, after crossing the rear of the beach at Mill Bay (toilets), passes the refreshment facilities at Gara Rock (call 01548 844810 for details), then follows a clear cliff path to Prawle Point. The path goes to the Coastwatch lookout at the very end, then descends to follow the "raised beach" shelf just above the waves before a short inland length to avoid a cliff fall leads to Lannacombe Beach. Beyond here a dramatic length goes along and up to the rocky ridge leading to Start Point, the path dropping to the lighthouse access road. From the car park at the top the path bears off right down the cliff face to Hallsands, passing above the old ruined village. A short diversion to the viewpoint is both instructive and interesting. The path continues over low cliffs to Beesands, where there is a pub, toilets and seasonal refreshments. Continue along the shingle ridge then behind an old quarry to descend into Torcross, with a panoramic view of Slapton Ley ahead on the descent. Torcross has all facilities, and buses to Plymouth, Kingsbridge and Dartmouth.

Gammon Head

Week 7 - Day 1

OS Maps: Landranger 202; Explorer OL20

	This Walk	Cumulative	This Walk	Cumulative	Grading	Timing
Ascent	1,493ft	89,225ft	455m	27,196m	Easy then strenuous	4.75 hours
Distance	10.2mi	476.7mi	16.4km	767.4km		

For detailed directions see our Torcross to Kingswear Path Description Booklet.

Something like a quarter of this Section consists of the low shingle ridge known locally as the Slapton Line, cutting off the freshwater lake of Slapton Ley from the sea. Most of the remainder of the Section is cliffs and coves, partly looking to the sea and partly to the outer reaches of the picturesque wooded Dart Estuary. This Section has some lengths a little more inland than is usual and some road lengths, one of which is frankly unpleasant, but in compensation there are also some splendid stretches.

Directions

A regular bus service runs along the coast road which is, for much of the Section, adjacent to the Coast Path. With stops at most obvious locations this gives numerous bus-walk options. There is also a very popular and scenic circular walk using the Coast Path between Dartmouth and the mouth of the Dart Estuary.

Blackpool Sands

From Torcross, with all facilities, the Coast Path runs along the shingle ridge. The official route is on the landward side but it is possible, if more tiring, to walk along the seaward side. At the end, Strete Gate, follow the narrow lane uphill to reach the A379 road. It is now necessary to walk along this and for the next 400 yards/365m **THE NEED FOR CAUTION ON THIS BUSY, NARROW AND DANGEROUS ROAD CANNOT BE OVERESTIMATED.**

Follow the main road through Strete village (pub and shop) then, just after the village end, take the path to the right which passes over fields and a footbridge to reach a high point above the sea. Continuing parallel to the coast for a while it then heads inland over a deep valley, crossing the main road and over more fields to a lane. Descend the lane then leave it across more fields until, after crossing the main road again, the picturesque cove of Blackpool Sands is reached. There are toilets and seasonal refreshments. Follow the path uphill through the woods then the route enters and meanders along various paths in the village of Stoke Fleming (pub, shop and toilets), arriving at the village hall. Cross the main road again and follow a lane to a National Trust car park. From here a scenic cliff path proceeds, latterly through woods, to reach the Dart Estuary and arrive at Dartmouth Castle. An estuary-side path passes the adjacent church and joins the road which is followed into the town. Look out for some steps on the right just after the public toilets before reaching the centre; the steps lead down to Bayards Cove through its little castle and on to the Embankment at the town centre. Dartmouth, of course, has all facilities.

Week 7 - Day 2

OS Maps: Landranger 202; Explorer OL20

	This Walk	Cumulative	This Walk	Cumulative	Grading	Timing
Ascent	2,992ft	92,217ft	912m	28,108m	Strenuous	5.75 hours
Distance	10.8mi	487.5mi	17.3km	784.7km		

For detailed directions see our Kingswear to Brixham Path Description Booklet.

This is a Section of superb cliff scenery, tough going in places and often quite lonely. In the west, near the mouth of the Dart, are substantial wooded areas but further along the cliffs become higher and more open. This makes for a dramatic, steeply undulating landscape ending at the sea in steep cliff faces.

Directions

A regular bus service links Brixham and Kingswear, on the east side of the Dartmouth Ferry, making a bus-walk possible. There is also a popular circuit using the Coast Path based on Kingswear.

Walkers have two ferry options from Dartmouth town centre to cross the river, the Lower Car Ferry, which also carries foot passengers, and the Dartmouth Passenger Ferry.

The Lower Car Ferry operates all year on a continuous service telephone 01803 752342.

The Dartmouth Passenger Ferry also operates all year on a continuous service telephone 01803 555872.

For ferry details see page 20.

From either ferry landing point in Kingswear cross the road and pass through an arch to ascend Alma Steps. Turn right along Beacon Road and continue out of the village. After some 1.25 miles/2km turn right down steps and undulate sometimes steeply into and through woodland to the old Battery buildings at Froward Point. Here the path descends steeply to the right from the corner of an old lookout building, passing World War II searchlight and gun positions before continuing along the cliffs. Pass Pudcombe Cove, by the National Trust Coleton Fishacre Gardens, and then on over Scabbacombe Head and past Scabbacombe Sands and Man Sands and over Southdown Cliff to Sharkham Point – this is a particularly strenuous length. Passing holiday accommodation the path arrives at Berry Head, a Napoleonic fortified area. Divert to the end of the headland to see the unusually squat lighthouse. Berry Head has toilets and seasonal refreshments. From here descend past an old quarry to a road, where there are further refreshment facilities at the Guard House Cafe (01803 855778). Turn right then go right again through the Shoalstone Car Park and along above the shoreline, returning to the road before descending steps to Brixham Breakwater. Follow the promenade to the harbour. Brixham has all facilities.

Week 7 - Day 3

OS Maps: Landranger 202: Explorer OL20 (western half); Explorer 110 (eastern half)

	This Walk	Cumulative	This Walk	Cumulative	Grading	Timing
Ascent	1,972ft	94,189ft	601m	28,709m	Moderate	6 hours
Distance	12.8mi	500.3mi	20.5km	805.2km		

For detailed directions see our Brixham to Torquay and Torquay to Shaldon Path Description booklets.

This is mostly an urban Section, passing along the shoreline of the "English Riviera", or Tor Bay. There is a mixture of grand terraces, open green parkland, amusement parks and the elegant white buildings overlooking the sea at Torquay. At the western end there is also the old fishing town of Brixham and at the other end the almost rural wooded cliffs around Babbacombe. All in all, this is a surprisingly diverse Section.

Directions

A range of bus routes runs throughout the Torbay area, including one which follows the coast road between Brixham and Torquay, and another linking Torquay to Babbacombe. As a result, a wide variety of bus-walks is possible.

Leaving Brixham by the fish market, the Coast Path initially passes a car park and gardens before passing two small coves and climbing into woodland which takes the path to Elberry Cove. From here it passes behind the sweep of Broadsands, climbing by the railway viaduct at the far end to proceed alongside the steam railway line to the promenade at Goodrington. At the far end climb through ornamental gardens and go down a road to Paignton Harbour and so along the promenade. Paignton's railway station is inland of the pier. Turn inland at Hollicombe, at the far end of Preston Sands, going through a park to the main sea-front road which is followed to Torquay Harbour. Torquay Station is inland a little before the harbour.

Cross the pedestrian bridge across the harbour and climb the hill, turning right at the Imperial Hotel on the signed path which leads to the open area at Daddyhole Plain. Descend to the sea-front road at Meadfoot Beach, climbing again at Ilsham Marine Drive. Take the cliff path round Thatcher Point to Hope's Nose. A cul-de-sac path goes to the end of this low headland.

From Hope's Nose follow the path inland of the road, crossing the road to the Bishop's Walk, which in turn arrives at a car park above Anstey's Cove. The path now goes round the edge of the grassy downs on Walls Hill, bearing off right to descend to Babbacombe Beach. Cross a wooden footbridge to Oddicombe Beach then climb by the cliff railway to reach Babbacombe's facilities at the top.

Corbyn Head Beach

Week 7 - Day 4 (half day)

OS Maps: Landranger 202; Explorer 110

	This Walk	Cumulative	This Walk	Cumulative	Grading	Timing
Ascent	2,090ft	96,279ft	637m	29,346m	Strenuous	3.75 hours
Distance	6.4mi	506.7mi	10.3km	815.5km		

For detailed directions see our Torquay to Shaldon Path Description booklet.

This is a tough Section of almost constant ups and downs. The characteristic red cliffs of this part of Devon are often quite high and quite sheer, though unfortunately the terrain is such that sea and cliff views are perhaps less frequent than would be wished. Its strenuous nature makes it a relatively quiet Section, except for the two ends, although it is never far from roads or housing.

Directions

A regular bus service links Babbacombe and Teignmouth, making a bus-walk an option.

From Babbacombe, a pleasant suburb of Torquay with all facilities, the Coast Path descends next to the cliff railway and then soon climbs again to avoid a cliff fall. This diversion takes the path up a grassy area to a main road where it turns right, then right again into Petitor Road.

Shaldon Ferry

At the bottom turn left on the Coast Path again, which soon descends onto a cliff face before reaching the wooded valley at Watcombe. Cross the track running down the valley and on through a wooded length to a short rocky stretch, turning right at a junction before reaching the car park at Maidencombe. There is a pub and toilets here. Turn right after the car park and keep on the rollercoaster path which eventually climbs to go alongside the coast road, then quickly leaves it to pass alongside fields to a track. Turn right and go round the wooded Ness headland, with super views ahead, descending to the promenade at Shaldon, on the estuary of the River Teign.

The ferry service across the River Teign operates throughout the year, weather permitting - mobile: 07896 711822.

For ferry details see page 20.

Walk, Shaldon-Teignmouth

If the ferry is not operating, continue inland along the riverside roads to Shaldon Bridge and cross the Teign. On the Teignmouth side turn right into Milford Park, through Bitton Sports Ground into Park Hill, cross into Bitton Avenue then into Clay Lane and right into Willow Street. At the end bear left then right into Quay Road, then right to go along the Strand and right to the Harbour Beach and the ferry point. Teignmouth has all facilities, including a mainline rail station and buses to Exeter.

Week 7 - Day 4 (half day)

OS Maps: Landranger 192; Explorer 110

	This Walk	Cumulative	This Walk	Cumulative	Grading	Timing
Ascent	488ft	96,767ft	149m	29,495m	Easy	3 hours
Distance	7.9mi	514.6mi	12.7km	828.2km		

For detailed directions see our Shaldon to Exmouth Path Description booklet.

This Section primarily comprises two fairly large seaside towns, flanked by a coastline of high red cliffs at one end and marshes and a sand bar at the other. Running through it, often next to the Coast Path, is possibly the most scenic part of Brunel's GWR railway line, the embankment of which forms the sea wall for much of this length. This is a busy, largely urban and much used Section with an historic importance to the tourist trade.

Directions

A regular bus service links Teignmouth and Starcross, the ferry point for Exmouth, and also passes through Dawlish and Dawlish Warren. As there are also stations on the railway line at these places, bus or train-walks are options here.

From the ferry point at Teignmouth, or from the town centre, go to the car park at The Point, jutting out into the Teign Estuary, and begin by walking along the promenade. Leaving the town the Coast Path continues between railway and sea below the red cliffs to the end, where it descends steps to pass under the railway and then up Smugglers Lane to the A379 road at the top.

High water route, Teignmouth-Smugglers Lane

With a high sea and an onshore wind the far end of the promenade can become very wet, and for about an hour either side of high tide the steps at Smugglers Lane become impassable. In these cases, immediately after leaving the town fork left and cross the railway on a footbridge on Eastcliff Walk, and this path eventually reaches the A379 which is then followed ahead to meet the official path at the top of Smugglers Lane.

Coast Path, Smugglers Lane-Dawlish Warren

Use the footway on the inland side of the A379 and walk for about 150 yards/135m before turning right into Windward Lane, going immediately left on a path which skirts fields before returning to the A379. Bear right into Old Teignmouth Road, which in turn returns to the A379 then, very soon, turn right by some railings on a path which zigzags down to the shoreline. Follow the sea wall through Dawlish, past the station – all facilities are found beyond the railway here. The best route is then to continue on the sea wall between railway and sea, again below the red cliffs, to Dawlish Warren. Just before the amusement area cross the obvious railway footbridge to a car park, turn right and follow to the main road.

High water route, Dawlish-Dawlish Warren

At high tides the sea wall becomes impassable between Dawlish and Dawlish Warren. In this case, go under the railway at Dawlish station to the station forecourt, turning left here up a narrow path then through an arch and up some steps. Continue past a housing area then through more arches to arrive at the A379. Continue ahead then right on the road signed to Dawlish Warren then immediately right again along a signed footpath which leads to Dawlish Warren and to join the more coastal path here.

Coast Path, Dawlish Warren-Starcross

The Coast Path does not go around the large sand spit at Dawlish Warren itself, jutting out into the mouth of the River Exe, or the marshes behind it, but if there is time this can be an exhilarating experience. Otherwise continue along Warren Road on the pavement, then opposite the entrance to Dawlish Warren Sandy Park join the cycleway and footpath to Cockwood Harbour. After following the road around the harbour join the A379. Cross the road and follow the footpath and cycleway to Starcross, and the ferry point to Exmouth. Starcross has all facilities.

The ferry operates mid-April – end October, telephone 01626 862452 or 07974 022536.

For ferry details see page 20.

If there is no ferry operating on arrival at Starcross, there are several options to reach Exmouth.

Option 1: Explorer Water Taxi – this runs daily 1st April until 31st October. Check their web site before travelling as times vary: www.exeplorerwatertaxis.co.uk

Option 2: Bus or train from Starcross to Exeter, bus or train from Exeter to Exmouth.

Option 3: Walk from Starcross to Turf Lock following the waymarked Exe Valley Way on the riverside road and footpath (3 miles/5km), then ferry Turf Lock-Topsham and bus or train from Topsham to Exmouth.

Ferry operates seasonally – telephone 07778 370582.

For ferry details see page 20.

Option 4: Walk from Starcross to Topsham Lock following the waymarked Exe Valley Way on the riverside road and footpath and Exeter Canal towpath (4.5 miles/7km), then ferry Topsham Lock-Topsham and bus or train from Topsham to Exmouth.

Ferry operates seasonally – telephone 01392 274306 (office) or 07801 203338 (ferryman).

For ferry details see page 20.

Cockwood Harbour

Week 7 - Day 5 (half day)

OS Maps: Landranger 192; Explorer 115

	This Walk	Cumulative	This Walk	Cumulative	Grading	Timing
Ascent	722ft	97,489ft	220m	29,715m	Moderate	3 hours
Distance	6.2mi	520.8mi	9.9km	838.1km		

For detailed directions see our Exmouth to Sidmouth Path Description booklet.

This is a well-used and popular Section, never far from houses and passing a large caravan site and a golf course on the way. Most of this length is on relatively low cliffs, and in the west these give excellent views over the mouth of the Exe and the great sandy bar of Dawlish Warren. Further east, the high point of West Down Beacon gives exceptionally fine panoramic views, while beyond the Beacon the path becomes more enclosed. It is an easy-going Section of some variety, ideal for those not wishing to explore remote or strenuous lengths.

Directions

A regular bus service links Exmouth and Budleigh Salterton, making this a good bus-walk option. In addition, a summer service links Exmouth with Sandy Bay, approximately mid-way along the section, giving another, shorter bus-walk.

Exmouth has all facilities, including a railway station on a branch line from Exeter. The obvious route for the Coast Path is to walk along the promenade from the former, now redeveloped, docks area at the mouth of the Exe, which is also the ferry landing point. Continue to the cliffs at Orcombe Point then climb the steps and continue on the cliff top, passing the Jurassic Coast marker and on to the Devon Cliffs Caravan Site at Sandy Bay. Follow the fence line inland of the Straight Point rifle range then climb to the high point at West Down Beacon. The path then descends steadily, seaward of the golf course though offering relatively few sea views on this stretch. Approaching Budleigh Salterton, a charming and traditional small town, the path turns inland then almost immediately, at a junction, goes right to descend to the end of the promenade. The shops, pubs and other facilities are immediately inland of the path, which continues towards the distinctive line of pine trees to the east of the town.

Geoneedle and Exe Estuary

Week 7 - Day 5 (half day)

OS Maps: Landranger 192; Explorer 115

	This Walk	Cumulative	This Walk	Cumulative	Grading	Timing
Ascent	1,037ft	98,526ft	316m	30,031m	Moderate then strenuous	3.5 hours
Distance	6.9mi	527.7mi	11.1km	849.2km		

For detailed directions see our Exmouth to Sidmouth Path Description booklet.

This pleasant Section is mostly on relatively low red cliffs with attractive views inland over an undulating pastoral countryside as well as to seaward. However, there are contrasts at both ends. The western end skirts the narrow, marsh-fringed estuary of the River Otter while the eastern end includes a wooded cliff top and high cliffs on the appropriately named High Peak and Peak Hill. This is a pleasant and quietly popular Section.

Directions

A regular bus service links Budleigh Salterton and Sidmouth, making a bus-walk a possibility.

Budleigh Salterton, a town with something of an olde-world air, has all facilities. The Coast Path goes along the promenade to the car park at the eastern end. Progress east seems tantalisingly close, but the River Otter, with no bridge at its mouth, bars the way. The path therefore passes through a gate at the rear riverside corner of the car park and follows the riverside path until it meets a road. Turn right and cross the River Otter on the road bridge, then bear right to follow the path back downriver to the sea, bearing round to the left on reaching the cliffs.

The path is clear to the caravan site at Ladram Bay, where there are toilets and seasonal refreshments. Here, descend across a field to the beach access track, going left then immediately right, past a pub and on to climb into woodland at High Peak. Here, the path goes behind the very top, emerging on a track. Turn right and climb again to the open land at Peak Hill. Follow the path down the cliff through woodland to a road, turn right then keep right along an old road length then onto a large grassy area down to a zigzag path next to the white Jacob's Ladder. At the bottom follow the seafront path to reach the main esplanade. Sidmouth is an elegant Regency town and has all facilities.

Sidmouth in Spring

Week 7 - Day 6

OS Maps: Landranger 192; Explorer 115 (most); Explorer 116 (eastern end)

	This Walk	Cumulative	This Walk	Cumulative	Grading	Timing
Ascent	2,408ft	100,934ft	734m	30,765m	Severe then strenuous	5.5 hours
Distance	10.4mi	538.1mi	16.7km	865.9km		

For detailed directions see our Sidmouth to Lyme Regis Path Description booklet.

This is a Section of lofty cliffs cut by deep and narrow valleys, making for a magnificent coastal landscape but a testing one to walk. In the west the cliffs are characteristically red, but this changes quite abruptly along the length as the Section reaches the most westerly chalk cliffs in England, appropriately bright white. Add an elegant Regency town, a charming picture-postcard village and a picturesque fishing town and the result is a length of great attraction.

Directions

A regular bus service links Sidmouth with Seaton, making a bus-walk an option. There are also regular, if less frequent, bus links to Branscombe and Beer, along the length, giving further options.

The Coast Path passes along the elegant esplanade at Sidmouth to the footbridge over the mouth of the River Sid at the eastern end. Some dramatic cliff falls have occurred just east of Sidmouth and a well-signed diversion is necessary past housing until, at the top of Laskeys Lane, it turns back to the cliff top. A steep climb up Salcombe Hill is soon followed by an equally steep descent and climb through the Salcombe Regis valley. The path skirts behind the hollow of Lincombe then descends to the beach at Weston Mouth. A short way along the beach the path leaves to climb steeply back to the cliffs and a good level stretch which eventually turns inland to meet a track. This descends to Branscombe Mouth, where there are refreshments and toilets. Beyond Branscombe the official path passes among some holiday chalets then along an undercliff path, with the cliffs rearing massively above, before climbing to the cliff top at Beer Head. These are the most westerly chalk cliffs in England. An alternative route from Branscombe Mouth climbs up the valley side and proceeds directly along the cliff top to Beer Head.

Follow the signed path from Beer Head, past a caravan site and into the village behind the beach. Beer, an attractive fishing village, has all facilities. Climb the path on the east side of the beach to the cliff top, descending to a road and down to Seaton Hole. If the tide is low, walk along the beach to the end of the promenade at Seaton. If not, an inland diversion must now be taken. A cliff fall caused by the extreme wet weather in 2012 has created a very large hole in Old Beer Road, necessitating permanent closure of the previous Coast Path route. At Seaton Hole one must now turn left on to Old Beer Road and walk approximately 330 yards/300m inland towards Beer. At the junction with the B3172 Beer Road, turn right towards Seaton. After approximately 1,100yards/1km, leave the Beer Road and take the path on the right through the chine and on to the promenade and so into Seaton, which has all facilities, including bus services to Exeter, Weymouth and Poole.

Week 8 - Day 1 (half day)

OS Maps: Landranger 193; Explorer 116

	This Walk	Cumulative	This Walk	Cumulative	Grading	Timing
Ascent	1,401ft	102,335ft	427m	31,192m	Moderate	3.5 hours
Distance	6.8mi	544.9mi	11.0km	876.9km		

For detailed directions see our Sidmouth to Lyme Regis Path Description booklet.

This unique length of the Coast Path was made impassable by the storms of winter 2013-14, which badly impacted on the still-active landslip which forms the National Nature Reserve of the Axmouth-Lyme Regis Undercliffs. It is proving very difficult to identify a safe alternative route through the landslip for the Coast Path. Check with the SWCP website at www.southwestcoastpath.com/faq/route-changes for the latest position. While there is a regular bus service between Seaton and Lyme Regis (X53), the Association recommends a very attractive inland alternative for use as a stop-gap until a coastal route can be re-established.

Directions

Leave Seaton on the Coast Path route which crosses the River Axe and turns right up the golf course access road and past the club house. Continue due east over the fairway and along a bridleway. Keep ahead where the Coast Path turns off to the right, soon arriving at a road (Stepps Lane).

Turn right along this quiet lane and continue for approximately 1.5 miles/2.5km to a junction in the hamlet of Dowlands. Follow the lane signed to Rousdon then turn right at a telephone box onto a public bridleway. Pass through a gate and under an arch into the Rousdon Estate. Follow the straight access road for 0.5 mile/0.8km and exit through the arch on the other side.

The bridleway then becomes a lane. At the junction after Charton Farm, by a large grey barn, turn left and continue to a crossroads. Cross this fairly busy road (A3052) and continue on the road opposite for another 0.5 mile/0.8km before turning right at a crossroads, signed to Shapwick. Keep on this lane to its end and here turn left, signed Uplyme.

After approximately 100 yards/91metres take the public bridleway on the right just past Shapwick House. Cross the field, heading for the cream coloured house, go through a gate and follow the bridleway to the left of the house. Follow this for approximately 0.25 mile/0.4km.

Just after some footpaths to the left, take the signed public footpath to the right, just past a cottage. Follow this up and round the cottage and over a stile then follow along the side of a field for about 100 yards/91metres before the path turns left and over another stile. After two more stiles the path emerges in Gore Lane. Turn right. At the Ware crossroads re-cross the A3052 and follow the lane opposite for just over 0.5 mile/0.8km, passing two paths leaving on the right. Turn right off the lane at the 30mph speed limit sign, just before a sharp left-hand bend, signed "to Coast Path – the Cobb 0.75 mile".

Follow the well-marked path down the valley, through a gate; bear right at the finger post marked "to Coast Path" and at the next junction of paths follow that signed for the Coast Path to Lyme Regis. Pass through a kissing gate and down the steps to the Cobb, Lyme Regis's harbour. Lyme Regis is a charming and attractive town and has all facilities.

Week 8 - Day 1 (half day)

OS Maps: Landranger 193; Explorer 116

	This Walk	Cumulative	This Walk	Cumulative	Grading	Timing
Ascent	1,883ft	104,218ft	574m	31,766m	Moderate then strenuous	3 hours
Distance	6.7mi	551.6mi	10.9km	887.8km		

For detailed directions see our Lyme Regis to West Bay Path Description booklet.

A major feature of this Section is the large number of cliff slippages caused by a combination of wet weather and geology. This means that as things currently stand there is effectively no proper coastal path between Lyme Regis and Charmouth (approximately 3 miles/4.5km), nor, indeed, immediately east of Charmouth. However, the remainder of this Section is a superb coastal experience, climbing as it does over the top of Golden Cap, the highest point on the entire south coast of England, with views to match as well as an energy requirement of a high level!

Directions

A regular bus service which could be used as a basis for a bus-walk links Lyme Regis, Charmouth and Chideock, which is about 0.75 mile/1.25km inland of Seatown.

Major diversions have had to be put in place in this Section, especially between Lyme Regis and Charmouth, to avoid the considerable cliff falls that have occurred. It looks likely that these diversions will remain in place for 2014. However, for up-to-date details check the Association's website (www.southwestcoastpath.org.uk).

Lyme Regis is a charming and attractive town with all facilities. From the Cobb Harbour proceed along the esplanade to the small car park at Cobb Gate and the Millennium Clock Tower: the town centre is on your left. Continue along the new sea wall for approximately 500m to steps on left. Go up the steps and continue on the footpath. Cross Charmouth Road car park to the main road (A3052), then turn right uphill past the Football Club, beyond which there is a gate at the corner of a lane to a footpath across fields to a lane where the route turns left for 100 yards/90m. Turn right at a sign up through woods and near the top is a path junction.

Official Coastal Route, Lyme Regis-Charmouth

If an official route is in place, and this is highly unlikely for 2014, turn right onto a path that runs between the cliff edge and the golf course. Take the track downhill to Charmouth and at the first junction (with Old Lyme Hill) turn sharp right to follow the signposted route back to the cliff edge. The old alternative route along the beach is also closed following a landslide.

Official Diversion, Lyme Regis-Charmouth

Dorset County Council have installed and waymarked their official diversion. At the path junction in the wood (at GR 3456 9330) turn left for 130 yards/120m to meet Timber Hill. Turn right here to join in some 440 yards/400m the A3052 road and continue on this for 110 yards/100m. Turn eastwards on a public footpath signposted to Fern Hill, crossing the golf course then north-east through woods to re-join the A3052. Turn right to the roundabout with the A35 and fork right, signposted to Charmouth, following the road into the village for 760 yards/700m. At the second road junction turn right into Higher Sea Lane. When the road bends right take a footpath south-east and continue for about 650 yards/600m to re-join the official Coast Path at GR3640 9305.

Official Diversion, Charmouth West

If the official route from Lyme Regis to the edge of Charmouth is in place, there may still be the necessity for a diversion at the western end of Charmouth. This will take the route from the west end of Old Lyme Hill north-eastwards to the main road through the village. It then turns right and, after 110 yards/100m right again into Higher Sea Lane as above.

Preferred Diversion, Lyme Regis-Charmouth

The Association recommends a preferable alternative to the official diversion above, which deviates from it at the A3052/A35 roundabout. Take the road signposted to Charmouth and shortly after the junction take steps on the right to a stile and public footpath. Follow the waymarked direction up the field to the former Lily Farm, now holiday accommodation. Cross a stile and pass between the buildings and the Dutch barn on the left and after the buildings cross a field to arrive at a tarmac lane (Old Lyme Hill). Turn right and after 90 yards/80m turn left to arrive at Old Lyme Road.

Go left along Old Lyme Road and after 80 yards/70m turn right into a private road, Westcliffe Road. Descend steeply for 330 yards/300m to a junction with Five Acres. Bear right here and at the end of the cul-de-sac take a footpath going forward into a narrow lane. Shortly it reaches a wider road (Higher Sea Lane). Turn right and continue ahead, ignoring various signs pointing off the lane, continuing round the bend to the west in the lane that rises for some 130 yards/120m to an oak signpost on the left. Here leave the lane through a metal gate to re-join the Coast Path, descending over grassy slopes to Charmouth Beach, with its toilets and refreshments.

Official Route, Charmouth East

The official route crosses a footbridge and climbs the obvious green path ahead. This is unlikely to be available for 2014.

Diversion, Charmouth East

From the approach to the footbridge go north-east along a tarmac lane (River Way) and at the end continue along a gravel path to Bridge Road. Continue to the main village road (The Street) then turn right, cross the bridge and fork right into Stonebarrow Lane. Continue up this narrow lane for nearly 0.75 mile/1.25km. At the car park at the top turn sharp right to a signpost then take a grassy track as signed south-westward to re-join the Coast Path.

Coast Path, Charmouth East-Seatown (Chideock)

There is a hefty climb to Golden Cap, the highest point on England's south coast, but the views from the top are spectacular. At the top go slightly left to the trig point which then leads to the long and steep descent. There is a minor diversion on the approach to Seatown, taking the Coast Path slightly inland then back to the coast along the access road. Seatown has toilets and refreshments. Other facilities are at Chideock, 0.75 mile/1.25km inland.

Golden Cap from Charmouth

Week 8 - Day 2

OS Maps: Landranger 193 (western half); Explorer 116 (western half)
Landranger 194 (eastern half); Explorer OL15 (eastern half)

	This Walk	Cumulative	This Walk	Cumulative	Grading	Timing
Ascent	1,489ft	105,707ft	454m	32,220m	Strenuous then moderate	6.25 hours
Distance	12.4mi	564.0mi	19.9km	907.7km		

For detailed directions see our Lyme Regis to West Bay and West Bay to Abbotsbury Path Description booklets.

This is a Section of two contrasting halves. West of West Bay is a rollercoaster of steep and high cliffs, giving far-reaching views along the coast and also inland, over the deeply dissected pastoral countryside. East of West Bay a sheer red sandstone cliff rises from the sea, looking almost artificial in its straight lines, and then the coastline subsides to a low level and the Coast Path loses its ups and downs, though not its hard work, as the shingle of what is the far western end of Chesil Beach tests the legs.

Directions

A regular bus service links Chideock, which is 0.75 mile/1.25km inland of Seatown, with Abbotsbury, and also calls at West Bay and Burton Bradstock which are along the length of this Section, giving various bus-walk options. A popular circular walk based on Abbotsbury uses the Coast Path as well as the South Dorset Ridgeway.

From the pub and toilets at Seatown the Coast Path climbs the cliff slope on its way to the high point of Thorncombe Beacon. There is a descent to the little beach at Eype then a further climb and descent to the harbour at West Bay, which has most facilities. Go round the back of the harbour, pass to the right of the church and ahead to the West Bay public house, opposite which is the Coast Path sign pointing to the surprisingly steep cliff. Arriving at Burton Freshwater the path runs between the caravan park and the beach and is well signed. Following major cliff falls in the summer of 2012 the Coast Path has been reopened along Burton Cliff, although a short inland diversion is necessary around the hotel leading to Burton Beach, where there are refreshments and toilets. Further on, the path passes inland of Burton Mere before coming to West Bexington, where there are toilets and seasonal refreshments.

See Section 71 for details of the alternative Inland Coast Path (South Dorset Ridgeway) between West Bexington and Osmington Mills.

The Coast Path continues along the back of the beach, later passing another car park with toilets and seasonal refreshments and some 200 yards/185m beyond this it turns inland to Abbotsbury. There are alternative routes either going into the village or going south and east of Chapel Hill and missing the village. A permissive path alternative leaves the Coast Path and leads direct to the famous Swannery. Abbotsbury is a beautiful stone-built village with much of historic interest and most facilities.

Back towards Seatown

Week 8 - Day 3

OS Maps: Landranger 194; Explorer OL15

	This Walk	Cumulative	This Walk	Cumulative	Grading	Timing
Ascent	955ft	106,662ft	291m	32,511m	Easy. Chesil Beach route strenuous	4 hours official route
Distance	10.9mi	574.9mi	17.5km	925.2km		

For detailed directions see our Abbotsbury to Ferry Bridge Path Description booklet.

This is an untypical Section of the Coast Path. In the west, there is an inland rural high-level field route, giving views over the unusual feature of Chesil Beach and the landlocked Fleet behind. To the east, the path runs along the banks of the Fleet, with pleasant views over this attractive feature, but with views of the sea largely cut off by the shingle bank of Chesil Beach. Although never far from houses or roads, this is often a very quiet Section.

Directions

Buses to and from Abbotsbury and Ferry Bridge link at Weymouth for a potential bus-walk.

Overlooking Chesil Beach

It is possible to walk direct from the beach near Abbotsbury to Ferry Bridge at Wyke Regis along the length of Chesil Beach. If this is intended, start at the beach at the inland turn (Day 2) to Abbotsbury, continuing along the beach. However, note that:

1. It is not possible to get off the beach before Ferry Bridge.

2. It is extremely hard and slow walking.

3. It is necessary to check that firing is not scheduled at the nearby Chickerell Rifle Range; telephone Major Hazard on 01305 783456, ext.8132.

4. The beach is closed to visitors from 1st May to 31st August for the bird nesting season.

Although the Coast Path does not pass through Abbotsbury most walkers will visit the attractive village and its facilities. From the village leave West Street on the path going south adjacent to Chapel Street Stores. Continue on to Nunnery Grove to the signed Coast Path, which now goes inland but is well signed and enjoyable with some excellent views. After Horsepool Farm on the edge of Abbotsbury the path climbs onto the ridge. After about a mile/1.5km turn right off the ridge then left after Hodder's Coppice. Cross a minor road then follow the field headland east then south to the north-east corner of Wyke Wood. The path then heads for the edge of the Fleet – be aware approaching Rodden Hive that the path suddenly goes through a hedge on the left. From here the path follows the edge of the Fleet. At Tidmoor Point follow the red and white posts, unless it is necessary to divert inland because of firing. The diversion is well marked. Approaching Wyke Regis there is a minor deviation behind an MOD Bridging Hard, then the path arrives at the A354 road adjacent to Ferry Bridge, the access for the Isle of Portland, at Wyke Regis, a suburb of Weymouth.

Week 8 - Day 4

OS Maps: Landranger 194; Explorer OL15

	This Walk	Cumulative	This Walk	Cumulative	Grading	Timing
Ascent	1,112ft	107,774ft	339m	32,850m	Moderate	6 hours
Distance	13.2mi	588.1mi	21.3km	946.5km		

For detailed directions see our Portland Path description booklet.

Portland is different. Different from the rest of Dorset and from the rest of the Coast Path. An almost-island, jutting out into the English Channel, joined to the mainland only by the end of Chesil Beach, it has an isolated air. Formed of limestone, it has been extensively quarried and these workings, some still operational, characterise much of the landscape. Elsewhere, former military buildings and those of Verne Prison and the Young Offenders' Institution are prominent. Portland is rugged rather than pretty, but it is well worth exploring with superb views and a rich natural and historic heritage.

Directions

Bus routes run the length of Portland, making a variety of bus-walks possible. This Section is, in any event, a circular walk in its own right. However, at the time of going to print there were suggestions that the service all the way to the Bill may be discontinued. Check on local bus information.

It is possible to omit this section and continue from Wyke Regis directly into Weymouth. However, Portland is officially part of the National Trail and its interest and sense of being different make it well worth the day's walk.

From Ferry Bridge cross the causeway onto Portland; this is done by simply following the shared footway/cycleway alongside the A354 road or alternatively by crossing the bridge on the A354 to beyond the boatyard and then walking along the raised bed of the old railway on the eastern bank to near the end of the causeway at the roundabout for the access road to Osprey Quay and here returning to the footway/cycleway. At the southern of the two roundabouts at Victoria Square take the main road south and shortly turn right into Pebble Lane then left just before the public toilets. Continue to the Cove House Inn and bear right up onto the promenade. About half way along, at the floodgates, cut back sharp left then right, following Coast Path signs up a steep tarmac path, past the school and up the steep path in the grass incline to the steps to the terraced path that was once the old road. Bear off right onto the signed path running between quarry banks and the cliff face, leading to 3 miles/5km of airy cliff-top walking to Portland Bill. Two short lengths of the Coast Path above West Wears have remained closed since January 2013 following movement in the cliffs. Follow the signed diversions as you proceed along the old quarrymen's tramway. At Portland Bill, as well as the lighthouse, are refreshments, toilets and buses (but see above).

Continue around the end of the low headland then start northwards, seaward of the wooden chalets, to follow a winding path along the top of low cliffs to join a road above Freshwater Bay after about 1.5 miles/2.5km. Turn right on the road (use the footway on the west side of the road) for 600 yards/550m, past Cheyne Weares car park to a signpost on the right. Follow the zigzag path into the undercliff area and follow the waymarking through disused quarry workings to Church Ope Cove.

Ascend the stepped and signed path up to Rufus Castle. Here the South West Coast Path also becomes the England Coast Path, the first section of which, from here to Lulworth Cove, was formally opened on 30th June 2012. The signposting now usually indicates simply "Coast Path". Some, but not all, of the improvements to

Looking back to Portland Lighthouse

the route that the Association sought on Portland can now be walked and the new route is described below. Unfortunately the major alignment around the north-east corner of Portland was not resolved because of legal complications with Portland Ports plc and security issues.

After Rufus Castle the Coast Path soon joins the track bed of the former Weymouth to Easton railway line. This is then followed northwards for some 1,585 yards/1,450m to a pair of signposts. Here turn left to follow a rocky path that climbs up the cliffs to what appears to be an isolated chimney seen on the skyline above. At the top turn sharp right along the prison road northwards and through a gap in a high wall. On the right is the Old Engine Shed, soon to be converted into a visitor centre. On reaching a narrow road the official route is signed across the road and takes a route across open ground passing disused quarries to reach the perimeter fence of the Verne prison. However, the Association's preferred route here, which is all on public rights of way, can be followed thus:-

At the road turn right and just over the brow of a hill turn left on an access track to compounds. Continue ahead on a grassy path towards a large pinnacle of rock (Nichodemus Knob) after which, at the "rock falls" sign, bear left steeply up onto the higher escarpment, heading for a large communications mast. At the high wire perimeter fence turn left and follow it along then round to the right, to reach the south entrance to Verne Prison. Here rejoin the route of the England Coast Path.

Take a path through a little gap to the left of the entrance, passing beside railings and down steep steps. Bear right along a path that traverses under the grassy banks.

The path drops downhill towards houses to a waymark post. Ignore the left fork and continue on the level on a grass path which then passes through an underpass below a road. Descend steeply down the Castletown Incline (a former quarry tramway), crossing two footpaths and a road. Pass under a footbridge and through another underpass to reach an access road and turn left to a roundabout.

Continue ahead for some 30 yards/27m and then cross to turn right down Liberty Road, signposted to Portland Castle. Go past the castle entrance to the car park and turn right towards the harbour, heading for five black posts. Here join the footway/cycleway to follow the harbour-side to the Sailing Academy, the venue of the sailing events at the 2012 Olympics. Continue on the footway/cycleway to reach the roundabout on the A354 road. From here follow the former railway trackbed to the boatyard before the bridge over the mouth of the Fleet and follow the footway alongside the road to Ferry Bridge.

Week 8 - Day 5

OS Maps: Landranger 194; Explorer OL15

	This Walk	Cumulative	This Walk	Cumulative	Grading	Timing
Ascent	2,385ft	110,159ft	727m	33,577m	Easy to moderate to strenuous	6.25 hours
Distance	14.1mi	602.2mi	22.7km	969.2km		

For detailed directions see our Ferry Bridge to Lulworth Cove Path Description booklet.

This section is part of the first section of the England Coast Path. The signposting generally only refers to "Coast Path".

The western part of this Section is an urban walk along the various lengths of Weymouth's sea front. East of the town is a length of relatively low cliffs but then at White Nothe, two thirds of the way along the section, the coastal geology changes. East of here is a rollercoaster of often sheer white cliffs, the length punctuated by the iconic landmarks of Durdle Door and Lulworth Cove. Both ends of this Section are busy, but in the centre is an often quiet and remote length.

Directions

A regular bus service links Weymouth with Lulworth Cove, also serving Osmington, close to the Coast Path mid-way along this Section, allowing some bus-walk options.

From Ferry Bridge the signed Coast Path follows the footway/cycleway on the old railway trackbed, passing behind the sailing centre. Shortly afterwards bear off right to continue into Old Castle Road. Ignore the footpath sign to the right, a cul-de-sac as the onward cliff path is closed due to a landslip. However, except at high tides the beach can be used to reach a flight of new timber steps that rejoin the former Coast Path beyond the landslip. Instead, continue along the road and 260 yards/240m beyond turn right into Belle Vue Road. Continue for about 600 yards/560m to a crossroads and turn right into Redcliff View. At the end of this road a path leads across a grassed area back to the coast at GR 682 781 (westbound walkers follow the path worn across the grassed area here). Continue on the path to Nothe Fort and bear sharp left then turn down steps on the right to Weymouth harbourside. This is followed to the Town Bridge, which is crossed and the opposite side of the harbour followed back to the Pavilion complex. Bear left to join the Esplanade.

From April, Ferries operate (rowing boats) to cross the harbour, slightly shortening the route, but they are weather dependant. Telephone 01305 838423.

For ferry details see page 20.

Leave Weymouth along the promenade then, at Overcombe, go up the minor road to Bowleaze Cove. After passing the Spyglass Inn the route now bears right to cross the crest of the grass public open space to reach the Beachside Centre. With the new public access rights now provided the Coast Path follows a signed route through the Beachside Leisure Centre to take a narrow path that squeezes between the Riviera Hotel and cliff edge and follows a new signed route to Redcliff Point. A little further on, beyond an education and adventure centre, follow the signed route on a re-established length of the Coast Path. On the downhill approach to Osmington Mills

St Oswald's Bay

the route avoids another landslip by bearing away from the cliff edge over a stile and down the edge of a field, then crosses two further stiles to meet a narrow road down to the coast.

See Section 71 for details of the alternative Inland Coast Path (South Dorset Ridgeway) between West Bexington and Osmington Mills.

The path goes slightly inland at Ringstead. Beyond the wooden church the route of the Coast Path near Holworth House is now signed to deviate north-east and south although the original route (which is a public right of way) can still be used as a more direct route.

Further on, at the coastguard cottages at White Nothe, take the left fork of the two yellow arrows. The path now traverses some quite severe gradients on its way to Lulworth Cove, passing behind Durdle Door to Hambury Tout. Follow the waymarking here – the route sometimes shown on older maps going south here is not usable. Approaching Lulworth Cove a stone-pitched path leads down through the car park to the Heritage Centre. Turn right here along the cliff past the view into Stair Hole. Pass the Jurassic Coast commemorative stone then turn down towards the Cove in front of the boathouse. Lulworth Cove has toilets and refreshments and most facilities are found here or at West Lulworth a little way inland.

Week 8 - Day 6 (half day)

OS Maps: Landranger 194 (most); Landranger 195 (eastern end); Explorer OL15

	This Walk	Cumulative	This Walk	Cumulative	Grading	Timing
Ascent	2,002ft	112,161ft	610m	34,187m	Severe	4 hours
Distance	7.3mi	609.5mi	11.8km	981.0km		

For detailed directions see our Lulworth to Kimmeridge Path Description booklet.

The coast of this Section is of geological interest and importance, largely having been formed by lines of relatively hard limestone having been breached at intervals to form coves and bays as the sea erodes the softer rocks behind. The result is a dramatic coastline of white cliffs and darker coloured coves, some prominent headlands and a succession of extremely steep slopes. Inland, the landscape of the military ranges has been unchanged by farming for some seventy years, though it is perhaps a little too obviously military in a few places.

Directions

Lulworth Cove and Kimmeridge village, about one mile/1.5km inland from Kimmeridge Bay, both have bus links to Wareham, which could provide a bus-walk option.

IMPORTANT: Note that this Section passes through the Lulworth Army Firing Ranges. Before deciding to walk this Section, check that the Ranges are open. PLEASE BE AWARE THE OFFICIAL COAST PATH FOR THIS SECTION MAY BE CLOSED TO WALKERS DURING THE WEEK. However most weekends and during school holidays it is normally open, but please read the section below to check the dates when walkers are allowed access along the official Coast Path.

The Lulworth Range walks, including the Coast Path between Lulworth Cove and Kimmeridge Bay, plus access to Tyneham village, are open to the public every weekend.

LULWORTH RANGE WALKS AND TYNEHAM VILLAGE - OPENING TIMES 2015

The Lulworth Range walks and Tyneham Villages are open to the public every weekend with the exception of the following:

1. 17th/18th January 2015
2. 7th/8th March 2015
3. 9th/10th May 2015
4. 4th/5th July 2015
5. 26th/27th September 2015
6. 14th/15th November 2015

In addition to the weekends they are open every day during the following times; all dates are inclusive:

• Christmas 20th December 2014 – 4th January 2015 • Easter 3rd – 12th April 2015

• Bank Holiday 2nd – 4th May 2015 • Spring 23rd May – 31st May 2015

• Summer 25th July – 30th August 2015 • Christmas 19th December 2015 – 3rd January 2016

Please note that the exhibitions in Tyneham School and Tyneham Church are open from 10.00 until 16.00. When no firing is taking place the gates to the walks are opened as near to 0900 hours on the Saturday morning as possible and remain open until 0800 hours on Monday morning. The Elmes Grove gate that allows vehicle access to Tyneham is opened at 0900 hrs daily when no firing is taking place and is closed at dusk each evening.

For any further information please phone 01929 404819

The abandoned village and its historical exhibition are 0.5 mile/800m inland of the Coast Path, and worth the diversion. The gates to the walks are opened as near to 09.00 on the Saturday morning as possible and remain open until 08.00 on the Monday morning when open only at weekends. The gate to Tyneham is locked each night at dusk. For any further information telephone 01929 404819 or 01929 404712, 0800-1700, Monday to Friday

If the Ranges are closed, it is strongly recommended that schedules are re-arranged so that the Coast Path is walked when open. If, however, this is not possible, two alternative inland diversions are shown below. If using these routes you are strongly advised to carry OS 1:25,000 Explorer Map OL15 (Purbeck and South Dorset).

Coast Path – Lulworth Cove-Kimmeridge Bay

The eastbound Coast Path from Lulworth Cove no longer leaves from behind the café adjacent to the beach – both the café and the adjacent cliffs were destroyed in the storms of the winter of 2013-14. Instead, take the road inland up through the village and after passing the entrance to the main car park and café take the narrow higher road northward past the properties on the east side of the road. After the last house take a signed footpath eastwards steeply uphill to join a path southwards that contours around the hill to re-join the old Coast Path route as it climbs around the cliff edge at the top of the cove. The Coast Path then turns south-eastwards and descends to the east side of the cove. As an alternative, tide permitting, walking the beach avoids considerable ascent and descent. At most states of the tide this is possible. Then take the path going up from the far side of the cove beach to re-join the Coast Path which rises steeply on the eastward cliff edge to the beginning of the Army Ranges. The route onward is straightforward – just follow the yellow topped posts through the ranges to arrive at Kimmeridge Bay. Here are toilets and seasonal refreshments (or all year refreshments in the village 0.6 mile/1km to the north).

If Ranges Closed – Alternative Option 1 (13.5 miles/22.0km)

This route is safer and quieter but more strenuous than Option 2; it uses mainly rights of way plus some permissive paths. It should be noted that this route is not specifically signed or waymarked as an official alternative to the Coast Path. However the Association is hopeful that some specific waymarking as an alternative route may be installed for 2015.

Leave Lulworth Cove as described above for the Coast Path and where the revised route of the Coast Path leaves to the east continue ahead on a footpath parallel to the B3070 road. At the end of the footpath return to the road and follow it inland, forking right, before taking the next road on the left just after a bus shelter (GR 825 807). In 100 yards/90m turn right on to a footpath that heads uphill for 0.75 mile/1.2km. At the second junction of paths turn right (east) and after 100 yards/90m turn left (north) to pass Belhuish Coppice and Belhuish Farm. On reaching the B3071 road at GR835 832 cross the road and take the track opposite. Ignore the first path junction to the north-east and continue downhill to the eastern boundary of Burngate Wood (GR 845 828). Turn north-east on a permissive path (blue) past Park Lodge and go across the road at GR 855 832 onto a bridleway. Continue along the bridleway for just over 2 miles/3.4km to GR 866 856 to join a minor road from Highwood veering north and later north-east to meet an east-west road at GR 871

861. Walk east along the road then fork right (signposted Stoborough) at GR 883 856. Go over the crossroads (seat) with the B3070 road at GR 886 855 (Route Option 2 joins this route at this location) and walk east for a further 1.5 miles/2.5km along Holme Lane to GR 909 854 (about 330 yards/300m before railway underbridge) and turn southwards onto diverted Doreys Farm bridleway (see Option 1A below), which is followed for 1.25 miles/2.1km before turning right onto Creech Road.

Turn right and after Creech Grange in 0.9 miles/1.5km the road climbs steeply to the Steeple viewpoint car park in another 0.6 miles/1.0km. Just before the car park turn left at GR 905 817 on a bridleway that falls steeply southwards to re-join the same road. As the road levels out, at a left hand bend at GR 907 812, take the bridleway/access road ahead that leads south through Steeple Leaze Farm. About 200 yards/185m south of the farm take the narrow footpath that heads up steeply south through woods to a bridleway on the ridge. Turn left through a gate and look for a narrow path on the right raking steeply downhill and then across three fields towards the coast ahead and Kimmeridge Bay, where the Coast Path is joined at a T-junction.

Option 1A (This avoids 0.6 miles/1.0km of road walking.)

On Doreys Farm bridleway (see above), after emerging from Bridewell Plantation (GR 914 839), where a fine house comes into view on the left, go through a field gate on the right onto the east side of Grange Heath. Initially the route is indistinct and the ground will be wet in and after inclement weather. However, look for short waymark posts that indicate the best route to follow to the south-west. In some 220 yards/200m a good gravel path will be found that winds its way across Grange Heath. Although this is described as a permissive path on some maps legal access is as shown, as this area is designated as Access Land. Follow the path south-west across the heath to join a bridleway that runs south-east to join Creech Road by a telephone box. Turn right on the road and in 0.3 miles/0.5km pass Creech Grange and then follow the details set out in the final paragraph of Option 1 above.

If Ranges Closed – Alternative Option 2 (12 miles/19km)

This option is mainly road walking, and care is needed on narrow bends. Leave the Cove to West Lulworth on the B3070, then turn right to East Lulworth and beyond, keeping to the B3070 for some 3 miles/5km to GR 886 855. Here turn right along Holme Lane to GR 911 854. From here, follow the route described from (*) in Option 1 above.

Taxi operators: Mike Whittle, Silver Cars, tel. 01929 400409, mobile 07811 328281 Adrian, Valley Taxis, tel. 01929 480507; and K Bay Taxi, tel.01929 480669, mobile 07545 776716, all offer their services in the Lulworth/Kimmeridge area.

Week 8 - Day 6 (half day)

OS Maps: Landranger 195; Explorer OL15

	This Walk	Cumulative	This Walk	Cumulative	Grading	Timing
Ascent	1,059ft	113,220ft	323m	34,510m	Severe	3.25 hours
Distance	5.2mi	614.7mi	8.3km	989.3km		

For detailed directions see our Kimmeridge to South Haven Point Path Description booklet.

This is a Section of steeply undulating cliffs, often with quite sheer faces and frequently with rock ledges at the cliff face. Houns-tout Cliff, near the eastern end of the Section, is especially steep. There are some very attractive bays formed by these cliffs, particularly at the eastern end. The tough terrain means that this Section often has a remote character, accentuated by the lack of neighbouring houses and roads.

Directions

Bus-walks are not easily undertaken on this Section. Circular walks using the Coast Path, based on inland villages such as Kimmeridge or Kingston, are possible.

The Coast Path from Kimmeridge Bay eastwards is straightforward, although care may be needed where small lengths have slipped, cracked or may be close to the cliff top. Just beyond Kimmeridge the Clavell Tower has been relocated 27 yards/25m inland and an improved Coast Path installed. There is a very steep climb to Houns-tout and the descent beyond turns inland to avoid dangerous terrain at Chapman's Pool. (For those aiming to end at Worth Matravers, which is about 1.2 miles/2km inland, the Coast Path is left where it crosses the valley at Hill Bottom Cottages. For the village head inland then turn right up a steep track past Renscombe Farm. Worth Matravers has a pub, shop and cafe.) The route up from Chapman's Pool is hazardous and is avoided by following the official Coast Path inland via Hill Bottom – see Section 69.

Clavell Tower

Week 8 - Day 7 (half day)

OS Maps: Landranger 195; Explorer OL15

	This Walk	Cumulative	This Walk	Cumulative	Grading	Timing
Ascent	1,195ft	114,415ft	364m	34,874m	Severe then Moderate	4 hours
Distance	8.1mi	622.8mi	13.1km	1,002.4km		

For detailed directions see our Kimmeridge to South Haven Point Path Description booklet.

The western part of this Section is dominated by St Aldhelm's Head, a flat-topped headland of limestone surmounted by an old chapel. There are extensive views, especially along the coast to the west. East of the headland the cliffs become increasingly disturbed by the remains of small-scale quarrying activity until the Country Park at Durlston Head marks the approach of Swanage.

Directions

Numerous footpaths cross the cliffs to the Coast Path from the outskirts of Swanage and the inland village of Langton Matravers. This allows for bus-walks which combine these link paths with the Coast Path.

(For those starting in Worth Matravers village, walk along the lane westwards past Weston Farm and Renscombe Farm then turn into the valley and on to the Coast Path at Hill Bottom Cottages.)

From the valley at Hill Bottom the Coast Path climbs on a well-signed route steeply up West Hill and on to Emmett's Hill. The path goes out round St Aldhelm's Head, with excellent coastal views west, and on as a fine high level walk to Durlston Head. Signing in Durlston Country Park is limited; keep on the low level path all the way round Durlston Head then, coming up on the north side take the second turning right (the first is a cul-de-sac to a quarry). Durlston Castle has now been converted to a Jurassic Coast Gateway Centre and includes refreshment facilities.

After leaving Durlston Castle follow a broad stony path north through the woods for some 760 yards/700m to a barrier and sign. From here there is a permanent diversion following a cliff fall. Turn left on a good path for some 125 yards/115m to reach Durlston Road at a gate. Turn right and in 185 yards/170m turn right again into Belle Vue Road. Follow the road north-eastwards to the grassed open space leading to Peveril Point. In bad weather or at high tides use the roadway and then down to the footpath at the end of the coastal buildings, otherwise use the foreshore. Continue along Swanage's sea front promenade. Swanage has all facilities.

Local taxi company Swanage & Purbeck Taxis' are offering a 10% discount to readers of this Guidebook. Contact Martin on 07969 927424.

Dancing Ledge

Week 8 - Day 7 (half day)

OS Maps: Landranger 195; Explorer OL15

	This Walk	Cumulative	This Walk	Cumulative	Grading	Timing
Ascent	492ft	114,907ft	150m	35,024m	Moderate	3.5 hours
Distance	7.6mi	630.4mi	12.2km	1,014.6km		

For detailed directions see our Kimmeridge to South Haven Point Path Description booklet.

This is an excellent and scenic Section. The southern, Swanage end comprises increasingly high cliffs, culminating in the length between Ballard Point and Handfast Point, with its offshore stacks. This is an exhilarating length with superb views over Poole Bay to Bournemouth and across the Solent to the matching cliffs of the Needles on the Isle of Wight. The northern end passes along a long sandy beach before arriving at the mouth of Poole Harbour, an enormous enclosed water area and the second largest natural harbour in the world.

Directions

A regular bus service, half hourly in summer and hourly in winter, links Swanage with South Haven Point, making a bus-walk a good option. There are also popular local circuits using the Coast Path in the Swanage-Ballard Down-Studland area.

Swanage has all facilities. The Coast Path passes along the town's sea front, following the main road (Ulwell Road) at the north end by the telephone box where it bears left and on ahead into Redcliff Road at a one-way system. At a shop and post-box turn sharp right into Ballard Way – do not be put off by "Private Estate" signs. Continue forward into the chalet area and follow signs for the Coast Path, to emerge on a grassed area on the cliff edge. However, from the sea front road, except at very high tides or in severe weather it is possible to keep along the narrow promenade then 200 yards/185m along the beach turn up some rough steps to re-join the official route in a little valley.

The path climbs out to Ballard Down, then the obvious high-level route continues out to Handfast Point and the much-photographed rocks of Old Harry before turning west towards Studland. Studland has toilets and refreshments. For the pub turn up the road from the toilets, otherwise turn right (east) on the outskirts of the village along the signed stony path to South Beach. On reaching the shore, turn left (north) along a terrace in front of beach huts to a seasonal cafe. The route ahead was diverted in 2013 inland up a track to join the road by the public toilets. Turn right here past the pub and right again to re-join the Coast Path above the beach huts. If this short diversion is no longer necessary then continue along the beach for another 90 yards/82m and look for a Purbeck stone waymark between beach huts numbers 59 and 60B, to find a narrow path that ascends steeply up the low cliff. At the top, at another sign, turn right and follow the cliff edge past Fort Henry to join the Middle Beach access road by a barrier. Turn sharp right down to the beach then left by another cafe.

The final 2.6 miles/4.3km are on the sandy beach. Note that further along this beach a length is used by naturists – do not be surprised if nobody else is wearing clothes! There is an alternative, the Heather Walk, through the dunes, marked by

Old Harry Rocks

yellow-topped posts, but the soft sand is tiring walking and part of the naturist area is still visible. The beach route curves round to the point at the mouth of Poole Harbour. This is South Haven Point, the end (or beginning) of the Coast Path, with an impressive commemorative marker. A ferry links the Point with Sandbanks on the opposite shore, which is linked to Poole and Bournemouth.

The ferry operates all year daily every 20 minutes, from Shell Bay (South Haven Point) 07:10 to 23:10; from Sandbanks 07:00 to 23:00; Christmas Day every half hour – telephone 01929 450203.; website www.sandbanksferry.co.uk.

Note that the ferry is usually scheduled to undergo maintenance during late October or November and may be closed for approximately four weeks. If you intend to use the ferry at this time check the Association's website under Path News or the ferry company's website above.

For ferry details see page 21.

Postscript

For those who have been with us all the way from Minehead, be it in one go or in bits and pieces over a period, a final few words seem appropriate. Alfred Wainwright, at the end of his work on the Pennine Way, said; "You have completed a mission and satisfied an ambition. You have walked the Pennine Way, as you have dreamed of doing. This will be a very satisfying moment in your life. You will be tired and hungry and travel stained. But you will feel great, just great." Just substitute the South West Coast Path for the Pennine Way and Wainwright's words will doubtless ring true. You will be glad and proud that you have walked and finished Britain's longest and finest footpath. As Wainwright said of the Pennine Way, it's a longer step than most take in their lifetime!

Alternative Inland Coast Path

OS Maps: Landranger 194; Explorer OL15

	This Walk	This Walk	Grading	Timing
Ascent	2,290ft	698m	Moderate	8 hours
Distance	16.8mi	27.0km		

For detailed directions see our West Bexington to Osmington Mills Path Description booklet.

This is a very scenic walk, parallel to the coast and a varying distance inland. For most of its length quite extensive coastal views are obtained beyond a green and rural foreground. Substantial lengths follow chalk ridges and these give impressive views north as well. Coastal features such as Portland and Chesil Beach are clearly seen, as are the flanks of the enormous Iron Age Maiden Castle inland. This is a quiet route, often feeling quite remote, and with usually no refreshments on its length it requires preparation. It is, nevertheless, a superb experience.

Directions

A regular bus service links Swyre (for West Bexington) and Osmington Mills, making this a perfect opportunity for a bus-walk.

The Dorset element of the Coast Path is unique in having an official alternative route for part of its length. This was often referred to by the apparently contradictory name of the "Inland Coast Path". It is, however, now known as the South Dorset Ridgeway (SDR) and the signposting now uses that name almost throughout. The waymarking has also been replaced and incorporates the name of the South Dorset Ridgeway. The length of the Section, and the fact that the two ends are linked by a regular bus service, make it an ideal long day's walk. However, be aware that other than one seasonal mobile refreshment van if the timing is right, no facilities are found anywhere along the route other than at the two ends, so it is necessary to be well prepared. A detailed route description is given below.

At West Bexington car park turn inland up the road and where the road turns left continue forward up the stony track, signposted "SDR. For Hardy Monument 6 Osmington Mills 16".

Near the top of the hill take the right-hand fork to reach a lay-by on the B3157 road. Take the gate or stile to the right and follow a faint path that follows the edge of the escarpment of the hill passing three waymark posts. After passing through a wall start to bear upwards to the left towards a signpost near the road. Continue eastwards through the field to reach a gate by the corner of a wall. Continue through the gate and almost immediately emerge on the B3157 road at a signpost. Cross and leave through a gate, again signposted "Hardy Monument".

Approaching Abbotsbury Castle prehistoric hill fort, where the grass path divides, take the upper, slightly right-hand fork along the top of the southern earthwork of the fort, past the trig point, from where there are superb views in all directions. It should be possible to see the Hardy Monument clearly in the distance.

Continue eastwards along the top of the earthwork and cross a minor road, signposted "SDR Hardy Monument". Proceed in an approximately easterly direction along the ridge of Wears Hill and the crest of White Hill for about 2 miles/3.2km, following the signing. Be careful not to follow any signs indicating routes down to the village of Abbotsbury in the valley below and its adjacent hilltop chapel. At the east end of White Hill bear north-east as signed and leave the field in the north-east corner through a gate on to a minor road. Continue north-east along this road for some 50 yards/46m and then turn right as signposted.

Follow the narrow and rough bridleway along the wire fence above the scrub to a path junction; where the bridleway bears right take the yellow waymarked footpath to the left and cross a stile. At the end of this short section take a headland path north-east. At the far side of the field the track then leads approximately 50 yards/46m to a further gate with a stile and waymark. Immediately adjacent to this gate is a prehistoric stone circle, a scheduled ancient monument. Continue forward on the track, leaving a small wood to the left, to reach the road between Portesham and Winterbourne Steepleton. Turn left along the road for about 60 yards/55m and then turn right over a stile into a field, signed "Hardy Monument". Continue eastwards through four fields. At a small wooded area before Black Down Barn (ruin) turn north at a signpost to Hardy Monument. Climb through the woods to the recently renovated monument. In season it may be possible to find a mobile refreshment van here.

To continue find a roadside signpost 30yards/32m east of the car park entrance. Cross the road and descend eastward on a narrow path through the bracken. Reaching the same road again, ignore the signpost "Bridleway to Coast Path" and the track opposite and turn left along the road then in another 30 yards/32m turn right, signposted "Inland Route or SDR to Bincombe" .

Now there is a good ridgeway path for some 3 miles/4.8km, with excellent views to seaward. At a point some 550 yards/500m after passing under the second set of HV power lines take the gate north of a large tumulus to stay on the north side of the fence running along the ridge. On reaching the B3159 road, marked by the Borough of Weymouth boundary stone, continue across as signposted and towards the A354 road.

Major road construction has now been completed and a new section of the busy A354 road opened over Ridgeway Hill. The former very difficult crossing of the old road has been replaced with a fine new bridleway bridge (locally known as Green Bridge). Cross the new bridge and take a new bridleway south, that at first rises and then falls, down the perimeter fence on the east side of the new road. About halfway down the hill look out for and take the old bridleway on the left.

Continue eastwards, then before the farm, with its adjacent radio mast, take care to go through the gate on the right, marked with a blue arrow. After crossing the field, leaving two tumuli on the left, reach a metalled road and turn right. At the junction at the corner of Came Wood turn right at the signpost "Bridleway to Bincombe".At the end of the path join a metalled lane and at the road junction turn left, signposted "South Dorset Ridgeway".

Drop down the road into the village of Bincombe and where the road turns right take the track forward leaving the small church on the right. Where the path splits take the left-hand fork, marked with a blue arrow and acorn. After the overhead HV power lines, pass through a small signposted wooden gate and then proceed forward through one field, into the next to a footpath sign. Here turn left and there is a choice of routes for the next couple of hundred yards/m.

For the best option, at a waymark post turn sharp right down a steep grassy slope to a stile at a road ahead. Cross the road to go over another stile to follow a grassy path that contours around the south and east sides of Green Hill. On reaching a road at a gate and stile turn left and in 50 yards/46m turn right through a gate signposted "White Horse Hill – Osmington Mills". The path is now easy to follow with extensive views to seaward over Weymouth and Portland. On passing a ruined building on the left the route reaches a broad track; here turn right, signposted "Osmington" and after about 200 yards/185m go through a gate as signposted. Shortly afterwards pass a trig point on the right and at the next field gate bear left and follow the field boundary along White Horse Hill. Just beyond the next gate fork right, signposted "For Osmington".

Descend to Osmington and follow the signs through the village. On reaching the main Weymouth road near the Sun Ray Inn turn left and in about 250 yards/230m turn right at a signpost, over a stile and footbridge. Follow the field boundary on the left through two fields - at the top look back to see the Hardy Monument in the distance and the white horse on the hillside. Go over the stile to the footpath sign, then turn half right to cross the field at an angle to a further stile. Cross it and turn left along the hedge side to the bottom. At the end of the field there is a very short length of enclosed footpath to the road; turn right along it, descending to Osmington Mills.

Hardy Monument

Portland Lighthouse

Accommodation

This list of accommodation has been prepared in path order.

The majority of our B&B addresses have been recommended by Coast Path walkers. The fact that they are included in this book does not indicate a recommendation by The South West Coast Path Association and their inclusion is merely for information purposes. We cannot, for financial and practical reasons, introduce vetting, inspection or any form of `Star' rating. We do have a system whereby addresses can be removed from the list. All the contact information in the following pages has been supplied by the accommodation providers themselves.

BUSINESS MEMBERSHIP

 Many of the accommodation addresses are highlighted with a red disc. This indicates that they have joined the Association as Business Members, with a large proportion of their membership fee going towards improvements on the Coast Path.

In return for their support for the Path, we urge you to support them and use their accommodation and facilities on your walk wherever possible. Your support for them will in turn encourage them to stay with us as Business Members, with all that means for our Path Improvement Funds.

B&B Key

Facilities:
O	Open All Year
EM	Evening Meal
CP	Car Parking
DW	Dogs Welcome
PD	Pick Up/Drop Service
D	Drying Facilities for wet clothes
PL	Packed Lunches
LSP	Long Stay Parking
KT	Kit Transfer
LT	Luxury Tent
W	Wifi
LF	Local Food

Room Type:
D	Double
T	Twin
F	Family
ES	Ensuite
S	Single
SS	Single Supplement

Campsite Key

Facilities:
T	Toilets
G	Grocery Shop
LSP	Long Stay Parking
O	Open All Year
S	Showers
CP	Car Parking
LY	Laundry
DW	Dogs Welcome
PD	Pick Up/Drop Service

Colour coding by walk regions

●	Exmoor	●	South Cornwall
●	North Devon	●	South Devon
●	North Cornwall	●	Dorset
●	West Cornwall		

Pick Up/Drop (PD)

This code denotes a facility whereby your host is willing to pick you up or drop you off at the Coast Path nearest their business. No fee should be charged for this service. They may offer to take your further, especially if you staying more than 1 night, but may ask you to pay for this service. Please remember that the distance from the path is only an estimate.

Kit Transfer (KT)

Where KT is offered, this is either through the company Luggage Transfers or is offered free of charge by the owner.

Listed Information

The part of the address in CAPITALS is an aid to location; it does not signify the postal town. The extreme left-hand column refers to the appropriate section in the 'Coast Path Walks'; we feel it may help you to find addresses quickly. The amount quoted gives an indication of the starting rate for bed and breakfast, and may well rise. **If working on a tight budget, it is best to ask first.**

Tourist Information Centres can be an additional source of accommodation addresses. We have provided a list of TICs along the Coast Path for your use on page 179.

Most of the B&B providers operate from their own private homes so do not expect plenty of staff as there are in hotels and large guesthouses. They work hard to make you comfortable, welcome, dry you out and make you feel like one of the family.

If your chosen address does not supply evening meals you should ask, when booking, how far it is to your evening meal – you can then decide if you want to stay there.

We wish to develop this list and suggestions for inclusion in our next guide will be welcome. Details of any new accommodation should be addressed to the Administrator. Our list is not comprehensive and walkers will find many B&Bs in towns and villages along the Coast Path that are not recorded in this book.

Although there are a lot of addresses that state they are 'open all the year', some of these close for the Christmas period. Walkers should remember that during the holiday season many of our accommodation addresses could be fully booked up in advance by holidaymakers staying for a week or two. Conversely a walker could book for one night only in good time, thus preventing a guest house proprietor from taking a week or more booking later on. Accommodation problems can be frustrating to all parties concerned so bear these facts in mind when hunting for one night only.

Campsites

Individuals - but we stress not parties - usually find no problem in obtaining leave to camp away from official camp sites if they request permission to do so. In fact, our correspondence has many examples of extra kindnesses extended by farmers and others to campers. We would, however, very much emphasise the requesting of permission first. It would be so easy for the thoughtlessness of a few to undo the good relationships of many others built up over some years.

The list of campsites is thin in many areas. Suggestions for inclusions in future lists will always be welcome. Information should be addressed to the Administrator.

Important

If having booked ahead, and for any reason you are unable to get to your accommodation address, please telephone and explain your absence to your intended host. We have known instances where the host has become so worried about the non-appearance of walkers that they have informed the emergency services. The last thing we want is the emergency services out on a wild goose chase.

Exmoor B&Bs

Walk No.	Contact name / Establishment name / Address	Telephone no. / Mobile no. / Email / Website	OS Map Ref. / Dist. from path	Starting price (£) / Months Open / Facilities / Info
1 BUSINESS MEMBER	Mrs J Bakker Beverleigh Beacon Road **MINEHEAD** TA24 5SE	01643 708450 www.beverleigh.co.uk beverleighminehead@gmail.com	968 469 200 mts	35 SS £10 PL D LSP CP KT PD O W D(2)(2ES) T(1)(1ES)
1	Mr & Mrs E & C Moulder Montrose Guest House 14 Tregonwell Road **MINEHEAD** TA24 5DU	01643 706473 www.montroseminehead.co.uk montroseminehead@btinternet.com	972 460 900 mts	40 Price based on 2 sharing, SS D CP KT O W D(4)(4ES) T(1)(1ES)
1	Mr & Mrs S Poingdestre Kenella House 7 Tregonwell Road **MINEHEAD** TA24 5DT	01643 703128 www.kenellahouse.co.uk kenellahouse@fsmail.net	972 462 500 mts	32.5 SS PL CP KT O D(6)(6ES) T(2)(2ES)
1	Mr & Mrs P Thompson Glendower House 30-32 Tregonwell Road **MINEHEAD** TA24 5DU	01643 707144 www.glendower-house.co.uk info@glendower-house.co.uk	972 460 1 km	35 D LSP CP W LF O(Feb - mid Dec) S(3)(3ES) D(4)(4ES) T(2)(2ES) F(2)(2ES)
1	N Bodd The Old Stables B&B Northfield Road **MINEHEAD** TA24 5QH	07435964882 www.theoldstablesminehead.co.uk info@theoldstablesminehead.co.uk	On path	45 SS PL D LSP CP KT O W LF T(1)(0ES) F(2)(2ES)
1	Mr & Mrs A Shaw Tudor Cottage **BOSSINGTON** TA24 8HQ	01643 862255 www.tudorcottage.net bookings@tudorcottage.net	898 479 100 mts	35 SS. Mob 07855 531593. AA 4* PL EM D LSP CP KT O() S(1)(0ES) D(2)(1ES) T(1)(0ES)
1 BUSINESS MEMBER	Mr & Mrs N Southwood Myrtle Cottage High Street **PORLOCK** TA24 8PU	01643 862978 www.myrtleporlock.co.uk enquiries@myrtleporlock.co.uk	885 467 1km	32.5 SS. DW D CP PD O W LF D(4)(4ES) T(2)(2ES) F(2)(2ES)
1 BUSINESS MEMBER	Mr & Mrs C Gladstone The Cottage High Street **PORLOCK** TA24 8PU	01643 862996 www.cottageporlock.co.uk cottageporlock@gmail.com	885 467 400 mts	35 £5 SS PL D LSP CP KT O W LF D(2)(2ES) T(2)(2ES) F(1)(1ES)
1 BUSINESS MEMBER	Mrs G Kenyon Sea View B & B High Bank **PORLOCK** TA24 8NP	01643 863456 www.seaviewporlock.co.uk seaview.porlock@btconnect.com	884 467 100m	32 Locally sourced award winning breakfast D LSP CP KT O W LF S(1)(1ES) D(2)(2ES) T()(1ES)
1	Mr & Mrs M Ley Reines House Parson Street **PORLOCK** TA24 8QJ	01643 862913 www.reineshouse.co.uk mmtley@yahoo.co.uk	885 465 1 km	32 SS £7 PL D KT PD O W LF D(1)(1ES) F(2)(2ES)
2 BUSINESS MEMBER	Mr & Mrs C Parker The Old Sea Captain's House 1 Tors Road **LYNMOUTH** EX35 6ET	01598 753369 www.thecaptainshouseinlynmouth.co.uk thecaptainshouse@btinternet.com	727 494 50 mts	28 PL DW D LSP CP KT W LF O(10 Jan-18 Dec) S(1)(1ES) D(6)(6ES) T(1)(1ES) F(1)(1ES)
2 BUSINESS MEMBER	Mrs C Sheppard River Lyn View 26 Watersmeet Road **LYNMOUTH** EX35 6EP	01598 753501 www.riverlynview.com carolriverlynview@talktalk.net	725 493 150 mts	30 SS PL DW D CP KT O W LF D(3)(3ES) T(2)(1ES)
2	Dr J Batch Bonnicott House 10 Watersmeet Road **LYNMOUTH** EX35 6EP	01598 753346 www.bonnicott.com stay@bonnicott.com	725 493 180 mts	30 £33 Apr-Sept PL EM D LSP CP LF O( ) S(3)(3ES) D(8)(7ES) T(1)(1ES) F(2)(2ES)

Walk No.	Contact name / Establishment name / Address	Telephone no. / Mobile no. / Email / Website	OS Map Ref. / Dist. from path	Starting price (£) / Months Open / Facilities / Info
2	Miss D Smith Hillside House 22 Watersmeet Road **LYNMOUTH** EX35 6EP	01598 753836 www.hillside-lynmouth.co.uk hillsidelynmouth@btinternet.com	725 493 200 mts	30 SS PL DW D KT O W S(0)(0ES) D(3)(3ES) T(1)(1ES)
2 **BUSINESS MEMBER**	Mr & Mrs J Tuck The Denes 15 Longmead **LYNTON** EX35 6DQ	01598 753573 www.thedenes.com enquiries@thedenes.com	715 494 400mts	35 SS £15. LSP by prior arrangement. Mob 07774 659223 PL EM D LSP CP KT W LF O(Mar to Dec) D(5)(5ES) T(2)(2ES) F(2)(2ES)
2 **BUSINESS MEMBER**	Mr & Mrs I Downing North Walk House North Walk **LYNTON** EX35 6HJ	01598 753372 www.northwalkhouse.co.uk walk@northwalkhouse.co.uk	718 497 on path	39 Also self-catering apartment PL EM DW D CP O W LF S(1)(1ES) D(4)(4ES) T(1)(1ES) SC(1)(1ES)
2 **BUSINESS MEMBER**	Mrs A Wilford Gable Lodge 35 Lee Road **LYNTON** EX35 6BS	01598 752367 www.gablelodgelynton.co.uk gablelodge@btconnect.com	717 495 400 mts PD	35 SS £10 PL EM D CP KT PD O W LF D(4)(4ES) T(1)(1ES) F(1)(1ES)
2 **BUSINESS MEMBER**	Mr & Mrs J Hodges Choughs Nest Hotel North Walk **LYNTON** EX35 6HJ	01598 753315 www.choughsnesthotel.co.uk relax@choughsnesthotel.co.uk	718 497 on path	48 SS PL EM D LSP CP PD O W LF D(5)(5ES) T(3)(3ES)
3 **BUSINESS MEMBER**	Mrs F M Dallyn Mannacott Farm Nr Hunters Inn **MARTINHOE** EX31 4QS	01598 763227 francesdallyn@gmail.com	662 481 800 mts	28 SS £4 PL D CP KT O(Easter - mid Oct) D(1)(1ES) T(1)(1ES)
3 **BUSINESS MEMBER**	Mr M Cowell Heddon's Gate Hotel Heddon Valley Kings Lane **PARRACOMBE** EX31 4PZ	01598 763481 www.heddonsgatehotel.co.uk stay@heddonsgatehotel.co.uk	1/2 mile	50 SS PL EM DW D LSP CP KT PD O W LF S(1)(1ES) D(7)(7ES) T(2)(2ES) F(1)(1ES)
3 **BUSINESS MEMBER**	Mrs R Brown Blair Lodge Moory Meadow **COMBE MARTIN** EX34 0DG	01271 882294 www.blairlodge.co.uk info@blairlodge.co.uk	579 473 on path	33 SS PL EM D LSP CP KT PD O W LF S(2)(1ES) D(5)(5ES) T(2)(2ES) F(1)(1ES)
3 **BUSINESS MEMBER**	Mrs P Palmer Mellstock House Woodlands **COMBE MARTIN** EX34 0AR	01271 882592 www.mellstockhouse.co.uk enquiries@mellstockhouse.co.uk	573 472 20 metres	30 SS £10 PL EM D LSP CP KT PD O W LF D(5)(5ES) T(2)(2ES) F(1)(1ES)
3 **BUSINESS MEMBER**	Mrs L Leyland Channel Vista Woodlands **COMBE MARTIN** EX34 0AT	01271 883514 www.channelvista.co.uk channelvista@btconnect.com	574 470 100 mts	35 SS. LSP by prior arrangement PL EM DW D LSP CP KT O S(2)(2ES) D(4)(4ES) T(2)(2ES) F(1)(1ES)
3	Mrs S Davey Fontenay Woodlands **COMBE MARTIN** EX34 0AT	01271 889368 www.visitfontenay.co.uk sarah@visitfontenay.co.uk	575 470 200 mts	25 PL by prior arrangement, mob 07814 769845. Child friendly PL DW LSP CP KT PD O W LF S(1)(0ES) D(1)(0ES) T(1)(0ES)

Walk No.	Contact name / Establishment name / Address	Telephone no. / Mobile no. / Email / Website	OS Map Ref. / Dist. from path	Starting price (£) / Months Open / Facilities / Info
4 BUSINESS MEMBER	Mr & Mrs D R & A Jenkins Avalon 6 Capstone Crescent **ILFRACOMBE** EX34 9BT	01271 863325 www.avalon-hotel.co.uk avalon_ilfracombe@yahoo.co.uk	522 478 01271 866543 on path	28 LSP low season only, Single £33 PL D LSP CP W O(5 Jan 14 to 19 Dec) S(1)(1ES) D(4)(4ES) T(3)(3ES) F(1)(1ES)
4 BUSINESS MEMBER	Mrs A Tappenden Ocean Backpackers Hostel 29 St James Place **ILFRACOMBE** EX34 9BJ	01271 867835 www.oceanbackpackers.co.uk info@oceanbackpackers.co.uk	522 478 25 mts	14 SS. Kitchen for SC. Weekend £15. 5 dorms sleeping 38 avail. DW D CP KT O W D(2)(1ES) T(1)(0ES) F(3)(1ES) SC(7)(6ES)
4	Mr & Mrs J Brown Avoncourt Hotel Torrs Walk Avenue **ILFRACOMBE** EX34 8AU	01271 862543 www.avoncourtilfracombe.co.uk johnbrown735@btinternet.com	513 476 on path	35 07974 212345 PL DW D CP KT PD O S(2)(2ES) D(4)(4ES) T(1)(1ES) F(1)(1ES)
4	Mr & Mrs C & J Pearson Lyncott House 56 St Brannocks Road **ILFRACOMBE** EX34 8EQ	01271 862425 www.lyncotthouse.co.uk	515 468 1 km	37.5 SS £7.50 D CP O D(4)(4ES) T(1)(1ES) F(1)(1ES)
4	Mrs S Furmston The Collingdale 13 Larkstone Terrace **ILFRACOMBE** EX34 9NU	01271 863770 www.thecollingdale.co.uk thecollingdale@gmail.com	526 475 30 mts	39 SS. PL D LSP CP KT W LF O(Mar-end Oct) D(9)(8ES) T(3)(3ES) F(3)(3ES)
4	Mr P Connors The Olive Branch Guesthouse 56 Fore Street **ILFRACOMBE** EX34 9DJ	01271 879005 www.olivebranchguesthouse.co.uk enquiries@olivebranchguesthouse.co.uk	100m	45 D LSP CP W LF O(1 Mar - 1 Nov) S(1)(1ES) D(3)(3ES) T()(1ES)
5 BUSINESS MEMBER	Mr P Milton Trimstone Manor Country House Hotel **TRIMSTONE** Nr Woolacombe EX34 8NR	01271 862841 www.trimstone.co.uk info@trimstone.co.uk	499 434 01271 863808 2 km	42 Also self catering & PD from Combe Martin to Barnstaple. PL EM DW D LSP CP KT PD O W LF S(1)(1ES) D(10)(10ES) T(2)(2ES) F(1)(1ES)
5	Frow Seacroft B&B Poole Lane **WOOLACOMBE** EX34 7AP	01271 870112 www.seacroftbbwoolacombe.co.uk info@seacroftbbwoolacombe.co.uk	2km	27.5 SS PL DW CP O W D(2)(2ES) T()(1ES)
6 BUSINESS MEMBER	Mrs G M Adams Combas Farm **PUTSBOROUGH** Croyde EX33 1PH	01271 890398 www.combasfarm.co.uk combasfarm@hotmail.co.uk	449 396 900 mts	35 SS high season PL D LSP CP KT W LF O( ) S(1)(0ES) D(2)(2ES) T(1)(1ES) F(1)(1ES)
6	Mrs V Learmonth Chapel Farm Guest House Hobbs Hill **CROYDE** EX33 1NE	01271 890429 www.chapelfarmcroyde.co.uk vall52@yahoo.co.uk	444 390 1 km	35 SS. Also self catering KT W LF O(Easter - Sept) D(1)(1ES) T(1)(1ES) F(1)(1ES)
6	Mr & Mrs F Cannock Sandbourne Down End **CROYDE** EX33 1QE	01271 890536 fredcannock@tiscali.co.uk	436 386 300 mts	35 PL D CP KT O W D(1)(1ES) T(1)(1ES)

For Combe Martin addresses see Exmoor B&Bs.

Walk No.	Contact name / Establishment name / Address	Telephone no. / Mobile no. / Email / Website	OS Map Ref. / Dist. from path	Starting price (£) / Months Open / Facilities / Info
7	Mr & Mrs Mrs B Watkins North Cottage 14 North Street **BRAUNTON** EX33 1AJ	01271 812703 www.northcottagebraunton.co.uk north_cottage@hotmail.com	485 367 750 mts	30 Mobile 07779 842367. SS £1.50. PL DW D CP KT O W LF S(2)(0ES) D(2)(2ES) T(1)(1ES)
7 BUSINESS MEMBER	Mrs A Benning The Firs Higher Park Road **BRAUNTON** EX33 2LG	01271 814358 www.bennings.co.uk alisonbenning@btinternet.com	498 364 2 km PD	35 SS PL DW D LSP CP KT O W D(1)(1ES) T(1)(1ES)
7 BUSINESS MEMBER	Mrs S Holker Silver Cottage 14 Silver Street **BRAUNTON** EX33 2EN	01271 814165 www.bedandbreakfast-braunton.co.uk silvercottage.braunton@gmail.com	487 367 400 mts PD	40 Mob 07974 017663 O D EM PL CP KT 2D
7 BUSINESS MEMBER	Mr C Brookes The Brookfield South Street **BRAUNTON** EX33 2AN	01271 812382 www.thebrookfield.co.uk info@thebrookfield.co.uk	487 362 400 mts	32.5 SS £12 PL D CP KT W O(Mid March to end Dec.) S(4)(4ES) D(5)(5ES) T(5)(5ES) F(1)(1ES)
8 BUSINESS MEMBER	Mr B Abell The Old Vicarage B&B Barbican Terrace **BARNSTAPLE** EX32 9HQ	01271 328504 www.oldvicaragebarnstaple.co.uk theoldvicaragebarnstaple@gmail.com	561 328 200 mts	40 D LSP CP KT O W LF S(1)(1ES) D(1)(1ES) T(1)(1ES) F(2)(2ES)
8 BUSINESS MEMBER	Mrs M Cumiskey The Poplars Rumsam Road **BARNSTAPLE** EX32 9EW	01271 378773 barnstaplebedandbreakfast.co.uk info@thepoplarsbarnstaple.co.uk		40 PL D LSP CP O W LF D(1)(1ES) T()(1ES)
8	Mr & Mrs P J Davis Cresta Guest House Sticklepath Hill **BARNSTAPLE** EX31 2BU	01271 374022 www.crestaguesthouse.co.uk contact@crestaguesthouse.co.uk	548 324 800 mts	30 PL CP O W S(2)(0ES) D(2)(2ES) T(2)(2ES) F(2)(2ES)
8	Mrs J Manning Herton Guesthouse Lake Hill **BARNSTAPLE** EX31 3HS	01271 323302 www.herton-guesthouse.co.uk janice@janicemanning93.wanadoo.co.uk	554 322 500 mts	29 SS Mob 07866236018 PL D LSP CP KT O D(3)(2ES) T(1)(1ES) F(1)(1ES) SC(1)(1ES)
8	Mrs S Svenson Yeo Dale Hotel Pilton Bridge **BARNSTAPLE** EX31 1PG	01271 342954 www.yeodalehotel.co.uk stay@yeodalehotel.co.uk	557 338 01271 344530 600 mts	42.5 EM & LSP by prior arrangement PL EM D LSP CP KT O S(3)(3ES) D(7)(7ES) T(2)(2ES) F(2)(2ES)
9	Mr P Day Lower Yelland Farm **FREMINGTON** Barnstaple EX31 3EN	01271 860101 www.loweryellandfarm.co.uk peterday@loweryellandfarm.co.uk	492 322 200 mts	35 £5 SS DW D CP KT O W LF S(2)(2ES) D(5)(5ES)
10 BUSINESS MEMBER	Mrs P & J Hills The Seagate The Quay **APPLEDORE** EX39 1QS	01237 472589 www.theseagate.co.uk info@theseagate.co.uk	10 yards	36 SS PL EM DW LSP CP O W LF S(1)(1ES) D(6)(6ES) T(2)(2ES) F(1)(1ES)
10	E Faramus 89 Abbotsham Road **BIDEFORD** EX39 3AQ	01237 472975 www.bobno89.co.uk bob.89@gmail.com	447 266 1km	30 SS £10. Mobile 07511 230030 PL D CP KT PD O W LF S(1)(0ES) D(2)(2ES)

Walk No.	Contact name / Establishment name / Address	Telephone no. / Mobile no. / Email / Website	OS Map Ref. / Dist. from path	Starting price (£) / Months Open / Facilities / Info
10 BUSINESS MEMBER	Mr & Mrs M Thomson Culloden House Fosketh Hill **WESTWARD HO!** EX39 1UL	01237 479421 www.culloden-house.co.uk cullodenhouse@gmail.com	432 289 100 mts	35 CP KT O W LF D(10)(5ES) T(6)(3ES)
9	Mrs S Clegg Mayfield Avon Lane **WESTWARD HO!** EX39 1LR	01237 477128 www.mayfieldbandb.co.uk mayfieldbandb@hotmail.co.uk	435 291 100 mts	35 PL D LSP CP KT PD O W LF D(1)(1ES) T(1)(1ES)
10	Mr & Mrs P Snowball Brockenhurst 11 Atlantic Way **WESTWARD HO!** EX39 1HX	01237 423346 www.brockenhurstindevon.co.uk info@brockenhurstindevon.co.uk	433 290 200 mts	45 SS CP O W S(3)(3ES) D(2)(2ES) T(1)(1ES)
11 BUSINESS MEMBER	Mr & Mrs Curtis Fuchsia Cottage Burscott Lane **HIGHER CLOVELLY** EX39 5RR	01237 431398 www.clovelly-holidays.co.uk tom@clovelly-holidays.co.uk	313 242 1km PD	32 SS PL D LSP CP KT PD W LF O(Closed Xmas & New Year) S(1)(0ES) D(1)(1ES) T(1)(1ES)
11 BUSINESS MEMBER	Mr & Mrs C West Pillowery Park Burscott **HIGHER CLOVELLY** EX39 5RR	01237 431668 www.clovellyaccommodation.com info@clovellyaccommodation.co.uk	312 241 1.5 km	28 £10 SS PL D LSP CP KT PD O W LF D(1)(1ES) T(2)(0ES)
11 BUSINESS MEMBER	Mrs M McColl 1 Southdown Cottage **HIGHER CLOVELLY** EX39 5SA	01237 431504 maryfmcoll@hotmail.com	297 236 3km	32.5 £14 SS PL EM DW D LSP CP KT PD O S(1)(0ES) D(1)(1ES) T(1)(1ES)
12 BUSINESS MEMBER	Mrs Y Heard West Titchberry Farm **WEST TITCHBERRY** Hartland Point EX39 6AU	01237 441287 westtitchberry@gmail.com	242 272 250 mts PD	27.5 £5 SS PL EM D LSP CP KT PD O W LF D(1)(0ES) T(1)(0ES) F(1)(1ES)
12 BUSINESS MEMBER	Ms M Chesterman 2 Harton Manor The Square **HARTLAND** EX39 6BL	01237 441670 www.twohartonmanor.co.uk merlyn@twohartonmanor.co.uk	258 245 3 km PD	30 PD Hartland Quay, Mobile 07771 610982. PL DW D LSP CP KT PD O W LF S(1)(0ES) D(1)(1ES) T(1)(1ES)
12 BUSINESS MEMBER	Mrs T Goaman Elmscott Farm **HARTLAND** EX39 6ES	01237 441276 www.elmscott.org.uk john.goa@virgin.net	231 215 01237 441076 400 mts PD	30 Also YHA Elmscott bookings PL EM D LSP CP KT PD O LF D(1)(1ES) T(1)(0ES)
12	Mrs K Clark Copps Castle B&B **HARTLAND** EX39 6AS	01237 441733 www.bandbhartland.co.uk coppscastle@gmail.com	1 1/2 miles	30 SS PL D LSP CP KT W LF O(East- er to Oct) D(2)(1ES) T(1)(1ES)
13	Mrs A Dart 1 Coastguard Cottages **STOKE** Hartland EX39 6DU	01237 441011 www.coastguardcottagestoke.com annajon@btinternet.com	235 246 500 mts	35 SS PL EM DW D LSP CP KT O W LF D(2)(2ES)
13	Mr & Mrs A Jones Cranham House **WELCOMBE** Hartland EX39 6ET	01288 331351 www.cranhamhouse.co.uk info2@cranhamhouse.co.uk	224 192 800 mts	37.5 SS, SC barn available PL EM D LSP CP PD O W D(2)(2ES) T(1)(1ES) SC(1)(1ES)

Walk No.	Contact name Establishment name Address	Telephone no. Mobile no. Email Website	OS Map Ref. Dist. from path	Starting price (£) Months Open Facilities Info
13 BUSINESS MEMBER	Mrs S Heywood Cornakey Farm **CORNAKEY** Morwenstow EX23 9SS	01288 331260 cornakeyfarm@hotmail.co.uk	208 160 300 mts	40 PL D LSP CP KT O W LF F(1)(1ES)
13 BUSINESS MEMBER	Mr C Fletcher The Bush Inn Crosstown **MORWENSTOW** EX23 9SR	01288 331242 www.thebushinnmorwenstow.com thebushinncrosstown@gmail.com	208 150 600 mts	50 Also self catering PL EM DW LSP CP KT O W LF D(2)(2ES) T(2)(2ES)
13	Mrs C White Trelawney Crosstown **MORWENSTOW** EX23 9SR	01288 331453	208 150 800 mts	30 SS £5 PL D CP O W LF S(1)(0ES) D(1)(0ES)
13	Mrs S Bramhill West Point Crimp **MORWENSTOW** EX23 9PB	01288 331594 www.budebedandbreakfast.co.uk bramhill@hotmail.co.uk	255 155 5.5 kms PD	40 PL LSP CP KT PD O D(1)(1ES) T(1)(1ES) F(1)(1ES)
13 BUSINESS MEMBER	Mrs J Steadman Tee-Side Guest House 2 Burn View **BUDE** EX23 8BY	01288 352351 www.tee-side.co.uk teeside.bude@gmail.com	208 066 400 mts	32.5 SS PL D KT O W LF D(4)(4ES) T(4)(4ES)
13 BUSINESS MEMBER	Mr M Safdar-Wallace Sea Jade 15 Burn View **BUDE** EX23 8BZ	01288 353404 www.seajadeguesthouse.co.uk seajadeguesthouse@yahoo.co.uk	209 065 450 mts	36.5 £3 SS, Rooms are D/T/F PL EM D KT PD O W LF D(7)(4ES)
13 BUSINESS MEMBER	Miss S Turner Brendon Arms Falcon Terrace **BUDE** EX23 8SD	01288 354542 www.brendonarms.co.uk enquiries@brendonarms.co.uk	214 061 as phone 20 mts	37 LSP CP O W LF S(1)(1ES) D(5)(5ES) T(3)(3ES)
13	Mrs E Payne Pencarrol Guest House 21 Downs View **BUDE** EX23 8RF	01288 352478 pencarrolbude@aol.com	209 070 300 mts	35 SS PL D W LF O(1st March to end Oct) S(1)(0ES) D(2)(2ES) T(1)(1ES) F(1)(1ES)
13	Mr M Fly Fairway Guest House 8 Downs View **BUDE** EX23 8RF	01288 355059 www.fairwayguesthouse.co.uk enquiries@fairwayguesthouse.co.uk	209 070 300 mts	30 SS. PL by prior arrangement PL D KT W LF O(Mar-Nov) S(3)(1ES) D(5)(5ES) T(3)(2ES) F(2)(2ES)
13	Mrs L Kelly Links Side 7 Burn View **BUDE** EX23 8BY	01288 352410 www.linkssidebude.co.uk linksidebude@hotmail.com	208 067 01288 352410 400 mts	30 PL D KT S(1)(1ES) D(4)(3ES) T(1)(1ES)

For addresses between Welcombe and Bude see North Cornwall B&Bs.

Walk No.	Contact name / Establishment name / Address	Telephone no. / Mobile no. / Email / Website	OS Map Ref. / Dist. from path	Starting price (£) / Months Open / Facilities / Info
14 BUSINESS MEMBER	Mr & Mrs F Mussell Trewartha St Gennys **CRACKINGTON HAVEN** EX23 0NN	01840 230420 www.bychy.co.uk francismussell@btinternet.com	145 967 as phone 750 mts	30 Some chalet accommodation £5 SS PL EM DW D CP KT PD O W S(1)(1ES) D(3)(3ES) F(1)(1ES) SC(4)(4ES)
14	Mr & Mrs J May Ludon Hill **CRACKINGTON HAVEN** EX23 0JZ	01840 230584 johnanniemay@btinternet.com	144 966 300 mts	35 D KT O D(1)(0ES) T(1)(0ES)
14	Mrs J Morris 14 Lundy Drive **CRACKINGTON HAVEN** EX23 0PA	01840 230106 www.crackingtonhavenbandb.co.uk julie@crackingtonhavenbandb. co.uk	154 959 1.5 km	30 PL D LSP CP KT PD O W LF D(1)(1ES)
14 BUSINESS MEMBER	Mr P Stedman Lower Meadows House Penally Hill **BOSCASTLE** PL35 0HF	01840 250570 www.lowermeadows.co.uk stay@lowermeadows.co.uk	101 913 350 mts	40 SS. Mob 07846242511. Farm shop produce. PL D CP KT PD O W LF D(4)(4ES) T(1)(1ES) F(1)(1ES)
15 BUSINESS MEMBER	Mr J Scott The Wellington Hotel The Harbour **BOSCASTLE** PL35 0AQ	01840 250202 www.wellingtonhotelboscastle.com info@wellingtonhotelboscastle.com	098 913 200 mts	45 PL EM DW D CP KT O W LF S(4)(4ES) D(7)(7ES) T(2)(2ES) F(1)(1ES)
15	Mr & Mrs J Tillinghast Valency Bed & Breakfast Penally Hill **BOSCASTLE** PL35 0HF	01840 250397 www.valencybandb.com tillinghast@btinternet.com	099 914 100mts PD	42.5 PD between Bude & Rock O D PL CP KT PD 3D[3]
15	Mr & Mrs G Barratt Orchard Lodge Gunpool Lane **BOSCASTLE** PL35 0AT	01840 250418 www.orchardlodgeboscastle.co.uk orchardlodgeboscastle@gmail.com	906 099 01840 298101 500 mts	37.5 PL D CP KT O D(3)(3ES) T(2)(2ES)
15	Mrs J Horwell The Old Coach House Tintagel Road **BOSCASTLE** PL35 0AS	01840 250398 www.old-coach.co.uk stay@old-coach.co.uk	098 906 400 mts	38 SS. PL D CP KT W LF O(March to October) D(4)(4ES) T(3)(3ES) F(1)(1ES)
16	Mrs A Jones Grange Cottage **BOSSINEY** Tintagel PL34 0AX	01840 770487	065 888 200 mts	33 SS £10 PL D CP W LF O(Mar - Sept) D(2)(1ES)
16	Mrs P Tinney Bossinney Cottage **BOSSINEY** Tintagel PL34 0AY	01840 770327 bossinney@tinney.org	066 888 200 mts	30 PL D CP KT W LF O(April - Oct) S(1)(0ES) D(1)(0ES) T(1)(0ES)
16 BUSINESS MEMBER	Mr K Walker Bosayne Guest House Atlantic Road **TINTAGEL** PL34 0DE	01840 770514 www.bosayne.co.uk enquiries@bosayne.co.uk	056 888 300 mts	30 PL D CP KT O W LF S(3)(0ES) D(3)(3ES) T(1)(1ES) F(1)(0ES) SC(1)(0ES)
16 BUSINESS MEMBER	Mr J Knight & Ms R Danger The Cornishman Inn Fore Street **TINTAGEL** PL34 0DB	01840 770238 www.cornishmaninn.com info@cornishmaninn.com	30 SS PL EM LSP CP KT O W LF S(1)(1ES) D(5)(5ES) T(3)(3ES) F(2)(2ES)

Walk No.	Contact name / Establishment name / Address	Telephone no. / Mobile no. / Email / Website	OS Map Ref. / Dist. from path	Starting price (£) / Months Open / Facilities / Info
17	Mrs V Mackay Trenowan B&B **TREKNOW** Tintagel PL34 0EJ	01840 770554 www.cornwall-online.co.uk/tre-nowanbandb trenowanbandb@btinternet.com	055 872 300 mts	30 Occasional DW O D PL CP LSP KT 1D[1] 1D/T[1] 1S
17 BUSINESS MEMBER	Mr & Mrs N Monk Lane End Farm Pendoggett **PORT ISAAC** PL30 3HH	01208 880013 www.laneendcornwall.co.uk nabmonk@tiscali.co.uk	026 793 2.5 km PD	36 Mobile: 07724 133820, also self catering PL D LSP CP KT PD W LF O() S(1)(1ES) T(1)(1ES)
16	Mr D Barnard Port Gaverne Hotel Port Gaverne **PORT ISAAC** PL29 3SQ	01208 880244 www.portgavernehotel.co.uk eat@portgavernehotel.co.uk	003 807 on path	75 SS £15 PL EM DW D CP KT PD O W LF S(2)(2ES) D(4)(4ES) T(6)(6ES) F(3)(3ES)
18	Mrs P White Seaways **POLZEATH** PL27 6SU	01208 862382 www.seawaysguesthouse.co.uk pauline@seaways99.freeserve.co.uk	939 788 350 mts	42 SS D LSP CP KT O W LF S(1)(0ES) D(1)(1ES) T(2)(1ES)
18	Mr & Mrs P Cullinan 4 Riverside **PADSTOW** PL28 8BY	01841 532383 www.southquaybedandbreakfast-padstow.co.uk cullinan@madasafish.com	920 754 190 mts	35 SS, DW in one room only DW O D(2)(1ES)
18	Mrs E Cortis 'Ere Tis 3 Egerton Road **PADSTOW** PL28 8DJ	01841 532320	920 748 100 mts	37.5 SS DW D LSP CP W LF O(Easter - Oct) S(1)(0ES) D(3)(1ES) T(1)(1ES)
20	Mrs E Kennerley Penhalonga **CONSTANTINE BAY** PL28 8JG	01841 521122 lizkennerley@btinternet.com	869 743	70 Price for 2 sharing; single £40, mobile: 07815 833158 PL LSP CP W LF O() S(1)(1ES) D(1)(1ES) T(1)(1ES)
20	Mrs R Barlow Treglos Hotel **CONSTANTINE BAY** PL28 8JH	01841 520727 www.tregloshotel.com stay@tregloshotel.com	865 743 01841 521163 300 mts	80 D EM PL CP DW 34 D/T 3S 5F ALL ES
20 BUSINESS MEMBER	Mrs M Neale Penlan **PORTHCOTHAN BAY** PL28 8LP	01841 520440 www.porthcothanbay.co.uk/pcb2_bandb.html mary@idenna.com	859 719 200 mts	35 Mobile 07525 940404 PL EM DW D LSP CP KT O W LF D(2)(2ES) T(1)(0ES)
20	Mr & Mrs J Nederpel Old MacDonald's Farm **PORTHCOTHAN BAY** PL28 8LW	01841 540829 www.oldmacdonalds.co.uk enquiries@oldmacdonalds.co.uk	867 877 1 km	40 PL EM CP KT O() T(1)(1ES) F(2)(2ES)
20	Mrs P Mcowen Greylands Treburrick **PORTHCOTHAN** PL27 7UR	01841 540451 www.greylands.moonfruit.com pam.mcowen@gmail.com	862 707 1km	32.5 SS. Mob 07791147597 PL EM DW D LSP CP KT PD O W LF D(1)(1ES)

Walk No.	Contact name / Establishment name / Address	Telephone no. / Mobile no. / Email / Website	OS Map Ref. / Dist. from path	Starting price (£) / Months Open / Facilities / Info
21 **BUSINESS MEMBER**	Mrs R Vickers Trevarrian Lodge Trevarrian **MAWGAN PORTH** TR8 4AQ	01637 860156 www.trevarrianlodge.com trevarrianlodge@gmail.com	850 661 400 mts	35 DW by prior arrangement only PL DW D LSP CP KT O W S(1)(1ES) D(1)(1ES) T(2)(2ES) F(2)(2ES)
21	Mrs B Bradley Dimora Gwel-an-Mor **MAWGAN PORTH** TR8 4DW	01637 860511 www.dimorabed.breakfast.co.uk abbholist@yahoo.co.uk	853 674 500 mts	Mobile 07712590509 PL DW D LSP CP O W D(1)(1ES) F(1)(1ES)
21 **BUSINESS MEMBER**	Mr G Dolan The Three Tees Hotel 21 Carminow Way **NEWQUAY** TR7 3AY	01637 872055 www.3tees.co.uk greg@3tees.co.uk	824 621 01637 820200 250 mts	34 PL DW D LSP CP KT O D(4)(4ES) T(2)(2ES) F(3)(3ES)
21 **BUSINESS MEMBER**	Mrs B Watts Tir Chonaill Lodge 106 Mount Wise **NEWQUAY** TR7 1QP	01637 876492 www.tirchonaill.co.uk tirchonailhotel@talk21.com	814 617 500m	32.5 Cornish, Irish, Gaelic & French spoken PL DW D LSP CP KT W LF O(March - Oct) S(2)(2ES) D(2)(2ES) T(2)(2ES) F(3)(3ES)
21	Mrs M Dewolfreys Dewolf Guesthouse 100 Henver Road **NEWQUAY** TR7 3BL	01637 874746 www.dewolfguesthouse.com holidays@dewolfguesthouse.com	828 620 500 mts	30 PL & DW by prior arrange- ment, £35 single also SC PL DW LSP CP KT O W LF S(3)(3ES) D(2)(2ES) T(2)(2ES) F(1)(1ES)
22	Mrs J Bunday La Reserve Treguth Close **NEWQUAY** TR8 5DD	01637 830519 www.lareservebedandbreakfast.co.uk jennyjehave@hotmail.co.uk	350 metres	30 SS £10 DW CP W LF O(Feb - Nov) D(1)(0ES) T(1)(0ES)
23 **BUSINESS MEMBER**	Mrs S Stirling & Mrs Sue Lawrie St Georges Country Hotel St Georges Hill **PERRANPORTH** TR6 0ED	01872 572184 www.stgeorgescountryhouse.co.uk info@stgeorgescountryhouse.co.uk	746 533 400 mts PD	45 SS £5 PL EM DW D CP KT PD O W LF D(5)(5ES) F(2)(2ES)
24	Mr & Mrs N York Kimberley West Polberro **ST AGNES** TR5 0SS	01872 552044 www.kimberleybedandbreakfast.co.uk kimberley_sta@hotmail.com	716 515 500mts	35 SS £15. mobile 07928893544. 4 night discount D LSP CP KT W O(Easter - Oct) D(2)(1ES) T(2)(1ES)

Wheal Coates

For Portreath addresses see North Cornwall B&Bs.

Walk No.	Contact name / Establishment name / Address	Telephone no. / Mobile no. / Email / Website	OS Map Ref. / Dist. from path	Starting price (£) / Months Open / Facilities / Info
25	Mr & Mrs S Haywood Cliff House Cliff Terrace **PORTREATH** TR16 4LE	01209 843847 www.cliffhouseportreath.co.uk cliffhousebookinginfo@gmail.com	656 455 On path	37.5 SS. Mob 07771523252 CP O W S(2)(0ES) D(2)(2ES) T(2)(2ES)
25 BUSINESS MEMBER	Mrs L Davies Nanterrow Farm **GWITHIAN** TR27 5BP	01209 712282 www.nanterrowfarm.co.uk nanterrow@hotmail.com	599 412 1.5km PD	35 SS D LSP CP PD W LF O(Feb-Nov) S(1)(0ES) D(1)(0ES) F(1)(0ES)
25	Mrs P Ellis The Mad Hatter 73 Fore Street **HAYLE** TR27 4DX	01736 754241 www.cornwall-online.co.uk/madhatter paulineellis-madhatter.org@tesco.net	566 378 1 km	32.5 Mobile: 07871 165381. SS PL EM DW D LSP CP PD O S(2)(1ES) D(2)(1ES) T(2)(1ES) F(1)(0ES)
26 BUSINESS MEMBER	Mrs O Parish Tamarisk Guest House Burthallen Lane **ST IVES** TR26 3AA	01736 797201 cornwall-online.co.uk/tamarisk-bandb-stives tamariskbb@gmail.com	508 406	40 D CP O W
26	Mr C England The Anchorage 5 Bunkers Hill **ST IVES** TR26 1LJ	01736 797135 www.anchoragestives.co.uk info@anchoragestives.co.uk	518 407 on path	45 PL D LSP KT O S(1)(0ES) D(3)(3ES) T(1)(1ES)
28	Mrs L Bowden Carlill 9 Porthminster Terrace **ST IVES** TR26 2DQ	01736 796738 www.carlillguesthouse.co.uk carlillguesthouse@hotmail.co.uk	300m	40 PL LSP CP KT O W S(2)(1ES) D(5)(2ES) T(4)(2ES) F(2)(1ES)
27	Mrs E Thompson Boswednack Manor **BOSWEDNACK** Zennor TR26 3DD	01736 794183 www.boswednackmanor.co.uk boswednack@ravenfield.co.uk	442 378 1.5 km	29 also SC PL CP KT O(Easter - end Sept) S(1)(0ES) D(2)(2ES) T(1)(0ES) F(1)(0ES)
28 BUSINESS MEMBER	Ms H Hurkett Gypsy Caravan B&B Primrose Cottage, Levant Road **TREWELLARD** Pendeen TR19 7SU	01736 787585 www.gypsycaravanbandb.co.uk holiday@gypsycaravanbandb.co.uk	373 339 300 mts	28 £5 per dog, cold hamper on request.Mob 07900631268/07765493398. SS if 1 nt D CP KT O LF S(1)(0ES) D(1)(0ES)
28	Mr E J Coak The North Inn **PENDEEN** TR19 7DN	01736 788417 www.thenorthinnpendeen.co.uk ernestjohncoak@aol.com	383 344 1 km	Also camping PL EM DW LSP CP O D(1)(1ES) T(3)(3ES)
28 BUSINESS MEMBER	Mrs J Hoather The Old Chapel **BOSCASWELL DOWNS** TR19 7DR	01736 786006 www.cornwallfarwest.co.uk geoffgoatherd@aol.com	385 344 1 km	32.5 Mobile 07789 547806, also self catering DW D LSP CP KT O W D(2)(0ES) T(2)(0ES) SC(3)(0ES)
28	Mr & Mrs T Dymond The Old Count House **BOSCASWELL DOWNS** Pendeen TR19 7EE	01736 788058 www.cornwallonline.co.uk dymondep@aol.com	383 344 1 km	30 PL LSP CP O(May - end Oct) D(2)(0ES)
28	Mrs J Eccleston Nanquidno Farm **ST JUST** Penzance TR19 7NU	01736 788463 www.nanquidnofarm.co.uk joeccleston3@hotmail.co.uk	363 292 695 mts	27 SS £3. Closed August EM DW D CP KT PD O W LF D(1)(0ES) T(1)(0ES)

Walk No.	Contact name / Establishment name / Address	Telephone no. / Mobile no. / Email / Website	OS Map Ref. / Dist. from path	Starting price (£) / Months Open / Facilities / Info
28 BUSINESS MEMBER	Mrs C Collinson Bosavern House **BOSAVERN** St Just TR19 7RD	01736 788301 www.bosavern.com info@bosavern.com	370 305 1 km	38 PL by prior arrangement, SS PL D CP KT O W LF S(1)(1ES) D(3)(3ES) T(2)(1ES) F(2)(2ES)
28	Mr & Mrs B Harrison Weavers **SENNEN** Penzance TR19 7AQ	01736 871565 www.cornwallfarwest/weavers weaversbb@btinternet.com	355 248 750 mts	38 SS D LSP CP KT O W LF T(1)(1ES)
28	Mrs J Pengelly Pengelly House **SENNEN COVE** Penzance TR19 7DF	01736 871866 www.pengellyhouse.com stay@pengellyhouse.com	352 265 40 mts	35 Continental breakfast in room, mobile 07810 361739 PL D LSP CP KT PD O W S(1)(1ES) D(1)(1ES) T(1)(1ES)
28 BUSINESS MEMBER	Mrs J Mitchell Mayon Farmhouse **SENNEN TR19 7AD**	01736 871757 www.mayonfarmhouse.co.uk mayonfarmhouse@hotmail.co.uk	356 257 400 mts	45 SS PL D LSP CP KT O W LF D(3)(3ES) T(1)(0ES) F(1)(1ES)
29 BUSINESS MEMBER	Mr J Hardman The Studio 3 Coastguard Cottage, Treen **ST LEVAN TR19 6LQ**	01736 810504 www.sennencornwall.com jeffrey_hardman@sky.com		37.5 SS. Mob 07713210489 PL DW D LSP CP KT O W LF D(1)(1ES) F(1)(1ES) SC(1)(1ES)
29 BUSINESS MEMBER	Miss & Mr Bance & Hicks Land's End Hostel Mill Barn, Trevescan **NEAR LAND'S END** TR19 7AQ	07519 309 908 www.landsendhostelaccommoda-tion.co.uk susie@landsendhostelaccommoda-tion.co.uk	355 248 400	25 Hostel Accommodation. £5 breakfast. DW CP KT O S(1)(0ES) D(1)(1ES) T(1)(1ES) F(2)(1ES)
29 BUSINESS MEMBER	Mrs P Willows Sea View House The Valley **PORTHCURNO TR19 6JX**	01736 810638 www.seaviewhouseporthcurno.com paulinewillows@hotmail.co.uk	383 227 400 mts PD	39 SS in Aug PL D LSP CP KT O(Open all year) S(1)(0ES) D(5)(3ES) T(1)(1ES) F(1)(1ES)
29	Mrs S Wear The Wearhouse The Valley **PORTHCURNO TR19 6JX**	01736 810129 susan.wear@me.com	383 226 200 mts	40 D LSP CP KT O D(4)(2ES) T(1)(1ES)
29	Mr & Mrs C Hatton Rose Cottage **PORTHCURNO TR19 6JY**	01736 810082 www.porthcurno.org.uk chris@chrisswcpa.co.uk	382 229 500 mts	35 SS. Mob 07926 084610 D CP PD O S(1)(0ES) D(2)(0ES)
31	Mrs D Waters White Gates Cliff Lane **MOUSEHOLE TR19 6PU**	01736 731691 www.chycor.co.uk	471 267 on path	35 SS DW CP W O(Easter-Sept) D(1)(0ES) T(1)(0ES) F(1)(1ES)
31 BUSINESS MEMBER	Mr & Mrs A Stott Glencree House 2 Mennaye road **PENZANCE TR18 4NG**	01736 362026 www.glencreehouse.co.uk stay@glencreehouse.co.uk	469 297 50 mts	33 PL KT PD O W LF S(2)(1ES) D(3)(3ES) T(1)(1ES) F(1)(1ES)
31 BUSINESS MEMBER	Mrs C Edwards Tremont Guest Accom-modation Alexandra Road **PENZANCE TR18 4LZ**	01736 362614 www.tremonthotel.co.uk info@tremonthotel.co.uk	465 300 200	35 SS PL D KT W LF O(March to Dec 20th) S(2)(2ES) D(3)(3ES) T(3)(3ES)

For Portreath addresses see North Cornwall B&Bs.

Walk No.	Contact name / Establishment name / Address	Telephone no. / Mobile no. / Email / Website	OS Map Ref. / Dist. from path	Starting price (£) / Months Open / Facilities / Info
31 BUSINESS MEMBER	Mrs F Brint Keigwin House Alexandra Road **PENZANCE** TR18 4LZ	01736 363930 www.keigwinhouse.co.uk fran@keigwinhouse.co.uk	500m	28 Mob 07557057773 PL D CP KT O W LF S(2)(0ES) D(2)(2ES) T(3)(2ES) F(2)(2ES)
31 BUSINESS MEMBER	Mr S Sprague Treventon Guest House Alexandra Place **PENZANCE** TR18 4NE	01736 332730 www.penzance-bed-and-breakfast.co.uk info@penzance-bed-and-breakfast.co.uk	01736 361873 100m	37.5 Local butcher, dairy & preserves PL D LSP CP KT O W LF D(5)(5ES) T(2)(2ES) F(1)(1ES)
31 BUSINESS MEMBER	Mr & Mrs Ruetsch Blue Seas Hotel 13 Regent Terrace **PENZANCE** TR18 5XX	01736 364744 www.blueseashotel-penzance.co.uk blueseapz@gmail.com		44 PL D LSP CP O W LF S(1)(1ES) D(7)(7ES) T()(3ES)
31	Mr & Mrs H Robinson Honeydew Guest House 3 Leskinnick Street **PENZANCE** TR18 2HA	01736 364206 www.honeydewguesthouse.co.uk info@honeydewguesthouse.co.uk	475 306 200 mts	35 SS. Mobile: 07817 531964 PL DW KT PD O S(1)(0ES) D(1)(1ES) T(1)(1ES) F(1)(1ES)
31	Mr & Mrs Cavanagh-Wilson Warwick House 17 Regent Terrace **PENZANCE** TR18 4DW	01736 363881 www.warwickhousepenzance.co.uk enquiry@warwickhousepenzance.co.uk	474 299 50 mts	44 SS, DVD library PL LSP CP O W LF S(2)(2ES) D(3)(3ES) T(2)(2ES) SC(1)(1ES)
31	C Care Downs Barn Farm **PENZANCE** TR19 6DG	01736 810295 www.downsbarnfarm.co.uk stay@downsbarnfarm.co.uk	419 245 1km	47.5 SS. Mob 07765576833 PL D CP PD O W LF D(2)(2ES) SC(2)(2ES)
31	Mr J Bolton Dunedin Guest House Alexandra Road **PENZANCE** TR18 4LZ	01736 362652 www.dunedinhotel.co.uk info@dunedinhotel.co.uk	466 299 200m	35 SS W LF O(Jan to end Oct) S(1)(1ES) D(4)(4ES) T()(1ES) F(2)(2ES)
32 BUSINESS MEMBER	Mrs M Foy Mzima Penlee Close **PRAA SANDS** TR20 9SR	01736 763856 marianfoy@prussia-cove-holiday.com	581 287 800mtrs PD	28 PL D CP KT PD O T(1)(0ES) F(1)(0ES)
32 BUSINESS MEMBER	Mrs B Rogers Wellmore End Cottage Methleigh Bottoms **PORTHLEVEN** TR13 9JP	01326 569310 www.wellmoreend-bandb.co.uk wellmoreend-bandb@tiscali.co.uk	200m	40 SS PL D LSP CP KT PD O W LF D(1)(1ES) F(1)(1ES)
33	Mr D Jeffery Strathallan Guest House 6 Monument Road **HELSTON** TR13 8HF	01326 573683 www.strathallangh.co.uk enquiries@strathallangh.co.uk		45 2 mins from town centre. Ideally situated to explore The Lizard. SS £10 PL EM D CP O W LF D(5)(5ES) T(1)(1ES)
33	Mrs T Payne Lyndale Cottage Guest House 4 Greenbank Meneage Road **HELSTON** TR13 8JA	01326 561082 www.lyndalecottage.co.uk enquiries@lyndalecottage.co.uk	662 269 3.5 km	35 SS CP O S(1)(1ES) D(3)(3ES) T(2)(2ES)

Walk No.	Contact name / Establishment name / Address	Telephone no. / Mobile no. / Email / Website	OS Map Ref. / Dist. from path	Starting price (£) / Months Open / Facilities / Info
33 **BUSINESS MEMBER**	Mr & Mrs I Paterson Tregathenan House B&B The Old Farmhouse, Tregathenan **HELSTON** TR13 0RZ	01326 569840 www.tregathenan.co.uk tregathenan@hotmail.com	654 306 6 km PD	30 SS £10. Mob 07796 697865 PL D LSP CP PD O W LF D(2)(1ES) T(1)(1ES) SC(3)(3ES)
33 **BUSINESS MEMBER**	Granary Barn Back-packers Nantrissack Farm **SITHNEY** Helston TR13 0AE	07740514188 www.cornwall-backpackers.co.uk tom@cornwall-backpackers.co.uk	638 298 3 miles	25 PD avail. Room only avail. Continental B'fast. D LSP CP KT O W D(2)(0ES) T(1)(0ES)
33	Mr and Mrs P W Savage The Mounts Bay Guest House & Inn Churchtown **MULLION** TR12 7HN	01326 241761 www.mountsbayguesthouse.co.uk mountsbaybandb@btinternet.com	678 192 1 km	35 SS EM D KT O W S(1)(1ES) D(4)(4ES) T(2)(2ES) F(1)(1ES)
33 **BUSINESS MEMBER**	Ms S Allen Mullion Cove Hotel **MULLION COVE** TR12 7EP	01326 240328 www.mullion-cove.co.uk enquiries@mullion-cove.co.uk	668 181 01326 240998 on path	60 SS PL EM DW LSP CP KT O W LF D(17)(17ES) T(10)(10ES) F(3) (3ES)
34 **BUSINESS MEMBER**	D Glosby Top House Inn **THE LIZARD** TR12 7NQ	01326 290974 www.thetophouselizard.co.uk mail@thetophouselizard.co.uk	704 125 1km	42.5 SS £27.50. Mob 07847604605 PL EM KT O W LF D(5)(5ES) T()(2ES) F(1)(1ES)
34	Mrs C Barker Stormfield **THE LIZARD** TR12 7NZ	01326 290184 0754 8847512 carol.annetts@hotmail.com	703 126 400 mts	35 SS PL D LSP CP KT PD O W LF D(1)(0ES) T(1)(0ES)
34	Mrs A Bunnetat Treluswell Main Road **THE LIZARD** TR12 7NZ	01326 290286 www.treluswellb&b.co.uk anniebunnetat@yahoo.co.uk	35	SS £15. Mobile 07967 193976 PL DW D CP KT O W LF S(1)(0ES) D(2)(0ES)
34	Mr & Mrs A H Pratt The Caerthillian **THE LIZARD** TR12 7NQ	01326 290019 www.thecaerthillian.co.uk caerthillian@hotmail.com	703 125 500 mts	35 SS from £10 PL DW D LSP CP KT O W LF S(1)(0ES) D(2)(2ES) T(1)(1ES) F(1)(1ES)
40	Mr G Cadgwith Cadgwith Cove Inn **CADGWITH** TR12 7JX	01326 290513 www.cadgwithcoveinn.com garryandhelen@cadgwithcoveinn.co.uk	On Path	19.5 O EM PL CP DW 5D 2T
35	Mrs A Rogers Fernleigh Chymbloth Way **COVERACK** TR12 6TB	01326 280626 www.fernleighcoverack.co.uk sudan-ann03@hotmail.co.uk	781 183 50 mts	38 PL EM DW D LSP CP KT O D(2)(1ES) T(1)(1ES) F(1)(1ES)
35	Mrs G Wood Arlyn Chymbloth Way **COVERACK** TR12 6TB	01326 280926 www.coverack.org.uk/pages/Arlyn.html woodpgs@tesco.net	781 183 300m	35 D LSP CP O() D(2)(1ES) F(1)(0ES)

Walk No.	Contact name Establishment name Address	Telephone no. Mobile no. Email Website	OS Map Ref. Dist. from path	Starting price (£) Months Open Facilities Info
36	Ms A Strickland Gallen-Treath Guest House **PORTHALLOW** St Keverne TR12 6PL	01326 280400 www.gallen-treath.com gallentreath@btclick.com	797 232 as phone 450 mts PD	38 EM single & DW supplement PL EM DW D CP KT PD O W LF S(1)(1ES) D(2)(2ES) T(2)(2ES) F(1)(1ES)
36	Mrs E Whale Porthvean **GILLAN** TR12 6HL	01326 231204 ewhale@hotmail.co.uk	782 252 on path	30 facilities to prepare own EM PL DW D LSP CP KT O T(1)(1ES)
36	Mr & Mrs J Moore Landre Vicarage Lane **MANACCAN** TR12 6JH	01326 231556 johnandwendymoor@gmail.com	767 251 500 mts	34 SS D CP O W D(1)(1ES)
36	Mrs P Royall **POINT** Helford TR12 6JY	01326 231083 pamroyall@btinternet.com	758 262 on path	37.5 SS D CP O W LF T(1)(1ES)
37	Mrs S P Annan Chynoweth Carwinion Lane **MAWNAN SMITH** TR11 5JB	01326 250534 www.chynoweth.helfordriver.net sallyannan2@gmail.com	781 283 800 mts	37.5 SS. Mobile 07900 274230 DW D CP KT PD O W LF D(1)(1ES) T(1)(1ES)
37	Mrs C Lake Gold Martin Carlidnack Road **MAWNAN SMITH TR11 5HA**	01326 250666 www.goldmartin.co.uk gold_martin@hotmail.com	779 291 1.6 km PD	38.5 Single only let with double room PL D CP KT PD O W LF S(1)(1ES) D(2)(2ES) T(1)(1ES)
37	Mr & Mrs G Williams Trevarn Carwinion Road **MAWNAN SMITH** TR11 5JD	01326 251245 www.trevarn.co.uk enquiries@trevarn.co.uk	777 284 as phone 800 mts	35 SS Mob 07877 580321 PL D LSP CP KT PD O W LF D(1)(1ES) T(1)(1ES)
37 BUSINESS MEMBER	Ms J Goodchild Falmouth Backpackers 9 Gyllyngvase Terrace **FALMOUTH** TR11 4DL	01326 319996 www.falmouthbackpackers.co.uk judi@falmouthlodge.co.uk	811 319 150 mts	19 3 DORMS, price includes simple breakfast D LSP CP KT O S(1)(0ES) D(1)(1ES) T(2)(0ES)
37 BUSINESS MEMBER	Mrs S Palin The Westcott Gyllyngvase Hill **FALMOUTH** TR11 4DN	01326 311309 www.thewestcottfalmouth.co.uk thewestcott@outlook.com	809 317	40 PL D CP KT O W LF S(1)(1ES) D(5)(5ES) T(2)(2ES) F(1)(1ES)
37 BUSINESS MEMBER	Mr A Oliver The Seaview Inn Wodehouse Terrace **FALMOUTH** TR11 3EP	01326 311359 www.seaviewinnfalmouth.co.uk seaviewinn@hotmail.co.uk	808 326 1/2 mile	35 Mobile 07805 171018, SS £20 PL EM DW D KT O W LF D(2)(2ES) T(1)(1ES)
37 BUSINESS MEMBER	Mr S Harris Camelot Guest House 5 Avenue Road **FALMOUTH** TR11 4AZ	01326 312480 www.camelotfalmouth.com hello@camelotfalmouth.com	811 320 200m	32.5 D CP PD O W S(2)(2ES) D(5)(5ES) T()(1ES)
37	Mr & Mrs S Davie Dolvean House 50 Melvill Road **FALMOUTH** TR11 4DQ	01326 313658 www.dolvean.co.uk reservations@dolvean.co.uk	809 319 01326 313995 300 mts	40 SS in D rooms, closed Xmas PL D CP KT O S(2)(2ES) D(6)(6ES) T(2)(2ES)

Walk No.	Contact name Establishment name Address	Telephone no. Mobile no. Email Website	OS Map Ref. Dist. from path	Starting price (£) Months Open Facilities Info
37	Mrs Kevern Lynford 20 Avenue Road **FALMOUTH** TR11 4AZ	01326 314258	811 320 200 mts	35 PL D CP KT O W LF S(2)(0ES) T(2)(2ES) F(1)(1ES)
37	Mrs R Riddette-Gregory Wellington House 26 Melvill Road **FALMOUTH** TR11 4AR	01326 319947 www.wellingtonhouse.co.uk info@wellingtonhousefalmouth.co.uk	01326 211533	30 DW D CP KT O W LF S(1)(1ES) D(3)(3ES) T()(1ES)
37	Mr & Mrs Kelly Telford Guest House 47 Melvill Road **FALMOUTH** TR11 4DG	01326 314581 www.telfordfalmouth.co.uk info@telfordfalmouth.co.uk	810 319 200m	35 PL CP O W LF S(1)(1ES) D(3)(3ES) T()(1ES) F(1)(1ES)

Porth Chapel

Walk No.	Contact name Establishment name Address	Telephone no. Mobile no. Email Website	OS Map Ref. Dist. from path	Starting price (£) Months Open Facilities Info
38	Mrs K Moseley Braganza Grove Hill ST MAWES TR2 5BJ	01326 270281 www.braganza-stmawes.co.uk braganzak@googlemail.com	846 331 as phone 300 mts	55 SS. Mob 078999 67367, PL, LSP & DW by prior arrangement. DW D CP KT O W S(1)(0ES) D(3)(3ES) T(4)(3ES)
39	Mr T Blasdale Treverbyn House Tollyfrank Hill VERYAN TR2 5QL	01872 501201 www.treverbyn.co.uk info@treverbyn.co.uk	914 393 2 km PD	35 SS PL D CP KT PD O S(1)(1ES) D(1)(1ES) T(1)(1ES)
39	Mrs S Treneary Jago Cottage Trewartha PORTLOE TR2 5QJ	01872 501491 www.roseland.me.uk jago@roseland.me.uk	925 396 400 mts	35 Also self catering for 5. Mob 07931 031575. PL EM DW D LSP CP KT O S(3)(3ES) D(3)(3ES) T(3)(3ES) F(1)(1ES)
39	Mrs B Leach Carradale PORTLOE TR2 5RB	01872 501508 barbara495@btinternet.com	935 394 300 mts	35 SS PL DW D LSP CP KT PD O W LF D(1)(1ES) T(3)(2ES)
39	Mrs W Penhaligon Trewithian Farm TRURO TR2 5EJ	01872 580293 www.trevithian-farm.co.uk enquiries@trewithian-farm.co.uk	1.5km	35 SS 07812994635 PL D LSP CP O W LF D(4)(3ES) T()(2ES) F(2)(2ES)
40	Mrs W Bennett 20 Perhaver Park GORRAN HAVEN PL26 6NZ	01726 843777 wendyann.bennett@talktalk.net	012 417 500 mts	30 PL DW D LSP CP W LF O( ) S(0)(0ES) D(2)(1ES)
40	Mr & Mrs I Soper Honeycombe House 61 Polkirt Hill MEVAGISSEY PL26 6UR	01726 843750 www.honeycombehouse.co.uk enquiries@honeycombehouse.co.uk	015 446 10 mts	35 Mobile 07710 593913. D LSP CP KT W LF O(mid Jan to mid Dec) S(1)(0ES) D(3)(3ES) T(1)(1ES)
40	Mrs J Conneely Mandalay Guest House School Hill MEVAGISSEY PL26 6TQ	01726 842435 www.mandalaybedandbreakfast. co.uk jillconneely@yahoo.com	014 452 400 mts	27 PL on request D PL CP DW KT 4D 2T 1S 2F ALL ES
40	Mrs F Thomas 35 Cliff Street MEVAGISSEY PL26 6QJ	01726 844656 www.trixology.com/cornwall franormthomas@btinternet.com	015 448 50	35 SS PL D KT PD O LF T(2)(1ES)
41	D Morley Tubbs Mill Lane Caerhayes ST AUSTELL PL26 6NB	01872 531852 www.sawdays.co.uk denise@goosebarn.net	1 mile	47.5 SS £5 PL EM DW D LSP CP KT PD W LF O(Mar to Sept) D(2)(1ES) T()(1ES)
41	D Best Broad Meadow House Quay Road AUSTELL PL25 3NX	01726 76636 stay@broadmeadowhouse.com		14 Posh Tent & Breakfast available or DIY pitch with bench & parasol DW CP O W LF
41	Mr & Mrs R & T Callis Ardenconnel 179 Charlestown Road CHARLESTOWN PL25 3NN	01726 75469 ardenconnel@tiscali.co.uk	036 520 400 mts	35 SS. Mob 07812915007 PL D CP O W LF S(4)(3ES) D(3)(2ES) T(3)(2ES) F(3)(2ES)

Walk No.	Contact name / Establishment name / Address	Telephone no. / Mobile no. / Email / Website	OS Map Ref. / Dist. from path	Starting price (£) / Months Open / Facilities / Info
42	Mr & Mrs P Dormand Emm's Cottage 19 St Austell Road **ST BLAZEY GATE** PL24 2EF	01726 817155 www.emmscottage.co.uk emmscot@aol.com	059 535	0
41	Mr M Bailey The Par Inn 2 Harbour Road **PAR** PL24 2BD	01726 815695 www.parinn.co.uk mattybailey1@hotmail.co.uk	25m	32.5 SS PL EM D LSP CP KT PD O W LF D(1)(1ES) T(1)(0ES)
41	Mrs K Allen Tremorvah, Southleigh Porthpean Beach Road **PORTHPEAN** PL26 6AU	01726 66889 kaa48@btinternet.com	031 510 300 mts	30 SS D LSP CP KT O W LF D(3)(1ES) T(1)(0ES)
42	Mr S Hardinge and Mrs A Davis Trevanion Guest House 70 Lostwithiel Street **FOWEY** PL23 1BQ	01726 832602 www.trevanionguesthouse.co.uk alisteve@trevanionguesthouse.co.uk	124 518 500 mts PD	37.5 Single £45, LSP by prior arrangement PL EM DW D LSP CP PD O() S(2)(1ES) D(3)(3ES) T(3)(3ES) F(2)(2ES)
42	Mrs S Hoddinott Trekelyn 3 Hanson Drive **FOWEY** PL23 1ET	01726 833375 suehoddinott@gmail.com	120 514 200 mts	40 SS £15 D CP O W LF D(1)(0ES) T(1)(0ES)
42	Mrs P Milbank Mazirah 51 Polvillion Road **FOWEY** PL23 1HG	01726 833339 paulamilbank@gmail.com	120 516 1 km	30 £40 single PL D LSP CP O LF D(1)(1ES)
43	Mrs B Alexander Hormond House 55 Fore Street **POLRUAN** PL23 1PH	01726 870853 www.hormondhouse.com bella@chrisbella.demon.co.uk	126 508 250 mts	40 PL DW D KT O W LF S(1)(1ES) T(2)(2ES) F(1)(1ES)
43	Mrs A Pidcock Penryn House The Coombes **POLPERRO** PL13 2RQ	01503 272157 www.penrynhouse.co.uk enquiries@penrynhouse.co.uk	205 511 500 mts	37.5 SS DW CP O W S(1)(1ES) D(7)(7ES) T(2)(2ES) F(2)(2ES)
44	Mrs C Neal Schooner Point 1 Trelawney Terrace **WEST LOOE** PL13 2AG	01503 262670 www.schoonerpoint.co.uk enquiries@schoonerpoint.co.uk	252 536 on path	30 SS in D room PL D LSP CP KT O W LF S(1)(0ES) D(3)(3ES) T(1)(1ES)
44	Mrs S Lever Sea Breeze Lower Chapel Street **EAST LOOE** PL13 1AT	01503 263131 www.seabreezelooe.com seabreezelooe@live.co.uk	256 531 100 mts	50 Price per room, LSP by prior arrangement. AA 4* LSP CP KT O W LF D(5)(5ES) T(1)(1ES)
44	Mr E Mawby Marwinthy Guest House East Cliff **EAST LOOE** PL13 1DE	01503 264382 www.marwinthy.co.uk eddiemawby@lineone.net	256 533 On Path	24 SS DW D O(Mar-Nov) D(2)(2ES) T(2)(2ES)
44	Mr & Mrs D Burton Deganwy Hotel Station Road **EAST LOOE** PL13 1HL	01503 262984 www.deganwyhotel.co.uk enquiries@deganwyhotel.co.uk	254 536 50 mts	34 SS LSP CP PD W LF O() S(4)(4ES) D(4)(4ES) T(3)(3ES) F(2)(2ES)

Walk No.	Contact name / Establishment name / Address	Telephone no. / Mobile no. / Email / Website	OS Map Ref. / Dist. from path	Starting price (£) / Months Open / Facilities / Info
44	Mr & Mrs P & C Calvert Meneglaze Shutta **EAST LOOE** PL13 1LU	01503 269227 www.looebedandbreakfast.com stay@meneglaze.com	255 540 500 mts	39.5 Mob 07708 808323 PL D CP O W LF D(3)(3ES) T(1)(1ES)
45	Mrs S Broad Treliddon Farmhouse **DOWNDERRY** PL11 3DP	01503 250288	324 551 1.4km	30 £10 SS PL DW D LSP CP KT PD O W LF S(1)(0ES) D(2)(2ES) F(2)(2ES)
46	Mrs F M Harvey The Bungalow Cliff Road **PORTWRINKLE** PL11 3BY	01503 230334 www.portwrinklebedandbreakfast.co.uk fiona.harvey334@btinternet.com	355 541 220 mts	30 PL by prior arrangement PL CP KT O W D(1)(0ES) T(1)(0ES)
46	Mrs J Pape Polhawn Cottage **POLHAWN COVE** Whitsand Bay PL10 1LL	01752 822657 www.polhawncovecottage.co.uk polhawn@btinternet.com	213 937 5 mts	35 SS PL LSP CP PD O D(2)(2ES) T(1)(0ES)
46	Mr N Meredith Cliff House Devonport Hill **KINGSAND** PL10 1NJ	01752 823110 www.cliffhouse-kingsand.co.uk chkingsand@aol.com	434 506 01752 822595 20 mts	37.5 SS. 2 SC cottages sleeping 2 and 8 PL EM D CP KT PD O D(2)(2ES) T(1)(1ES) SC(2)(2ES)
46 BUSINESS MEMBER	Mrs J A Southward The Edgcumbe Arms **CREMYLL** PL10 1HX	01752 822294 www.edgcumbearms.co.uk info@edgcumbearms.co.uk	453 534 on path	45 SS. Also SC EM CP O W LF D(3)(3ES) T(1)(1ES)

Towards Rame Head

Walk No.	Contact name / Establishment name / Address	Telephone no. / Mobile no. / Email / Website	OS Map Ref. / Dist. from path	Starting price (£) / Months Open / Facilities / Info
47 BUSINESS MEMBER	Mrs J Kirsop-Taylor Rusty Anchor 30 Grand Parade **PLYMOUTH** PL1 3DJ	01752 663924 www.therustyanchor-plymouth.co.uk enquiries@therustyanchor-plymouth.co.uk	473 534 on path	42.5 SS. Mobile 07855 333993. Group discounts PL EM DW D CP KT O LF D(3)(3ES) T(1)(1ES) F(2)(2ES)
47 BUSINESS MEMBER	Ms C M Williams Edgcumbe Guest House 50 Pier Street **PLYMOUTH** PL1 3BT	01752 660675 www.edgcumbeguesthouse.co.uk enquiries@edgcumbeguesthouse.co.uk	473 537 01752 395975 10 mts	38 Mobile: 07941 242228 SS also SC PL DW D CP KT O LF S(3)(2ES) D(4)(4ES) T(2)(2ES) F(2)(2ES)
48	Mrs G Shelford Heybrook Bay Guest House Beach Road, **HEYBROOK BAY** PL9 0BS	01752 862345 www.heybrookguesthouse.co.uk heybrookgh@btinternet.com	496 488 On path	32 SS PL LSP CP KT W O() D(2)(0ES) T(2)(0ES)
48 BUSINESS MEMBER	Mr & Mrs J Pitcher 1 Barton Close **WEMBURY** PL9 0LF	01752 863710 lorraine.pitcher123@btinternet.com	527 494 1 km	30 Mob 07712576757 PL D LSP CP KT PD O W T(1)(1ES)
48	Mrs M R Denby 107 Southland Park Road **WEMBURY** PL9 0HH	01752 862036 daviddenby@btinternet.com	523 489 500 mts	30 PL EM D LSP CP O S(1)(0ES) D(1)(1ES) T(1)(1ES)
48	Mrs J Mills 11 Valley Drive **WEMBURY** PL9 0EZ	01752 862581	523 493 750 mts	25 SS D CP KT O F(1)(1ES)
48	Mr P Greenwood Muskejaat 2 Warren Close **WEMBURY** PL9 2AF	01752 863392 pwgreenwood59@gmail.com		30 SS. Mob 07554 919295 D CP O W D(1)(0ES) T()(1ES)
49 BUSINESS MEMBER	Mrs J Rogers Worswell Barton Farmhouse **WORSWELL BARTON** Noss Mayo PL8 1HB	01752 872977 www.worswellbarton.co.uk info@worswellbarton.co.uk	537 470 800 mts	42.5 SS also SC PL D LSP CP KT W LF O(end Feb - end Oct) D(4)(2ES) T(1)(0ES) SC(3)(0ES)
49	Mrs S Spooner Rogers Cellars Passage Wood Road **NOSS MAYO** PL8 1EU	01752 872771 suespoonerrogers@btinternet.com	534 475 on path	40 SS £5 PL DW D LSP CP KT PD O W LF S(1)(1ES) D(1)(1ES) T(1)(1ES) F(1)(1ES)
49	Mrs J Barnett Revelstoke Coombe Hannaford Road **NOSS MAYO** PL8 1EJ	01752 872663 www.nossmayobandb.net mrandmrsbarnett@gmail.com	546 469 850 mts	40 D Rooms can be Twin or Singles. SS £10. PL DW D LSP CP KT PD W LF O() D(3)(1ES)
49	Mr G Smith The Dolphin Inn **KINGSTON** TQ7 4QE	01548 810314 www.dolphin-inn.co.uk info@dolphininn.eclipse.co.uk	635 478 2 km	39.25 SS. PD O()

Walk No.	Contact name / Establishment name / Address	Telephone no. / Mobile no. / Email / Website	OS Map Ref. / Dist. from path	Starting price (£) / Months Open / Facilities / Info
49 BUSINESS MEMBER	Mr R Baker Kimberley **RINGMORE** Near Kingsbridge TQ7 4HJ	01548 811115 www.kimberley-annex.co.uk info@kimberley-annex.co.uk	652 462 1500 mts	40 Pick up Mothecombe, boat across R. Erme charged, T room let with D room as family suite D LSP CP KT PD O D(1)(1ES) T(1)(0ES)
50	Ms H Vanstone Holywell Bigbury B&B Holywell Stores, St Ann's Chapel **NEAR BIGBURY ON SEA** TQ7 4HQ	01548 810308 www.holywell-bigburybe-dandbreakfast.co.uk holywellstores@msn.com		20 PL DW D LSP CP KT PD O W LF D(2)(1ES) T(1)(1ES)
50	Mrs J Griffiths The Old Post Office **SOUTH MILTON** TQ7 3JQ	07760 225717 www.theoldpostofficesouthmilton.co.uk toposouthmilton@hotmail.co.uk	1 mile	26 PL D CP KT PD O W LF D(2)(2ES) T()(1ES)
49	Mr A J Roberts Summer Winds Marine Drive **BIGBURY-ON-SEA** TQ7 4AS	01548 810669 pritchard212@btinternet.com	651 443 on path	37.5 SS. Mob 07540 533854 PL CP W O(Shut Xmas & NY) D(2)(2ES) T(1)(1ES) F(1)(1ES)
50 BUSINESS MEMBER	Miss S Ireland The Cottage Hotel **HOPE COVE** TQ7 3HJ	01548 561555 www.hopecove.com info@hopecove.com	675 401 01548 561455 25 mts	56 Price includes dinner, Dbl rooms can be twin PL EM DW D LSP CP KT W LF O() S(2)(2ES) D(24)(24ES) F(5)(5ES)
50	Miss S Ireland Tanfield B & B **HOPE COVE** TQ7 3HJ	01548 561555 www.hopecove.com info@hopecove.com	675 401 01548 561455 300 mts	27 Book in EM & LSP at Cottage Hotel, PL ordered at hotel PL EM D LSP CP KT O() S(1)(1ES) D(5)(5ES) T(2)(2ES)
51	Miss M L Coleman Sun Bay Hotel **INNER HOPE COVE** Kingsbridge TQ7 3HH	01548 561371 www.sunbayhotel-hopecove.co.uk sunbayhotel@btconnect.com	676 399 on path	30 Phone for single prices PL EM DW CP D(6)(6ES) T()(6ES) F(2)(2ES)
51 BUSINESS MEMBER	The South Sands Hotel South Sands Hotel **SALCOMBE** TQ8 8LL	01548 845900 www.southsands.com donna.mccheyne@southsands.com	728 376 on path	80 15% walker discount avail. PL EM DW D LSP CP KT O W LF D(8)(8ES) T(2)(2ES)
51	Mr & Mrs R Petty-Brown Rocarno Grenville Road **SALCOMBE** TQ8 8BJ	01548 842732 www.rocarno.co.uk rocarno@aol.com	736 389 500 mts	35 SS PL D CP KT PD O W LF D(1)(1ES) T(1)(1ES)
51	Mrs P Snelson Waverley Devon Road **SALCOMBE** TQ8 8HL	01548 842633 www.waverleybandb.co.uk pauline@waverleybandb.co.uk	738 388 500 mts	35 SS. Mob 07980 012608 also SC PL DW D CP W LF O(Feb to Nov) S(1)(1ES) D(6)(5ES) T(6)(5ES) F(3)(3ES)

Walk No.	Contact name / Establishment name / Address	Telephone no. / Mobile no. / Email / Website	OS Map Ref. / Dist. from path	Starting price (£) / Months Open / Facilities / Info
51	Ms A Woodhatch Rainbow's End 11 Platt Close **SALCOMBE** TQ8 8NZ	01548 843654 annwoodhatch@btinternet.com	730 393 1.5 km	32 SS Mobile: 07974 773451 PL D LSP CP KT PD O W T(1)(1ES) F(1)(1ES)
51	Mr R Moore Egremont Trust The Yard, **Island Street** **SALCOMBE** TQ8 8DD	01548 844300 www.egremonttrust.org.uk info@icc-salcombe.co.uk		30 You will be sleeping on the boat. All rooms are bunk. EM O()
51	Mrs P Jackson 33 Knowle House Close **KINGSBRIDGE** TQ7 1AN	01548 853820 trish.j@hotmail.co.uk	735 446 5 km	35 Mobile: 07792 152750, £5 SS in D room PL D LSP KT PD O() S(1)(0ES) D(1)(0ES)
51	C Riley Paxhaven Organic B&B **KINGSBRIDGE** TQ7 3HH	01548 562342 www.paxhavenbandb.co.uk info@paxhavenbandb.co.uk	200m	25 PL D CP W LF O(Feb to Nov) D(2)(2ES) T()(1ES)
52	Mrs J Foss Down Farm **START POINT** Kingsbridge TQ7 2NQ	01548 511234 www.downfarm.co.uk downfarm@btinternet.com	806 377 600m	38 SS. Self catering available. PL EM D LSP CP O W LF D(1)(1ES) T(1)(1ES) F(1)(1ES)
52	Mrs V Johnston Valseph The Green **BEESANDS** TQ7 2EJ	01548 580650 www.beesands-bedandbreakfast.co.uk valseph@btinternet.com	819 406 on path	35 mobile 07890 197673 LSP CP KT O(Mar-Nov) D(1)(1ES)
53	Mrs V Mercer Old Walls **SLAPTON** TQ7 2QN	01548 580516 www.slaptonbandb.co.uk val.slapton@gmail.com	823 449 500mts	35 PL DW D O W LF S(1)(0ES) D(1)(0ES) T(1)(0ES) F(1)(1ES)
53	Mrs I Sidell Roxburgh House Dartmouth Road **STRETE** TQ6 0RW	01803 770870 www.roxburghhouse.co.uk ingrid@roxburghhouse.co.uk	841 467 on path	40 SS £5 PL DW D LSP CP KT PD O W LF S(1)(0ES) D(1)(0ES) T()(1ES)
53 BUSINESS MEMBER	Mr & Mrs C Tonkin Fairholme Bay View Estate **STOKE FLEMING** TQ6 0QX	01803 770356 www.fairholmedartmouth.co.uk stay@fairholmedartmouth.co.uk	863 488 As Phone 100 mts	30 £40 single occupancy CP O D(2)(2ES) T(1)(1ES)
53 BUSINESS MEMBER	Mrs V Ruddle Estuary View 11 Horn Hill **DARTMOUTH** TQ6 9RA	01803 834066 www.estuaryview.co.uk valerieruddle@yahoo.com	876 513 200 mts	35 SS £5. Mob 07950 852014 D KT PD O W T(1)(1ES)
53 BUSINESS MEMBER	Mr & Mrs C Helyer Eight Bells South Embankment **DARTMOUTH** TQ6 9BB	01803 839506 www.dartmouthbandb.com lizhelyer20@gmail.com	878 511 200 mts	37.5 SS £7.50. Mobile: 07813 803472. D CP O S(2)(2ES) D(2)(2ES) T(1)(1ES) F(1)(1ES)
53	Mrs J Wright Camelot 61 Victoria Road **DARTMOUTH** TQ6 9RX	01803 833805 jjwright@talktalk.net	875 514 500 mts	32.5 SS. Mobile: 07870 665863 D KT O W LF D(3)(2ES)

Walk No.	Contact name / Establishment name / Address	Telephone no. / Mobile no. / Email / Website	OS Map Ref. / Dist. from path	Starting price (£) / Months Open / Facilities / Info
53	Mr & Mrs M Cairns-Sharp Valley House B&B 46 Victoria Road **DARTMOUTH** TQ6 9DZ	01803 834045 www.valleyhousedartmouth.com enquiries@valleyhousedartmouth.com	872 512 400 mts	40 SS. D CP O W LF D(2)(2ES) T(1)(1ES)
54 BUSINESS MEMBER	Mr N Makin Beacon House B&B, Prospect Steps South Furzeham Road **BRIXHAM** TQ5 8JB	01803 428720 www.beaconbrixham.co.uk nigel.makin@btconnect.com	925 5 150m	35.5 D LSP CP O W LF S(4)(4ES) D(4)(4ES) T()(1ES)
54	Mr & Mrs K Colby Melville Guesthouse 45 New Road **BRIXHAM** TQ5 8NL	01803 852033 www.themelville.co.uk info@themelville.co.uk	920 559 500 mts	30 SS PL CP KT O W S(2)(2ES) D(8)(8ES) T(2)(2ES) F(2)(2ES)
54	Mr & Mrs A Watson Midhurst B&B 132 New Road **BRIXHAM** TQ5 8DA	01803 857331 www.midhurstbnb.co.uk midhurst_bookings@btinternet.com	917 556 1km	35 PL by prior arrangement. PL CP KT O W LF S(1)(1ES) D(2)(2ES) T(1)(1ES)
54	Mrs C Robinson Westbury Guesthouse 51 New Road **BRIXHAM** TQ5 8NL	01803 851684 www.westburyguesthouse.com westburyguesthouse@gmail.com	919 560 300	30 £5 SS PL CP O W LF D(6)(6ES) T(4)(4ES) F(2)(2ES)
54	Wilson Brixham House 130 New Road **BRIXHAM** TQ5 8DA	01803 853954 www.brixhamhouse.co.uk stay@brixhamhouse.co.uk	916 555 1.8km	35 PL DW D O LF S(2)(2ES) D(3)(3ES) T()(1ES)
55	Mr & Mrs F Bam-ford-Dwane The Clifton Hotel 9 & 10 Kernou Road **PAIGNTON** TQ4 6BA	01803 556545 www.cliftonhotelpaignton.co.uk stay@cliftonhotelpaignton.co.uk	891 607 01803 556545 100 mts	35 SS £7 PL EM D CP W O(April to end Sept) S(2)(2ES) D(4)(4ES) T(3)(3ES) F(3)(3ES)
55	Mrs T Whytock Cherry Tree Hotel 10-11 Esplanade Road **PAIGNTON** TQ4 6EB	01803 557056 www.cherrytree-hotel.com info@cherrytree-hotel.com	892 604	40 07598928130 PL CP O W LF S(2)(2ES) D(14)(14ES) T()(5ES) F(7)(7ES)
55 BUSINESS MEMBER	Mrs J Frost Garway Lodge Guest-house 79 Avenue Road **TORQUAY** TQ2 5LL	01803 293126 www.garwaylodge.co.uk info@garwaylodge.co.uk	905 646 850 mts	35 Mobile: 07790 783997 PL D LSP CP KT O S(3)(3ES) D(3)(3ES) T(2)(2ES)
55	Mr Ashman The Haytor Hotel Meadfoot Road **TORQUAY** TQ1 2JP	01803 294708 www.haytorhotel.com enquiries@haytorhotel.com	922 634 300 mts	42 SS. LSP CP O W LF S(8)(8ES) D(15)(15ES) T(3)(3ES)
55 BUSINESS MEMBER	Mrs D Blenkinsopp Aveland House Aveland Road **BABBACOMBE** TQ1 3PT	01803 326622 01803 328940 avelandhouse@aol.com www.avelandhouse.co.uk	921 652 800 mts	38 Business Member for 2014 & 2015 O D EM PL CP LSP KT 4D 2T 2S 2F ALL ES

Walk No.	Contact name / Establishment name / Address	Telephone no. / Mobile no. / Email / Website	OS Map Ref. / Dist. from path	Starting price (£) / Months Open / Facilities / Info
55 BUSINESS MEMBER	Mrs T Howell The Babbacombe Palms Guesthouse 2 York Road **BABBACOMBE** TQ1 3SG	01803 327087 www.babbacombepalms.com reception@babbacombepalms.com	922 655 100 mts	35 DW D KT PD O W LF D(5)(4ES) T(1)(1ES) F(2)(2ES)
55 BUSINESS MEMBER	Mr C Dunn Headland View 37 Babbacombe Downs Road **BABBACOMBE** TQ1 3LN	01803 312612 www.headlandview.com reception@headlandview.com	926 655	35 AA 4* D CP KT W LF O(Shut Dec) S(6)(4ES) D(6)(4ES) T(1)(1ES)
55	Mr J Hannan Babbacombe Guest House 53 Babbacombe Road **BABBACOMBE** TQ1 3SN	01803 328071 www.babbacombeguesthouse.com info@babbacombeguesthouse.com	925 654 300 mts	31 PL CP KT O W LF S(1)(1ES) D(3)(3ES) T(1)(1ES) F(1)(1ES)
55	Mrs S Brewer Coastguard Cottage 84 Babbacombe Downs Road **BABBACOMBE** TQ1 3LU	01803 311634 sheila.besidethesea@googlemail.com	927 653 100 mts	30 mobile 07780 661381 PL D O W S(1)(1ES) D(1)(1ES) F(1)(1ES)
55	M Stubbs Seabreeze 39 Babbacombe Downs Road **BABBACOMBE** TQ1 3LN	01803 322429 www.seabreezebabbacombe.co.uk reception@seabreezebabbacombe.co.uk	20m	37.5 D CP W LF O(Mar to Nov) D(5)(5ES)
56	Ms J Beckett West Wing Ringmore Lodge, Salty Lane **SHALDON** TQ14 0AP	01626 872754 ringmorelodge@hotmail.co.uk	927 722 1 km	38 SS £5. Mobile 17805 993890 PL D CP KT PD O W D(1)(1ES) F(1)(1ES)
56	Mrs P Burdett 10 The Strand **SHALDON** TQ14 0DL	01626 873315 maggieburdett@yahoo.com	934 722 on path	35 mobile: 07976 978742, SS D KT W LF O(March - Sept) D(1)(1ES)
56	Mrs J Benjamin Port View Riverside **SHALDON** TQ14 0DJ	01626 872277 www.shaldonholiday.com jenni.benjamin@btinternet.com	933 724 on path	40 07887384276. SS £5 O(0) T(2)(1ES)
56	Mrs D Loach Coombe Bank Guest House Landscore Road **TEIGNMOUTH** TQ14 9JL	01626 772369 www.coombebankhotel.net dianne.loach@btopenworld.com	935 732 01626 774159 450 mts	29.5 mobile: 07860 782415 SS PL D LSP CP KT O S(2)(1ES) D(4)(3ES) T(2)(2ES) F(1)(1ES)
56	Mr & Mrs J Allan Thomas Luny House Teign Street **TEIGNMOUTH** TQ14 8EG	01626 772976 www.thomas-luny-house.co.uk alisonandjohn@thomas-luny-house.co.uk	939 729 500 mts	52.5 SS £22.50 CP O W LF D(2)(2ES) T(2)(2ES)
57 BUSINESS MEMBER	Mrs A Ferris The Blenheim The Seafront, 1 Marine Parade **DAWLISH** EX7 9DJ	01626 862372 www.theblenheim.uk.net blenheimholidays@btconnect.com	962 765 10mts	38 SS DW LSP CP KT O W LF S(3)(3ES) D(6)(6ES) T(4)(4ES) F(4)(4ES)

Walk No.	Contact name / Establishment name / Address	Telephone no. / Mobile no. / Email / Website	OS Map Ref. / Dist. from path	Starting price (£) / Months Open / Facilities / Info
58	Mrs H Morrish Appletree Cottage 23 Victoria Place **BUDLEIGH SALTERTON** EX9 6JP	01395 445433 www.appletreecottagebudleigh.co.uk hilary@appletreecottagebudleigh.co.uk	061 818 150 mts	27 SS PL D CP KT O T(3)(1ES)
59 BUSINESS MEMBER	Mr B Gardner The Kings Arms Fore Street **OTTERTON** EX9 7HB	01395 568416 www.kingsarmsotterton.co.uk info@kingsarmsotterton.co.uk	081 853 1/2 mile	35 SS PL EM DW D LSP CP KT PD O W LF D(9)(9ES) T(2)(2ES) F(3)(3ES)
60	Mr & Mrs M White Durham House Fore Street **BEER** EX12 3JL	01297 20449 www.durhamhouse.org info@durhamhouse.org	227 894 300 mts	30 Seasonal CP O D PL CP 6D[5] 1T[1] 1F[1]
60	Mrs E D Jordan Lyndhurst Manor Road **SEATON** EX12 2AQ	01297 23490 davidjordan367@btinternet.com	244 902 80 mts	30 DW CP O(April - Oct) S(1)(0ES) D(1)(0ES) T(1)(0ES)
60	Mr & Mrs B Rosewarne Sea Glimpses 8 Burrow Road **SEATON** EX12 2NF	01297 22664 liz@seaglimpses.fsnet.co.uk	250 899 01297 22664 20 mts	35 SS. Mobile 07527 636687 CP KT O W S(1)(0ES) D(1)(0ES) T(1)(0ES)
60	Mr & Mrs D & S Jamieson Bay tree House 11 Seafield Road **SEATON** EX12 2QS	01297 21966 www.baytreedevon.co.uk info@baytreedevon.co.uk	250m	30 Mob 07760222080 D LSP CP KT W LF O(Closed Xmas & NY) S(1)(0ES) D(1)(1ES) T(1)(1ES) F(2)(2ES)
61	Mrs J Thomson Westley Bed and Breakfast Lyme Road **UPLYME** Lyme Regis DT7 3UY	01297 445104 www.westleybedandbreakfast.wordpress.com westleybandb@btinternet.com	324 934 1.8 km	32.5 SS. Mobile: 07982 302038 D CP PD O W LF D(2)(2ES) T(1)(0ES)
61	Mr O Lovell Lucerne View Road **LYME REGIS** DT7 3AA	01297 443752 www.lucernelyme.weebly.com lucernelyme@btopenworld.com	338 923 500 mts	39 SS PL D CP O S(1)(1ES) D(3)(3ES) T(1)(1ES) SC(1)(1ES)

Walk No	Contact name / Establishment name / Address	Telephone no. / Mobile no. / Email / Website	OS Map Ref. / Dist. from path	Starting price (£) / Months Open / Facilities / Info
62	Mr & Mrs C Crawford Mervyn House **CHIDEOCK** Near Bridport DT6 6JN	01297 489578 www.chideockandseatown.co.uk callbrig@gmail.com	422 928 500 mts	40 D LSP CP KT O W S(1)(1ES) T(1)(1ES)
62	Mr & Mrs Tuck Broadlands B&B Dog House Lane **CHIDEOCK** DT6 6HX	01297 489543 enquiries@broadlandschideock.co.uk	2km	40 PL D CP O W LF D(2)(2ES)
63	Mrs P A Bale Highway Farm West Road **BRIDPORT** DT6 6AE	01308 424321 www.highwayfarm.co.uk bale@highwayfarm.co.uk	443 928 01308 424321 1.5 km	40 Mobile: 07791 915228 on bus route, Self catering also available PL D LSP CP KT O D(2)(2ES) T(1)(1ES) F(1)(1ES)
63	Mr A Hardy Britmead House 154 West Bay Road **BRIDPORT** DT6 4EG	01308 422941 www.britmeadhouse.co.uk britmead@talk21.com	465 912 500 mts	40 Mob 07973 725243 CP KT O(Closed Xmas & New Year) D(4)(4ES) T(2)(2ES) F(2)(2ES)
63	Mr W Vickers & Ms D Clarke Seacroft 24 West Bay **WEST BAY** DT6 4HD	01308 423407 www.seacroftbandb.co.uk seacroft24@btinternet.com	461 905 50 mts	32.5 SS. Mob 07855 457875 PL D W P CP KT O S(1)(1ES) D(2)(2ES) T(1)(1ES) F(1)(1ES)
63 BUSINESS MEMBER	Mr A Bailey Barn Cottage Graston Farm, Annings Lane **BURTON BRADSTOCK** DT6 4NG	07778 261796 www.grastonfarm.co.uk ababredy@fwi.co.uk	503 899 1750m	35 PL EM DW D LSP CP KT PD O W LF D(2)(1ES) T(1) (1ES)
63	Mrs L Comley Bridge Cottage Guest Rooms 87 High Street **BURTON BRADSTOCK** DT6 4RA	01308 897222 www.bridgecottagebedandbreakfast.co.uk lizcomley@aol.com	487 893 300 mts	32.5 SS also SC PL DW D CP KT O D(2)(2ES) T(1)(1ES) F(1)(1ES)
63	Mrs E M Edwards Sea Fret House Coast Road **PUNCKNOWLE** DT2 9DQ	01308 897435 www.seafret.co.uk enquiries@seafret.co.uk	537 874 800m	35 100 mts from inland alternative route Section 80 PL DW D LSP CP KT PD O W LF D(1)(1ES) F(1)(1ES)
63 BUSINESS MEMBER	Mrs I Donnelly Cowards Lake Farmhouse 13 West Street **ABBOTSBURY** DT3 4JT	01305 871421 www.abbotsbury.co.uk/cowardslake cowards-lake@btconnect.com	573 853 800 mts	37.5 SS £12.50. DW LSP CP KT PD O W LF D(1)(1ES) T(1)(1ES)
63	Mrs P Crockett 21 Rodden Row **ABBOTSBURY** DT3 4JL	01305 871465 pat21rr01@hotmail.co.uk	579 855 750mts	27.5 Mobile 07925 350023. Prior booking preferred PL O W D(1) T(1)

Walk No.	Contact name / Establishment name / Address	Telephone no. / Mobile no. / Email / Website	OS Map Ref. / Dist. from path	Starting price (£) / Months Open / Facilities / Info
63	C Rawlings Upalong 8 West Street **ABBOTSBURY** DT3 4JT	01305 871882 www.upalongwestdorset.co.uk candcrawlings@gmail.com	573 853 500 mts	30 EM by prior arrangement, mobile 07887 981850, £10 SS CP O W LF D(1)(0ES) T(1)(0ES)
63	Mrs M Peach 6 Market Street **ABBOTSBURY** DT3 4JR	01305 871364 www.abbotsburybandb.co.uk enquiries@abbotsburybandb.co.uk	576 853 1200 mts	37.5 £10 SS KT O W S(1)(1ES) D(1)(1ES)
65	Mrs J Hunter Turnstones B&B 6 Ventnor Road, **FOR-TUNESWELL** Isle of Portland DT5 1JE	01305 824291 www.turnstones.net info@turnstones.net	687 735 500 mts	35 SS. Mobile: 07969 040811. D CP KT O W LF D(3)(3ES)
65	Mr G Bisogno Alessandria House 71 Wakeham Road, Easton **PORTLAND** DT5 1HW	01305 822270	694 716 01305 820561 20 mts	35 Please call to book. PL DW D CP KT O W S(5)(2ES) D(3)(2ES) T(2)(2ES) F(4)(4ES)
65	K Wallace Portland Lodge Easton Lane **PORTLAND** DT5 1BW	01305 820265 info@portlandlodge.com	690 725 600m	32 Mob 07980388789 LSP CP O W S(4)(4ES) D(12)(12ES) T() (10ES) F(4)(4ES)
65	Mrs K Smith Fairview Cottage 14 Old Coastguard Cottages **PORTLAND BILL** DT5 2JT	01305 820368 www.portlandbill.net grahamsmith.14@btinternet.com	678 688 on path	40 Mob 07832219420 D CP KT O W S(1)(ES) D(1)(ES)
66	Mrs D Quick Harbour Lights Guest House 20 Buxton Road **WEYMOUTH** DT4 9PJ	01305 783273 www.harbourlightsguesthouse.com harbourlights@btconnect.com	673 779 200 m	35 O(March-Nov inc) S(4)(2ES) D(5)(5ES) T(2)(2ES) F(2)(2ES)
66	Ms S Arnold Greenwood Guest House 1 Holland Road **WEYMOUTH** DT4 0AL	01305 775626 www.greenwoodguesthouse.co.uk enquiries@greenwoodguesthouse.co.uk	673 793 1 km PD	35 PL D CP KT O S(1)(0ES) D(3)(2ES) T(2)(1ES) F(1)(1ES)
66	Mr M Clark Oaklands Edwardian Guesthouse 1 Glendinning Avenue **WEYMOUTH** DT4 7QF	01305 767081 www.oaklands-guesthouse.co.uk stay@oaklands-guesthouse.co.uk	678 800 500 mts	34 SS PL EM D CP O(February to November) D(6)(6ES) T(2)(2ES) F(1)(1ES)
66	Mrs M Acton Maribels Bed And Breakfast 28 Alma Road **WEYMOUTH** DT4 0AJ	01305 781921 www.maribelsweymouth.co.uk maribelacton@gmail.com	100m	30 SS £10 CP KT O W LF S(1)(1ES) D(2)(2ES) F(1)(1ES)
66	Ms J Rolph The Beach House 2 Brunswick Terrace **WEYMOUTH** DT4 7RR	01305 789353 www.thebeachhouseweymouth.co.uk stay@thebeachhouseweymouth.co.uk	01305 300300 10metres	36 PL D CP O W S(3)(1ES) D(4)(4ES) T(1)(1ES) F(1)(1ES)

BUSINESS MEMBER — rows 65 (Mr G Bisogno), 66 (Mrs D Quick), 66 (Ms S Arnold), 66 (Mr M Clark), 66 (Mrs M Acton), 66 (Ms J Rolph)

Walk No.	Contact name / Establishment name / Address	Telephone no. / Mobile no. / Email / Website	OS Map Ref. / Dist. from path	Starting price (£) / Months Open / Facilities / Info
66 BUSINESS MEMBER	Mr Saxton Gloucester House B & B 96 The Esplanade WEYMOUTH DT4 7AT	01305 785191 www.gloucesterhouseweymouth.co.uk gloucesterhouse@hotmail.co.uk	15metres	PL CP KT O W S(3)(3ES) D(6)(6ES) T(2)(2ES) F(4)(4ES)
66	Mr & Mrs P Vincent Old Harbour View Trinity Road WEYMOUTH DT4 8TJ	01305 774633 www.oldharbourviewweymouth.co.uk info@oldharbourview.co.uk	on path	49 mobile: 079744 22241. SS D CP KT W LF O(Shut Xmas & NY) D(1)(1ES) T(1)(1ES)
66	Portland Pebble B&B 9 Smallmouth Close WEYMOUTH DT4 9XS	07799204848 www.portland-pebble.com bookings@portland-pebble.com		35 PL D LSP CP O W D(2)(2ES) F(1)(1ES)
66	Ms L Dagostino Riverhouse B&B 54 Church Street UPWEY VILLAGE	01305 812740 www.riverhousebedandbreakfast.co.uk enquiries@riverhouseinn.co.uk	665 849	42.5 SS PL LSP CP KT O W LF D(3)(3ES)
66	Mrs J Selfe The Dairy House CHALDON HERRING DT2 8DN	01305 852138 www.chaldonherringpc.org joanneselfe@hotmail.com	795 835 1 1/2 miles	30 EM DW D LSP CP KT PD O W LF S(1)(0ES) D(1)(0ES) F(1)(0ES)
66	Mr & Mrs Horvath 1 Old Coastguard Cottages OSMINGTON MILLS DT3 6HQ	01305 832663 hope.horvath68@live.co.uk	736 817 20 mts	40 Excellent cooked breakfast. PL DW LSP CP KT PD O W S(2)(1ES) D(2)(1ES)
64 BUSINESS MEMBER	Mrs J Furlong Swallows Rest Marleaves Farm South Road WYKE REGIS DT4 9NR	01305 785244 www.swallowsrestselfcatering.co.uk jane.furlong@swallowsrestselfcatering.co.uk	662 770 300m	37.5 Disabled access Bungalow sleeps 5. Mobile: 07747753656 PL DW D LSP CP KT O W LF S(1)(1ES) D(2)(1ES) T(1)(1ES) F(1)(1ES) SC(8)(8ES)
66	Mrs J Laing Tewkesbury Cottage 28 Main Road WEST LULWORTH BH20 5RL	01929 400561 jackie.laing@tiscali.co.uk	823 806 700 mts	37.5 SS. Mobile: 07971 426027 DW D CP KT O W LF D(2)(1ES) T(1)(0ES)
67	Mrs G Hole Bradle Farm CHURCH KNOWLE Kimmeridge BH20 5NU	01929 480712 01929 481144 www.bradlefarmhouse.co.uk info@bradlefarmhouse.co.uk	930 806 4 km PD	42.5 SS, EM at café owned by farm, Mobile: 07764 950920 PL D CP KT PD O W LF D(2)(2ES) T(1)(1ES)
68	Mrs S Mitchell Alford House 120 East Street CORFE CASTLE BH20 5EH	01929 480156 www.alfordhouse.com info@alfordhouse.com	963 816 2 km PD	37.5 07918 056728. Free collection from Kingston. Small petrol charge otherwise. PL DW D CP PD O W LF D(2)(2ES) T(1)(1ES)
68 BUSINESS MEMBER	Mr D Ensor Chiltern Lodge 8 Newfoundland Close WORTH MATRAVERS BH19 3LX	01929 439337 www.chilternlodge.co.uk densor@btopenworld.com	976 778 1 km	32 SS £9. Mobile: 07906 508125 PL EM D CP KT PD O W LF D(1)(0ES) T(1)(0ES)

Walk No.	Contact name / Establishment name / Address	Telephone no. / Mobile no. / Email / Website	OS Map Ref. / Dist. from path	Starting price (£) / Months Open / Facilities / Info
68	Mr & Mrs Arnold Post Office Cottage Worth matravers **SWANAGE** BH19 3LQ	01929 439442 www.worthmytravels.co.uk office@worthmytravels.co.uk	900m	40 SS. Mobile: 07917 003817 PL DW D CP O W LF D2 (2) T1 (1)
78	Mrs A Styles Langton Manor Farmhouse **LANGTON MATRAVERS** BH19 3EU	01929 421247 www.langtonmanorfarmhouse.co.uk alexstyles999@aol.com	003 789 2 km	O D PL CP PD W 1F[1]
69	Mrs L Fegan The Limes 48 Park Road **SWANAGE** BH19 2AE	01929 422664 www.limeshotel.net info@limeshotel.net	033 783 250 mts	46 LSP by prior arrangement only. Families welcome PL DW D LSP CP O S(4)(1ES) D(2)(2ES) T(4)(4ES) F(3)(3ES)
69	Mr & Mrs A Preston Sunny Bay House 17 Cluny Crescent **SWANAGE** BH19 2BP	01929 422650 www.sunnybay.co.uk gillgc@aol.com	031 784 1 km	30 Mobile 07799298767 D CP O W S(1)(0ES) D(1)(1ES) T(1)(1ES) F(1)(1ES)
69	Mrs K Gibson Harmony House 93 Kings Road West **SWANAGE** BH19 1HN	01929 427255 harmonyhouse-swanage@hotmail.com	022 789 800 mts PD	35 Mobile: 07837 403892 PL D KT PD O D(2)(2ES) T(1)(0ES)
69	Miss L Wall Footsteps Pitstop 38 Quarry Close **SWANAGE** BH19 2QY	01929 421441 www.swanagefootsteps.com lou@shojjy.orangehome.co.uk	022 787 1.5 km	20 Breakfast £3. Mobile 07796050402 PL CP KT PD O W S(1)(0ES) T(1)(0ES)
69	Mr & Mrs M Anderson Danesfort Hotel 3 Highcliffe Road **SWANAGE** BH19 1LW	01929 424224 www.danesforthotel.co.uk reception@danesforthotel.co.uk	031 798 25 mts	35 EM by prior arrangement PL LSP CP KT O W S(1)(1ES) D(3)(3ES) T(1)(1ES) F(3)(3ES)
70	Mrs North The Laurels 60 Britannia Road **POOLE** BH14 8BB	07837 737368 www.thelaurelsbandb.com info@thelaurelsbandb.com	032 913 3.5 km	45 D CP O W D3 T3 S3 F2(ES)

BUSINESS MEMBER

South Haven Point

SOUTH
WEST

COAST
PATH

Walk No.	Contact name Establishment name Address Region/Postcode	Telephone no. Fax / Reservation / Mobile no. Website Email	OS Map Ref. Dist. from path	Starting price Months Open Facilities Info
1	Mr P R Weaver Sparkhayes Farm Camp Site Sparkhayes Lane **PORLOCK** Somerset TA24 8NE	01643 862470 www.porlock.co.uk	886 469 on path	£7.00 O T S LY G CP LSP DW on 300 coast bus route
2	Mr C Onley Sunny Lyn Camp & Caravan Site **LYNBRIDGE, LYNTON** North Devon EX35 6NS	01598 753384 www.caravandevon.co.uk info@caravandevon.co.uk	719 485 800 mtrs	£6.00 Open 15/3 to 31/10 T S LY G CP DW
3	Mr & Mrs A Mortimer Lower Campscott Farm **LEE** Devon EX34 8LS	01271 863479 www.lowercampscott.co.uk holidays@lowercampscott.co.uk	495 455 2 km	£6.00 O T S LY G CP LSP DW

Minehead Start/Finish Point

For Combe Martin addresses see Exmoor Campsites.

Walk No.	Contact name Establishment name Address Region/Postcode	Telephone no. Fax / Reservation / Mobile no. Website Email	OS Map Ref. Dist. from path	Starting price Months Open Facilities Info
5	Mr & Mrs B Gilbert North Morte Farm Campsite **MORTEHOE** Devon EX34 7EG	01271 870381 www.northmortefarm.co.uk info@northmortefarm.co.uk	459 455 500 mtrs	£6.00 Open April to Oct T S LY G DW
5	Mrs H Lethbridge Damage Barton **MORTEHOE** Woolacombe, Devon EX34 7EJ	01271 870502 www.damagebarton.co.uk enquiries@damagebarton.co.uk	476 457 2 km	£11.00 Open Mar - Nov T S LY G DWCP

Castle Rock from Valley of Rocks

Walk No.	Contact name Establishment name Address Region/Postcode	Telephone no. Fax / Reservation / Mobile no. Website Email	OS Map Ref. Dist. from path	Starting price Months Open Facilities Info
15	Mr C Heard Lower Pennycrocker Farm **BOSCASTLE** Cornwall PL35 0BY	07967 605392 01840 250613 www.pennycrocker.com karyn.heard@yahoo.com	124 925 500 mtrs	£6.00 O T S CP DW LSP
20	Mrs C Pawley Carnevas Farm Holiday Park **PORTHCOTHAN BAY** Cornwall PL28 8PN	01841 520230 www.carnevasholidaypark.com carnevascampsite@aol.com	862 728 800 mtrs	£11.00 Open 1/4 to 31/10 T S LY G CP DW
21	Mrs L Lightfoot Magic Cove Touring Park **MAWGAN PORTH** Newquay, Cornwall TR8 4BD	01637 860263 www.magiccove.co.uk magic@magiccove.co.uk	850 679 300 mtrs	£6.00 Open Easter-end Sept T S LY DW G 250 mts from site
22	Mrs S Eastlake Treago Farm Caravan & Camping **CRANTOCK** Newquay, Cornwall TR8 5QS	01637 830277 www.treagofarm.co.uk info@treagofarm.co.uk	781 600 400 mtrs	£5.00 Open Easter to early Oct T S LY G CP DW PD
24	Ms J Sawle Beacon Cottage Farm Touring Park, Beacon Drive **ST AGNES** Cornwall TR5 0NU	01872 552347 07879 413862 www.beaconcottagefarmholidays.co.uk beaconcottagefarm@lineone.net	705 505 400 mtrs	£8.00 Open 1 April to 1 Oct T S LY CP LSP DW
24	Mrs P Williams Presingoll Farm Caravan & Camping Park **ST AGNES** Cornwall TR5 0PB	01872 552333 www.presingollfarm.co.uk pam@presingollfarm.co.uk	720 495 1.6 km	£7.50 Open 1 April - end Oct T S LY CP LSP DW

Near Porthcothan

Walk No.	Contact name Establishment name Address Region/Postcode	Telephone no. Fax / Reservation / Mobile no. Website Email	OS Map Ref. Dist. from path	Starting price Months Open Facilities Info
28	Miss K Morgan Ayr Holiday Park **ST IVES** Cornwall TR26 1EJ	01736 795855 01736 798797 www.ayrholidaypark.co.uk recpt@ayrholidaypark.co.uk	511 405 350 mtrs	£15.50 price based on 2 sharing O T S LY CP LSP DW
28	Mr E J Coak The North Inn **PENDEEN** Cornwall TR19 7DN	01736 788417 www.thenorthinnpendeen.co.uk ernestjohncoak@aol.com	383 344 1 km	£4.00 O T S CP LSP DW (Also B&B)
28	Mr & Mrs A Collinson Secret Garden Caravan & Camping Park Bosavern House **ST JUST IN PENWITH** Cornwall TR19 7RD	01736 788301 www.secretbosavern.com mail@bosavern.com	371 305 1 km	£18.00 Open 1/3 to 31/10 T S LY CP (Also B&B)
32	Mrs L Garthwaite Kenneggy Cove Holiday Park Higher Kenneggy **ROSUDGEON** Penzance, Cornwall TR20 0AU	01736 763453 www.kenneggycove.co.uk mgarthwa@aol.com	561 287 500 mtrs	£12.00 Open mid May to end Sep T S LY G DWCP
33	Mr S Cook National Trust, Teneriffe Farm Campsite Predannack **MULLION** Cornwall TR12 7EZ	01326 240293 www.nationaltrust.org.uk teneriffefarmcampsite@nationaltrust.org.uk	672 167 1km	£6.50 Open 27/3 to 31/10 T S LY G CP DW
33	Mr & Mrs N Whittle Silver Sands Holiday Park Gwendreath **HELSTON** Cornwall TR12 7LZ	01326 290631 www.silversandsholidaypark.co.uk info@seliversandsholidaypark.co.uk	729 169 1km	£12.50 Open mid Mar-early Nov T S LY G DW
34	Mr & Mrs R H Lyne Henry's Campsite Caerthillian Farm **THE LIZARD** Cornwall TR12 7NX	01326 290596 www.henryscampsite.co.uk	701 125 500 mtrs PD	£9.00 O T S LY G CP LSP DW PD KT Dogs off peak only
35	Mr & Mrs R Flynn Little Trevothan Caravan and Camping Park **COVERACK** Cornwall TR12 6SD	01326 280260 www.littletrevothan.com sales@littletrevothan.co.uk	770 180 750 mtrs	£8.00 Open Mar - Oct T S LY LSP CP DW

Near Zennor

South Cornwall Campsites

Walk No.	Contact name / Establishment name / Address / Region/Postcode	Telephone no. / Fax / Reservation / Mobile no. / Website / Email	OS Map Ref. Dist. from path	Starting price / Months Open / Facilities / Info
40	Dr J Whetter Trelispen Caravan & Camping Park **GORRAN HAVEN** Cornwall PL26 6NR	01726 843501 www.trelispen.co.uk trelispen@care4free.net	005 421 1 km	£10.00 Open 1/4 to 31/10 T S LY CP DW
41	Mrs L Bowler The Meadows Campstie **PENTEWAN** Cornwall PL26 6DL	01726 844383 www.themeadowspentewanvalley.co.uk lynn@themeadowspentewanvalley.co.uk	007 482 1 mile	£7.50 Open May to Oct T S LY G CP DW
43	Mr & Mrs K Cox Polruan Camping & Caravanning **POLRUAN** Cornwall PL23 1QH	01726 870263 www.polruanholidays.co.uk polholiday@aol.com	132 507 250 mtrs	£14.00 Open Apr-Oct T S LY G CP LSP DW
43	Mr & Mrs Stanbury Great Kellow Caravan & Campsite **POLPERRO** Cornwall PL13 2QL	01503 272387 www.bestofsecornwall.co.uk kellow.farm@virgin.net	200 521 500 mtrs	£6.00 Open 1/3/15 to 3/1/16 T S CPDW
44	Mr D Byers Looe Country Park Caravan & Campsite, Bucklawren Road **LOOE** Cornwall PL13 1QS	01503 240265 www.looe-caravan-campsite.co.uk info@looecountrypark.co.uk	283 555 2 km	£11.00 O T S LY G CP DW (DW, certain breeds)
44	Mr. E A P & Mrs. J Jourdan Fat Apples Cafe The Old Vineyard **NEAR HELSTON** Cornwall TR12 6QH	01326 281559 fatapplescafe@gmail.com Tripadvisor: Fat Apples Cafe, Porthallow	On the path	£5.00 O T LY G CP LSP DW Showers tbc for 2015 Wild camping and Cafe
44	Mr S R Cox Camping Caradon Park, Trelawne **LOOE** Cornwall PL13 2NA	01503 272388 www.campingcaradon.co.uk enquiries@campingcaradon.co.uk	542 218 2.4 km	£13.00 O T S LY G CP LSP DW

Polperro Harbour

Walk No.	Contact name / Establishment name / Address / Region/Postcode	Telephone no. / Fax / Reservation / Mobile no. / Website / Email	OS Map Ref. / Dist. from path	Starting price / Months Open / Facilities / Info
52	Mrs M Tucker Higher House Farm Little Holloway **EAST PRAWLE** Devon TQ7 2BU	01548 511422 www.eastprawlefarmholidays.co.uk marilynjtucker@btinternet.com	781 365 250 mtrs	£5.00 Open 23/5 to 20/9 T CP LSP DW (Dogs must be tethered)
54	Mr & Mrs W Hosking Upton Manor Farm Camping St Mary's Road **BRIXHAM** Devon TQ5 9QH	01803 882384 www.uptonmanorfarm.co.uk uptoncamp@btconnect.com	549 926 1/2 mile	Open Easter to end Sep T S LY CPLSP Parking charged Grocery nearby
56	Mrs A Mann Long Meadow Farm Combe Road **SHALDON** Devon TQ14 0EX	01626 872732 01626 872323 www.longmeadowfarm.co.uk anne@longmeadowfarm.co.uk	922 721 2 kms	£10.00 Open Easter-end Sept T S LY CP LSP DW
57	Mr A Bulpin Leadstone Camping Warren Road **DAWLISH** Devon EX7 0NG	01626 864411 www.leadstonecamping.co.uk post@leadstonecamping.co.uk	974 782 800 mtrs	£8.00 Open 22/5 to 6/9 T S LY G CP DW
57	Cofton Country Holidays **STARCROSS** Devon EX6 8RP	01626 890111 01626 890160 www.coftonholidays.co.uk info@coftonholidays.co.uk	1km	£14.50 O T S LY G CP LSP DW
58	Prattshayes Farmhouse **LITTLEHAM** Devon EX8 5DB	01395 276626 mary.marsden@nationaltrust.org.uk	025 807 1.5 km	£12.00 Open Mar to Oct T S CP LSP DW Tuck shop

Anchor off MSC Napoli at Branscombe

Dorset Campsites

Walk No.	Contact name / Establishment name / Address / Region/Postcode	Telephone no. / Fax / Reservation / Mobile no. / Website / Email	OS Map Ref. / Dist. from path	Starting price / Months Open / Facilities / Info
62	M R Loosmore Manor Farm Holiday Centre **CHARMOUTH** Dorset DT6 6QL	01297 560226 www.manorfarmholidaycentre.co.uk enquiries@manorfarmholidaycentre.co.uk	368 937 500 mtrs	£12.00 O T S LY G CP LSP DW
62	Mr M J Cox Golden Cap Holiday Park **SEATOWN** Chideock Dorset DT6 6JX	01308 422139 01308 425672 www.wdlh.co.uk holidays@wdlh.co.uk	425 919 50 mtrs	£13.70 Open 20/3 to 2/11 T S LY G CP DW
63	Mr & Mrs M Cox Highlands End Holiday Park **EYPE** Dorset DT6 6AR	01308 422139 01308 425672 www.wdlh.co.uk holidays@wdlh.co.uk	453 916 100 mtrs	£16.00 Open 6/2 to 30/11 T S LY G DW CP
63	Mrs K Batten Freshwater Beach Holiday Park **BURTON BRADSTOCK** Dorset DT6 4PT	01308 897317 01308 897336 www.freshwaterbeach.co.uk enquiries@freshwaterbeach.co.uk	898 479 on path	Open 20/3 to 8/11 T S LY G CP LSP DW On-site restaurant
63	Mr R Cox Graston Copse Holiday Park Annings Lane Dorset DT6 4QP	01308 426947 01308 425672 www.wdlh.co.uk holidays@wdlh.co.uk	497 899 2 km	£12.35 Open 23/4 to 29/9 T S LY CP DW
69	Mr & Mrs J Wootton Toms Field Campsite & Shop Toms Field Road **SWANAGE** Dorset BH19 3HN	01929 427110 www.tomsfieldcamping.co.uk tomsfield@hotmail.com	995 785 1.5 km	£7.00 Camping Mid Mar to end Oct T S LY G CP LSP DW Walkers Barn and Stone Room also available, open all year.

Durdle Door

View of Chesil Beach

Youth Hostels

There is an amazing variety of Youth Hostels along the South West Coast Path, 20 in total and all offering comfortable, friendly accommodation.

You don't have to be a member of the YHA but membership enables you to take advantage of more than 4000 Youth Hostels world wide, and discounts online and high street retailers as well as local tourist attractions.

YHA annual membership costs are currently:

Under 26 - £10, Individual - £20, Household £30. Discounts for direct debit payments.

Buffet breakfasts, lunches and evening meals all available, but you can still prepare your own food in most of the hostels.

Book directly with the Youth Hostel of your choice or for further assistance, please contact YHA Customer Services, Tel: 0800 0191700. Website at www.yha.org.uk

Email: customerservices@yha.org.uk

Youth Hostels

Town	Address	Phone	OS Ref
Minehead	Alcombe Combe MINEHEAD TA24 6EW	0845 371 9033	973 442
Ilfracombe	Mullacott Farm, ILFRACOMBE EX34 8NA	01271 866 877	513 452
Westward Ho!	Fosketh Hill, WESTWARD HO! EX39 1UL	01237 479766	430 290
Elmscott	Hartland, BIDEFORD EX39 6ES	0845 371 9736	231 217
Boscastle	Palace Stables BOSCASTLE PL35 0HD	0845 371 9006	096 915
Tintagel	Dunderhole Point TINTAGEL PL34 0DW	0845 371 9145	047 881
Treyarnon	Tregonnan Treyarnon PADSTOW PL28 8JR	0845 371 9664	859 741
Newquay	Mor Lodge, Mount Wise NEWQUAY TR7 2BP	01637 877776	809 613
Perranporth	Droskyn Point PERRANPORTH TR6 0GS	0845 371 9755	752 544
Portreath	Nance Farm, Illogan, PORTREATH TR16 4QX	01209 842244	668 443
Land's End	Letcha Vean ST JUST TR19 7NT	0845 371 9643	364 305
Penzance	Horneck, PENZANCE TR20 8TF	0845 371 9653	457 302
Lizard	The Lizard HELSTON TR12 7NT	0845 371 9550	704 116
Coverack	Parc Behan, School Hill HELSTON TR12 6SA	0845 371 9014	782 184
Boswinger	GORRAN PL26 6LL	0845 371 9107	991 411
Beer	Bovey Combe, Townsend SEATON EX12 3LL	0845 371 9502	223 896
Litton Cheney	Litton Cheney DORCHESTER DT2 9AT	0845 371 9329	548 900
Portland	Castle Road, Castle Town PORTLAND DT5 1AU	0845 371 9339	685 741
Lulworth Cove	School Lane WEST LULWORTH BH20 5SA	0845 371 9331	832 806
Swanage	Cluny Crescent SWANAGE BH19 2BS	0845 371 9346	031 785

Tourist Information Centres

Town	Address	Phone	Website/Email
Minehead	The Beach Hotel, The Avenue, Minehead TA24 5AP	01643 702624	www.minehead.co.uk
Porlock	West End, Porlock TA24 8QD	01643 863150	www.porlock.co.uk
Lynton	Town Hall, Lee Road, Lynton EX35 6BT	01598 752225	www.lynton-lynmouth-tourism.co.uk
Combe Martin	Museum, Cross Street EX34 0DH	01271 889031	www.visitcombemartin.com
Ilfracombe	The Promenade, Ilfracombe EX34 9BZ	01271 863001	www.visitilfracombe.co.uk
Woolacombe	The Esplanade, Woolacombe EX34 7DL	01271 870553	www.woolacombetourism.co.uk
Braunton	Bakehouse Centre, Caen Street EX33 1AA	01271 816688	www.visitbraunton.co.uk
Barnstaple	The Square, Barnstaple EX32 8LN	01271 375000	www.staynorthdevon.co.uk
Bideford	Burton Art Gallery, Kingsley Rd EX39 2QQ	01237 477676	www.burtonartgallery.co.uk
Bude	The Crescent, Bude EX23 8LE	01288 354240	www.visitbude.info
Boscastle	The Harbour, Boscastle PL35 0HD	01840 280010	www.visitboscastleandtintagel.com
Padstow	North Quay, Padstow PL28 8AF	01841 533449	www.padstowlive.com
Newquay	Marcus Hill, Newquay TR7 1BD	01637 854020	www.visitnewquay.org
Perranporth	Westcott House, St Pirans Road TR6 0BH	01872 575254	www.perranporthinfo.co.uk
Hayle	Hayle Library, Commercial Road TR27 4DE	01736 754399	www.hayle.co.uk
St Ives	The Guildhall, Street An Pol TR26 2DS	01736 796297	www.stivestic.co.uk
Penzance	Station Approach, Penzance TR18 2NF	01736 335530	www.purelypenzance.co.uk/tourism
Falmouth	Prince Of Wales Pier, 11 Market Strand TR11 3DF	01326 741194	www.falmouth.co.uk
Mevagissey	St George's Square, Mevagissey PL26 6UB	01726 844440	www.mevagissey-cornwall.co.uk
Fowey	5 South Street, Fowey PL23 1AR	01726 833616	www.fowey.co.uk
Looe	The Guildhall, Fore Street, Looe PL13 2AA	01503 262072	www.visit-southeastcornwall.co.uk
Plymouth	3-5 Plymouth Mayflower, Barbican PL1 2LR	01752 306330	www.visitplymouth.co.uk
Ivybridge	The Watermark, Ivybridge PL21 0SZ	01752 897035	www.ivybridgewatermark.co.uk
Salcombe	Market Street, Salcombe TQ8 8DE	01548 843927	www.salcombeinformation.co.uk
Kingsbridge	The Quay, Kingsbridge TQ7 1HS	01548 853195	www.welcomesouthdevon.co.uk
Dartmouth	The Engine House, Mayors Ave TQ6 9YY	01803 834224	www.discoverdartmouth.com
Brixham	Hobb Nobs Gift Shop, The Quay TQ5 8AW	08444 742233	www.englishriviera.co.uk
Paignton	Garfield Road, Paignotn, TQ4 6ED	01803 551959	www.ukinformationcentre.com
Torquay	5 Vaughan Parade, Torquay TQ2 5JG	01803 297428	www.englishriviera.co.uk
Shaldon	Shaldon Car Park, Ness Drive TQ14 0HP	01626 873723	www.visitsouthdevon.co.uk
Teignmouth	The Den, Sea Front, Teignmouth TQ14 8BE	01626 215666	www.visitsouthdevon.co.uk
Dawlish	The Lawn, Dawlish EX7 9PW	01626 215665	
Exmouth			www.exmouth-guide.co.uk
Budleigh-Salterton	Fore Street, Budleigh Salterton EX9 6NG	01395 445275	www.visitbudleigh.com
Sidmouth	Ham Lane, Sidmouth EX10 8XR	01395 516441	www.visitsidmouth.co.uk
Seaton	The Underfleet, Seaton EX12 2TB	01297 21660	www.seatontic.com
Lyme Regis	Guildhall Cottage, Church Street DT7 3BS	01297 442138	www.lymeregis.org
Bridport	Town Hall, South Street, Bridport DT6 3LF	01308 424901	www.visit-dorset.com
Swanage	The White House, Shore Road BH19 1LB	01929 422885	www.swanage,gov.uk
Wareham	Trinity Church, South Street BH20 4LR	01929 552740	www.visit-dorset.com
Poole	Poole Welcome Centre, The Quay BH13 1HJ	08452 345560	www.pooletourism.com
Not on Coast Path			
Truro	Municipal Buildings, Boscawen St, Truro TR1 2NE	01872 274555	www.truro.gov.uk
Weston Super Mare	The Winter Gardens, Royal Parade BS23 1AJ	01934 417117	www.visitsomerset.co.uk

Towards Wembury

We are sometimes asked what we have achieved and have set out below some of the things in which we have been involved in one way or another. We do as well send a steady flow of reports on path deficiencies, both as regards maintenance and the route of the path to the local authorities and the Natural England and the South West Coast Path Team.

1973 Official Formation in May. Attendance Cornish opening at Newquay.

First information sheets produced.

1974 Attendance at South Devon and Dorset opening in September at Beer.

Registration as a Charity.

1975 Clematon Hill, Bigbury, small new section of Coast Path agreed at SWWA's instigation.

Attendance at opening of so-called Exmoor Coast Path.

Bideford Public Enquiry - successful opposition to golf course on the Coast Path at Abbotsham.

Hartland Point success in getting path south from Hartland Point over Blagdon and Upright Cliffs.

Lulworth walk the new range Coast Path.

1976 First Footpath Guide issued. Thurlestone Diversion opposed.

North Cliffs improvements between Portreath and Hayle secured, thanks to National Trust.

Watermouth consulted by Devon County Council. Abbotsbury consulted by Dorset County Council.

1977 Evidence presented to Lord Porchester's Exmoor study.

Evidence given to Devon County Council for Taw/Torridge Estuary survey.

1978 Westward Ho! Attendance at Somerset/N. Devon opening.

Hartland new path seaward of radar station obtained, thanks to South West Way Association.

1979 Evidence given at Public Enquiries at Abbotsbury and Lulworth Cove.

First printed News Letters and Descriptions (illustrated)

1980 Dialogues with Countryside Commission about path deficiencies.

Alternative Coast Path open Glenthorne Estate, Somerset

1981 Path improvements at Watermouth; Braunton to Barnstaple; Dean Quarry; Clematon Hill; Bigbury; Mothecombe and Maidencombe.

1982 Further openings at: Cleave Farm (N Cornwall) Pentewan and Mount Edgcumbe, (S Cornwall) Higher Brownstone Farm, Kingswear and a short section west of Berry Head in South Devon.

Also agreement for a high tide route at Mothecombe (S Devon).

1983 Opening of the Widmouth Head section (N Devon), Kingswear and Mansands (S Devon) Crackington Haven (N Cornwall) with major improvements to path on the western side.

1984 New Sections of path opened on the east bank of the mouth of the River Dart near Kingswear giving access to Mill Bay Cove. And Trebarwith Strand to Backways Cove (N Cornwall).

1985 Culbone - Foreland Point - path at the Glenthorne Estate waymarked as official route.

Pinehaven - Port Quin (N Cornwall) new path opened.

1986 Minehead - Porlock Weir New path between North Hill and Hurlstone Point waymarked.

Black Head (Cornwall) purchased by the National Trust so allowing a coastal route.

1987 Barnstaple/Bideford/Northam new route completed along old railway track.

Bude - attendance at Public Enquiry to prevent development adjacent to footpath.

Chynhalls Point path moved to seaward of hotel.

Branscombe - Attendance at Public Enquiry for true coast path - route adopted.

Bidna/Northam - sea wall breached, acceptable diversion negotiated.

1988 Woody Bay- Trentishoe - Devon County Council adopts our recommended, nearer the coast route.

1989 Fire Beacon Point/Pentargon Cornwall County Council installs new path.

Wembury - attend public meeting to successfully oppose erection of locked gates across Coast Path by Royal Navy.

1991 Buckator - at our request Cornwall County Council re-route official path around the headland.

1992 Watcombe and Maidencombe Our recommended route installed by Devon County Council.

Worthygate Wood - our suggested path installed by National Trust.

1993 Foreland Point - successful opposition to stop closure of path on west side.

Buck's Mills - success with our request for a Path to avoid the holiday complex.

Port Quin - our suggested path installed by National Trust.

Reverse Guide from Poole to Minehead introduced.

1994 Invited by Countryside Commission to become a member of the South West Coast Path Steering Group to review the management of the South West Coast Path.

1995 Culbone - section re-opened by Exmoor National Park.

Association details on the Internet. See details on page 2.

1996 Path Descriptions for the whole Coast Path published.

Lyme Regis - golf course route reinstated by Dorset County Council.

1997 The SWCP Project published its strategy for the future management of the Coast Path.

The Association becomes a member of the SWCP Management Group.

1998 Our Silver Jubilee Year (25 years old).

The Association launches its Silver Jubilee Appeal to raise funds towards markers at each end of the Coast Path.

Mount Batten, Plymouth – Coast Path opened

1999 Name changed to South West Coast Path Association.

2000 Crock Pits - Exmoor National Park installs a coastal route recommended by Association.

2001 Eight Winter Cliff Falls Disrupt Dorset Coast Path.

Celebratory marker installed at Minehead.

Foot & Mouth Crisis - whole Coast Path closed for 3 months.

11 August - Whole Coast Path walked on one day by Association members to celebrate the re-opening of the Coast Path.

Improvements made

2002 Celebratory marker installed at South Haven Point, Poole Harbour.

St German's Beacon - True coastal route installed between Downderry & Portwrinkle.

2003 South West Coast Path Association is 30 years old.

Easter Saturday - Association arranges 'Walk the whole path in one day' to celebrate the 25th anniversary of the official inclusion of the Somerset and North Devon sections.

Chynhalls Cliff –desired realignment is installed by Cornwall County Council.

Isle of Portland – Countryside Agency accepts the route around the Island.

Tregantle Cliff – desired realignment throughout the rifle ranges is installed by the MoD as permissive path. For this we award the MoD our Annual Award.

2004 Annual award presented to Brian Muelaner and National Trust Team for their work at Lansallos.

2005 Strete to Stoke Fleming – realigned Coast Path opened.

Wembury Point –Association donates £1000 to National Trust fundraising to buy this land.

2006 After 33 years in members' homes, our Administration department moves to new office at Lee Mill.

Cain's Folly –Path reinstated after 6 years of an unsatisfactory diversion.

2007 Minehead - Porlock Marsh - Thatcher Point –our requested realignments installed.

Watermouth – Major funding pledged by Association for off road Path realignment.

Porthallow – Design and artists chosen for the halfway marker.

2008 Association On-Line Shop opened.

5000th Member - Jill Fletcher, of Portishead given a presentation at Minehead.

2009 Honorary Secretary, Eric Wallis, listed in New Year's Honours, to receive MBE for his voluntary service to this registered charity.

Porthallow Halfway marker unveiled in May.

2010 Death of Eric Wallis MBE Hon Secretary since 1986 after short illness.

Coast Path re-routed around Cape Cornwall.

Planning for new style Annual Guide.

Planning and surveying the first stretch of the new English Coast Path from Portland to Lulworth commenced by Natural England.

2011 Association moves to larger office at Lee Mill.

2012 Association funding is used to help progress no fewer than twelve improvement projects around the Coast Path, at Baggy Point, near Northam, between Westward Ho! and Bucks Mills, at Hartland, at Trevaunance Cove (St Agnes), in West Cornwall at Trevega, Tregerthen and Trevean Cliffs, near Millendreath (Looe), at Challaborough (South Devon), at St Mary's Bay (Torbay) and at Durlston near Swanage.

2013 Association celebrates its 40th anniversary with the Great South West Walk. Sponsorship of this walk along the whole length of the Coast Path by local holiday companies, providers of accommodation and other facilities, as well as the walkers themselves, raises over half a million pounds for Coast Path improvements when match funding is added in, enabling over 100 improvements. A fitting birthday present!

Eric Wallis Memorial Steps opened at Royal William Yard, Plymouth.

Watermouth improvements opened. Path moved off busy A399 to give walkers a safe walk regardless of the state of the tide.

2014 With financial contributions from Local Authority partners and the National Trust, the Association appoints a Business Development Manager.

Great South West Walk 2014 takes place in September, organised jointly with Children's Hospice South West. The event raises £40,000, shared between the two organisations, allowing for £20,000 worth of improvements to the Coast Path.

The Association's South Hams Appeal is successful in raising £40,000 for storm damage repairs, to be match-funded by Devon County Council.

The Association makes a successful bid to the Coastal Communities Fund for £1 million, with half for storm damage repairs at 30+ sites around the Coast Path and half for funding for promotional work and engaging with businesses and community groups.

Work begins on setting up a new network of Association volunteers to monitor the Coast Path and liaise with the Path managers.

FUNDING IMPROVEMENTS TO THE SOUTH WEST COAST PATH

A wide range of over 100 improvements to the Coast Path has been funded by the Great South West Walks of 2013 and 2014. In addition, funds from members' subscriptions have enabled improvement works to be undertaken at a further 28 sites around the Coast Path in the last three years. And now, with the successful application to the Coastal Communities Fund and the success of the South Hams Appeal, over 30 more improvements will be under way over the next year. We would like to thank all our members for their support, both financially through subscriptions and also as membership numbers give us "clout" when bidding for funds. With ever decreasing financial support available from traditional sources of central and local government because of their funding cuts, the help of members of the Association is vital in enabling us to provide improvements to the fantastic resource which is the South West Coast Path.

The Association Shop

- This is just a small selection of products available. Please refer to our website for full shop listings and colour availability. Alternatively, we would be happy to take your order over the phone, or answer any query you may have regarding any of our products.

- Order at **www.southwestcoastpath.org.uk** or by telephone **01752 896237**.

Hoodie

Available as one block colour or two-colour with contrasting hood, embroidered SWCPA logo in over 50 assorted colours - be as colourful as you dare! 80% cotton, 20% polyester. Also available in children's sizing.

£25.00/£27.50 (Adult) plus postage
£18/£20 (Children) plus postage

Front Row Top

Half Zip neck sweatshirt, 100% cotton. Contrast tape to neck and left hem. Panel detail to body sides. Available in navy/white or red/navy both with embroidered logo. Sizes: XS, S, M, L, XL, XXL

£35.00 plus postage

Sweat Shirt

In a range of colours embroidered with the embroidered logo. (70% polyester/30% cotton). Sizes: S, M, Large, XL, XXL.

£25.00 plus postage

Sleeveless Fleece

Available in a range of colours, with embroidered with embroidered logo and two zip pockets. 100% pill resistant polyester and unlined. Sizes: S, M, L, XL, XXL.

£25.00 plus postage

Bobble Hat

8 fun colours (embroidered with the new SWCPA logo). The perfect accessory to keep the head warm. 100% soft touch acrylic, heavy gauge knit with ribbed cuff. Also available in children's sizing.

£10.00 (Adult) plus postage
£8.00 (Children) plus postage

Baseball Cap

Available in Dark Green or Stone. 100% cotton with embroidered logo. One size adjustable to fit.

£9.95 plus postage

Metal Badge

30mm quality enamel badge suitable for clothing, rucksacks etc.
Secure with 'butterfly' pin.

£3.50 plus postage

Light waterproof and windproof Jacket

With SWCPA logo available in 6 enticing colours.
100% polyester, microfleece body and sleeve lining, concealed waterproof hood, 2 side pockets and safety tape across lower back panel.

£30.00 plus postage

Fleece Jacket

Available in various colours with embroidered logo and two zip pockets. 100% pill resistant, unlined, elasticated hem and cuffs.
Sizes: S, M, L, XL and XXL.

£29.00 plus postage

Morf Snoods

Morf Suprafleece multi-function snood/hat/neckwarmer/headband. 100% polyester microfibre, anti-microbial. Available in Black, Royal Blue, Red, Grey or Navy Blue. Embroidered with the Coast Path logo.

£9.00 plus postage

Polo Shirt

Polo Shirt available in various colours with embroidered logo. A good quality garment, easy to wash (65% polyester/35% cotton).
Sizes: S, M, L, XL and XXL.

£19.25 plus postage

Tea Towel

Full cotton tea towel 48cm x 78cm, depicting the end markers and scenes and flowers from locations on the trail. In the centre is a clear map of the whole South West Coast Path.

£4.25 plus postage

Cloth Badge

Good quality cloth badge, showing the Peninsula map, with 'South West Coast Path' embroidered below, approximate size 4" x 3" (10cm x 8cm). Suitable for sewing onto shirt or rucksack.

£3.00 plus postage

To order:

• Order at **www.southwestcoastpath.org.uk** or by telephone **01752 896237**.

Membership As A Gift

Complete with covering letter which can be sent out to the recipient on your behalf.

£14.50 Single / £16.00 Joint Membership includes postage
£22.00 Overseas Membership includes postage

Map Poster

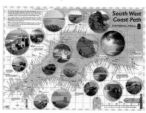

A large sized map poster showing the South West Coast Path with the path printed in white enabling walkers to mark off sections walked.
Size 64cm x 45cm (251/4" x 173/4").

£5.75 plus postage

Boot Bag

With handle for easy transportation with 4 plastic stud feet, made from polyester easy to sponge clean. Sizing 33x26x18.5cm

£15.00 plus postage

Backpack

With SWCPA logo available in 11 colours, the perfect accompaniment for any activity. Dimensions 40x28x14cm. Zip front pocket, adjustable padded and reinforced straps, padded back.

£15.00 plus postage

Glassware

Cut glass Tumblers or Tankards with the Peninsula map sand-blasted on the glass. Suitably packaged.

£16.00 Tumbler plus postage
£15.00 Tankard plus postage

Completion Certificate and Badge

Celebrate your achievement with our Completion items.

FREE to members
£5.00 to non-members plus postage

We accept the following credit/debit cards:

To order:
- Order at www.southwestcoastpath.org.uk or by telephone **01752 896237**.

A-Z Maps

A collection of 5 Maps in the South West Coast Path series - simply turn the pages!

£7.95 each plus postage

Coast Path Notelets

Pack of 8 Notelets in 4 designs with white envelopes, all depicting Coast Path images. Approximate size 15cm x 10.5cm.

£3.75 plus postage

Log Book

Keep a day by day record of your walk in an easy to carry, pocket size booklet, with a page per section in which to record your journey around some of the most beautiful countryside in the British Isles. Supplied with Waterproof Cover.

£3.50 plus postage

Reverse Guide

REVISED 2011 A trail description of the whole 630 miles in the direction Poole to Minehead.

£4.00 plus postage

Also available direct from the artist...

A Calligraphic Map of the South West Coast Path

This quality calligraphic map of the South West Coast Path has been designed, illustrated and written by James Skinner of Gloucester.

The printed calligraphic map has been written entirely by hand, complemented by fine pen and ink drawings illustrating many of the sights to be found whilst walking the path.

The calligraphic map would make a superb gift, or an ideal memento for anyone having walked part or all of the path.

Overall size: approx 560 mm deep x 760 mm wide

£10.99 including free postage and packing

A £5 donation is made to the SWCPA for each map sold

View the map at www.jamesskinnercalligrapher.co.uk or telephone 01452 611614 for further details

Membership

You may be one of those who have either bought this guide from us or a book shop. You can guarantee receipt of next year's updated, revised edition by joining the Association.

The South West Coast Path Association is a charity which represents all users of the Coast Path, be they serious hikers or afternoon strollers.

As well as producing information guides about the Coast Path, the Association raises money to help the authorities provide the best possible standard for Coast Path walkers.

If you would like to join the Association, and see your subscription go towards improving the path and its publications, you would be very welcome. Membership includes a free copy of the updated annual guide each year.

This annual guide is updated every year and published at the end of February.

Annual Subscriptions:

Single £14.50
Joint £16.00
Life Membership £220.00
Joint Life Membership.................. £250.00
Non-UK Membership £22.00

To join online visit www.southwestcoastpath.org.uk or telephone 01752 896237

Near Gunver Head

Application Form

I wish to join the South West Coast Path Association.

Name_____

Address _____

_____

_____

Postcode _____

Telephone _____

Email _____

Payment Details:

Payment made by:

☐ Cheque   ☐ Visa/Mastercard

Expiry _____/_____   Security Number _____

Card Number _____

PLEASE DETACH HERE

Gift Aid

Under the Gift Aid Scheme the Association can reclaim the income tax paid on any donation or membership subscription received, provided you are a UK tax payer. If you would like to help us in this way then please indicate below and sign. All that we ask is if you cease to pay income tax in the future, please let us know.

I am a UK tax payer and would like South West Coast Path Association to reclaim the tax paid on any subscriptions or donations that I make to them.

Signature(s) Date

Please send completed form to:
The Administrator, South West Coast Path Association, Bowker House,
Lee Mill Bridge, Ivybridge PL21 9EF • Tel: 01752 896237

NOTES

Whilst walking on the path, or on any other occasion, should you meet someone interested in this book, the Association, or the Coast Path, do not worry if no one has a pencil and paper, just tear off one of these:

The South West Coast Path Association was formed 41 years ago to promote the interest of users of our Coast Path. We continue to press the authorities to maintain it properly and to complete the path. An annually updated guide to the whole 630 miles (1014km) of the South West Coast Path is issued to members every Spring. They also receive newsletters that provide the latest news about the state of the path.

For information about membership and how to obtain this annual guide contact:
South West Coast Path Association, Bowker House, Lee Mill Bridge, Ivybridge PL21 9EF
T: 01752 896237 E: info@swcp.org.uk W: www.southwestcoastpath.org.uk

---

The South West Coast Path Association was formed 41 years ago to promote the interest of users of our Coast Path. We continue to press the authorities to maintain it properly and to complete the path. An annually updated guide to the whole 630 miles (1014km) of the South West Coast Path is issued to members every Spring. They also receive newsletters that provide the latest news about the state of the path.

For information about membership and how to obtain this annual guide contact:
South West Coast Path Association, Bowker House, Lee Mill Bridge, Ivybridge PL21 9EF
T: 01752 896237 E: info@swcp.org.uk W: www.southwestcoastpath.org.uk

---

The South West Coast Path Association was formed 41 years ago to promote the interest of users of our Coast Path. We continue to press the authorities to maintain it properly and to complete the path. An annually updated guide to the whole 630 miles (1014km) of the South West Coast Path is issued to members every Spring. They also receive newsletters that provide the latest news about the state of the path.

For information about membership and how to obtain this annual guide contact:
South West Coast Path Association, Bowker House, Lee Mill Bridge, Ivybridge PL21 9EF
T: 01752 896237 E: info@swcp.org.uk W: www.southwestcoastpath.org.uk

---

The South West Coast Path Association was formed 41 years ago to promote the interest of users of our Coast Path. We continue to press the authorities to maintain it properly and to complete the path. An annually updated guide to the whole 630 miles (1014km) of the South West Coast Path is issued to members every Spring. They also receive newsletters that provide the latest news about the state of the path.

For information about membership and how to obtain this annual guide contact:
South West Coast Path Association, Bowker House, Lee Mill Bridge, Ivybridge PL21 9EF
T: 01752 896237 E: info@swcp.org.uk W: www.southwestcoastpath.org.uk

---

The South West Coast Path Association was formed 41 years ago to promote the interest of users of our Coast Path. We continue to press the authorities to maintain it properly and to complete the path. An annually updated guide to the whole 630 miles (1014km) of the South West Coast Path is issued to members every Spring. They also receive newsletters that provide the latest news about the state of the path.

For information about membership and how to obtain this annual guide contact:
South West Coast Path Association, Bowker House, Lee Mill Bridge, Ivybridge PL21 9EF
T: 01752 896237 E: info@swcp.org.uk W: www.southwestcoastpath.org.uk

PLEASE CUT ALONG DOTTED LINES